HUGH KENNEDY

The Caliphate

A PELICAN INTRODUCTION

PELICAN
an imprint of
PENGUIN BOOKS

PELICAN BOOKS

UK | USA | Canada | Ireland | Australia
India | New Zealand | South Africa

Penguin Books is part of the Penguin Random House
group of companies whose addresses can be found at
global.penguinrandomhouse.com.

Penguin
Random House
UK

First published 2016
001

Text copyright © Hugh Kennedy, 2016

The moral right of the author has been asserted

Book design by Matthew Young
Set in 10/14.664 pt FreightText Pro
Typeset by Jouve (UK), Milton Keynes
Printed in Great Britain by Clays Ltd, St Ives plc

A CIP catalogue record for this book is
available from the British Library

ISBN: 978-0-141-98140-6

To my young grandchildren, Ferdie, Ronja and Aurora
in the hope that they may grow up in a world where
people of different religions and cultures can live
together in peace and mutual respect.

Contents

ACKNOWLEDGEMENTS

It is now fifty years since I began researching and writing about the history of caliphs from different eras and areas of Muslim history, starting with the Abbasids, the subject of my PhD at Cambridge under the enthusiastic guidance of the great Martin Hinds, a brilliant scholar who died far too young, and moving on to write about Umayyads, both in Syria and the Iberian peninsula, and the Almohads. The half-century which has passed since I began work has seen the subject of caliphate moving from the status of a historical relic to the forefront of modern political debate, and this transformation has encouraged me to explore beyond my comfort zone to examine the way in which ideas the office has been used and exploited through the ages.

Inevitably in such a long sweep of history, I have been 'standing on the shoulders of giants' and using the works of scholars more learned and distinguished than myself. I have tried to acknowledge at least some of these debts in the notes and bibliography and I must apologise to any I have inadvertently omitted.

Much of this book was written on the beautiful Greek island of Amorgos, looking out from the terrace of Marco's house over the olive groves to the white houses of the little port of Aigiali, with the wine-dark sea and the islands beyond. But however important the calm and peace may be for writing, the book was conceived and formed in the busy cross-current of ideas and debates in the School of Oriental and African Studies in the University of London, where I work. There cannot be an academic environment on the planet where so many ideas and cultures come into daily contact, and ideas of history and community are explored with such vigour. I have benefitted enormously from my interactions with staff and students and perhaps especially by discussions with my numerous Muslim students about the nature and ethics of political power in an Islamic context.

This book has also benefitted from the enthusiasm of colleagues in publishing, my wonderful agent Georgina Capel who is so enthusiastic about my ideas, Laura Stickney at Penguin Books who has supported this project from the beginning and my copy-editor Claire Péligry who has saved me from so many errors and confusions.

And finally from the support of my wife Hilary and my growing family, Katharine, Alice and James and the next generation, Ferdie, Ronja and Aurora, all of whom have supported me (and distracted me in the nicest possible way) in the course of writing.

INTRODUCTION

What is caliphate? What does the term mean? What is the history of the idea? Is it an ancient irrelevance, only interesting as a voice from a past which is safely consigned to history? Or is it a concept that we can interpret and use today? In this book I shall try to answer these questions. The concept of caliphate has had many different interpretations and realizations through the centuries, as we shall see, but fundamental to them all is that it offers an idea of leadership which is about the just ordering of Muslim society according to the will of God. Some have argued that the caliph is the shadow of God on earth, a man whose authority is semi-divine and whose conduct is without blame; many more would accept that the caliph was, so to speak, the chief executive of the *umma*, the Muslim community, an ordinary human with worldly powers, and there is a wide spectrum of ideas in between. All are informed by the desire to see God's will worked out among all Muslims.

This is not a book, primarily, about contemporary politics. It is rather a history book and much of the historical material it deals with dates to the period which historians in the Anglo-Saxon tradition call the early Middle Ages or even the Dark Ages, the four centuries between the death of the

Prophet Muhammad in 632 and the coming of the Crusaders to the Middle East in 1097, though some of the narrative discussion goes through to the twenty-first century. It is easy to imagine that this period has little or no bearing on the position we, Muslims and non-Muslims alike, find ourselves in today and indeed most accounts of the so-called Islamic State, for example, begin with recent history and see the movement as a response to western influence and twenty-first-century pressures. I would argue, on the contrary, that in order to understand Islamic State's idea of caliphate, and why it should prove relevant and important to many, we have to understand its roots deep in the Muslim tradition. Islamic State has made the revival of the caliphate a centrepiece, a keystone of its project for Islamic renewal and the response this has generated shows the potency of the idea almost fourteen centuries since it first emerged. For modern Islamists searching for a basis to construct a viable political vision for the revival of the Muslim *umma*, the events of these centuries are at once an inspiration and a justification.

These events continue to be an inspiration partly because they recall a world in which the caliphate was the most powerful and advanced polity in the whole of western Eurasia, when Baghdad had a population of some half a million while London and Paris could only boast a few thousand inhabitants, when the caliphate administered huge areas with a standing army and a literate and numerate bureaucracy and Baghdad and Cairo were huge centres of trade and culture. To anyone within the Muslim tradition or outside it, knowledge of the history of this period can encourage that cultural self-confidence which is essential to any civilization if it is to live at peace with itself and with its neighbours. At this level my book is aimed at Muslims and non-Muslims who want to inform themselves, as everyone should, about the real glories and achievements of a vibrant civilization.

But it goes further than that. For some Muslims, the history of the caliphate points to a time when Muslims were God-fearing and devout, puritanical and self-disciplined, and always willing to sacrifice their lives in the path of Allah. This vision is not simply a nostalgic memory. To a degree not found in any other contemporary political discourse, this ancient past justifies the present for certain Islamist groups. Reading such contemporary propaganda as the Islamic State periodical *Dabiq*, it is impossible not to be struck by the constant references to the acts of the Prophet Muhammad, the *sahāba* who were his companions and disciples, and the early caliphs. If they did something, the argument goes, then we should follow their example. No further justification is needed, and even the most apparently cruel and barbaric actions require no further legitimization if they can be shown to be following the examples of such great heroes. We cannot understand what these loud and insistent voices are saying, still less argue against them, unless we too go down the road into the ancient past.

History has a power for this tradition which we do not find elsewhere. No one in Britain looks to the Anglo-Saxon Chronicle, a work which dates from the same centuries as the early Arabic sources, and uses it as a way of justifying political behaviour today. It may intrigue us, it may give important insights into the ways our ancestors conducted themselves and the deeds of King Alfred may even, in a general way, be inspirational, but they will not be normative, nor will they provide instructions or excuses for today's and tomorrow's behaviour. That is why any discussion of the concept of caliphate has to be a history book, and why we need to understand properly these complex memories and traditions.

I have sought to enliven the book by quoting original texts translated from Arabic and Persian, which can give us insight into the lived experience of caliphate, records of what people saw and heard at the time unfiltered by later attitudes and preoccupations. Such texts make the point that many Muslims looked to their caliphs, and expected their caliphs, to produce dazzling displays of opulence and be a focus of cultural activities which would redound to the credit of not just the ruling dynasty but the whole Muslim community. By reading these descriptions we can perhaps recover something of the delight and *joie de vivre* which attended the performance of the caliphate, but which is often lost in dry narrative history.

I have made use of modern historical works, starting with that of my illustrious predecessor as Professor of Arabic at SOAS, Sir Thomas Arnold, whose book *The Caliphate* (1924) was the first volume in English devoted to the subject. Fellow academics will recognize many of my debts. The main ones I have acknowledged in the Notes and Further Reading, and my apologies go to any I have inadvertently missed. Fundamentally, however, what I write stems from within the Muslim tradition. The material is derived not from orientalist outsiders but from the wealth of intelligent and perceptive Muslim historical writing, mostly in Arabic but some in

Persian and Turkish, which is one of the great glories of the Islamic cultural tradition. I cannot pretend to have covered all the various manifestations of caliphate throughout the Muslim world; in particular, some readers may feel that I have neglected developments in south and south-east Asia in the nineteenth and twentieth centuries, but I feel that would have made the work too long and diffuse and these should be the subject of another study.

This coming from within the tradition generates a respect for political and religious actors and writers. The early Muslims, who struggled to create institutions which would express Islamic values while also providing a safe and orderly framework in which they could practise their faith, did not, in the main, act in fanatical or irrational ways, nor were the writings in which they recorded their deeds, debates and disputes fundamentally dishonest. They wrestled with political and religious dilemmas which are common to many human societies: how to live the good life; how to construct a community which enables people to live together even if they do not have the same opinions; what offences are so grave that a person must be expelled from the community or put to death; and, perhaps most fundamentally, how to understand the will of God and what He expects of mankind. If we treat their arguments, fears, hopes and visions with respect, we will come much closer to understanding their deeds and attitudes than if we dismiss their concerns or feel that their writings are too partisan and tendentious to be taken seriously.

This book is quietly polemical. The message which runs through it is that the idea of caliphate is a rich and varied tradition. Many Muslims have embraced the argument that such an institution is the best way of ordering human society, but caliphate is a many-splendoured thing. There is no one way, no single template or legal framework which defines caliphate. History tells us that there have been caliphs of many different sorts, warrior caliphs, pious caliphs, intellectual caliphs, pleasure-loving caliphs, incompetent caliphs, cruel and tyrannical caliphs. They are all part of the caliphal tradition. There has never been one generally agreed view of what powers the office should have, who is qualified to be caliph and how caliphs should be chosen. Perhaps it is this flexibility, even uncertainty, which has enabled the idea to survive so long and have traction in so many different Muslim societies.

My aim here is to show something of the variety of caliphal experience. You can choose what you want to take from this tradition, but the choice is yours. If you want a caliphate which is aggressive and fiercely controlling of the Muslim population, you can find precedents in the vast historical records. If you want a caliphate which is generous and open to different ideas and customs while, of course, remaining true to its vision of God's will and purpose, then you can find that in the historical tradition too. The past bears many different messages.

There are those who see caliphate as a vehicle for imposing their particular and often very narrow view of Islam on the *umma*; there are others who see caliphate as a justification for aiming at world conquest; but there are equally those who see caliphate as simply providing a framework in which Muslims can strive to live a godly life and make up their own minds about the best way to this. There are those who have looked to the caliph as God's representative on earth with semi-divine powers; others who have seen his role as protecting the Muslim community from its enemies by collecting taxes and raising armies. And we should not forget those who remember with pride the open, broad-minded and inclusive societies presided over by the great Abbasid and Fatimid caliphs and the superb intellectual and artistic achievements they encouraged. The history of the caliphate, and Islamic history more generally, must not be the possession of one interpretation or one narrow view, rather we should all, Muslim and non-Muslim alike, rejoice in the richness and variety of the experience of caliphate through the ages.

The history of the idea of caliphate has endured and been used and adapted from the death of the Prophet Muhammad in 632 until the present day, a period of almost fourteen centuries. It has been discussed, adopted and rejected in countries stretching from as far as South East Asia to Portugal and Morocco. It is no surprise, then, that the concept has been put into practice in many different ways and expressed in many different languages. The variety of the caliphal experience is therefore one of the themes I shall explore in the following chapters. At the same time, these different practices and expressions of the idea of caliphate have a common historical basis, or rather they derive from a memory of historical circumstances which have important elements in common, even though their interpretation may vary wildly. The way in which this tradition was expounded, developed and invented in different eras and in different political and social environments will be one of the main themes of this work.

Three Questions

Three questions will dominate the discussion in this volume and run through its chapters like a connecting thread. The first of these is: how was a caliph to be chosen? Three possible answers to this question emerged. The first option was that the caliph would be chosen by the Muslims themselves. This apparently simple idea, however, could be worked out in many different ways. Who were the choosers to be? Should there be many or could just one be enough? Was any sane and sound adult male (the idea of a female caliph being one which is never entertained in these historical debates) eligible for the office, an idea espoused by the Kharijites, or did the caliph have to be of a certain family or lineage; above all did they have to be of the Prophet's tribe, Quraysh, for the Sunnis, or even his direct descendants through his daughter Fātima, his son-in-law Alī and their children, Hasan and Husayn, for the Shi'ites?

The second option was that the caliphate should be hereditary within one Holy Family, that of Alī and Fātima, daughter of the Prophet Muhammad. But this led to further questions and possibilities. Should all of the family be considered eligible or just one branch? Within that branch, should the office be decided by primogeniture, the succession of the eldest son, even if that son was apparently incapable or failed to obey the established laws and customs of the Muslims? Should he still be chosen or passed over in favour of a more suitable candidate? And, of course, as the years and centuries wore on, more and more people could claim to be descended from the holy lineage until their numbers seemed to be as great as the sands of the sea. In these circumstances it was possible, even likely, that individuals invented their genealogies, either because they were frauds who hoped to accrue some of the benefits of such a prestigious connection, or because they were deluded and genuinely felt that the blood of the Prophet ran through their veins.

The third option was that of *nass*. *Nass* essentially means choice or designation by the previous ruler. It often meant in practice the choice by a ruler of one or more (an heir and a spare) of his sons, but not necessarily so, as when the caliph Ma'mūn chose a member of the family of Alī instead of one of his own Abbasid sons and relatives. *Nass* had very little theoretical or ideological underpinning compared with either election or heredity, but in practice it was the most common way in which the office was passed down through the generations. It gave the green light, so to speak, for the concept of dynastic succession.

The first question – how was the caliph to be chosen – was inextricably bound up with the second: what should the caliph do and how extensive should his powers be? There was a whole spectrum here between those who held that the caliph was essentially a God-king, the equal or even superior of the Prophet Muhammad, and those who believed that he should be more of a *primus inter pares* or chief executive of the Muslim community, with no more direct connection with the Almighty than any other Muslim. This difference was connected with the question of the method of choice. If the succession was hereditary within the Holy Family, it was essentially a choice made by God and therefore the leader had divine approval, he was God's chosen instrument in the ordering of human affairs and had the power to interpret, or even modify, the Qur'ān and the *sunna* (the practice and sayings of Muhammad). This is essentially the Shi'i view. If, on the other hand, the caliph was to be chosen by humans, however pious and learned, then he was necessarily fallible: all humans can make mistakes. He would certainly have no direct line to God, no status to interpret the Qur'ān or decide law. That would have to be left to the scholars and intellectuals (*ulama*) who devoted their lives to the study and understanding of the Qur'ān and the *hadīth* (sayings of the Prophet). This is essentially the Sunni view.

The third fundamental question was: what was the evidence on which these issues could be decided and how should it be interpreted? After the death of Muhammad in 632, the Muslim community was confronted with an unprecedented situation. There were no guidelines to be sought in the past for the mission of Muhammad, and his reception by the Muslims had made the pre-Islamic past irrelevant anyway, except as an awful warning of how not to behave and order society. Equally the practices of the great Roman and Persian monarchies could not be adduced because they had rejected the teachings of the Prophet and been defeated and, in the case of the Persian monarchy, destroyed by the Muslims with God's support. In fact, as time wore on some Muslims did incorporate ideas from the ancient monarchies about how things should be done, but such ideas could never be the basis of an argument, since they would otherwise impugn the unique validity of the Prophet's message and hence of Islam itself. Only the ancient prophets sent by God, all 144,000 of them, were possible exemplars, but, with the important exceptions of Moses and Jesus, the lives and policies of these shadowy or even unknown figures could provide little guidance.

In the absence of ancient or foreign models, the Muslim community soon began to develop a body of precedent based on its own early history, as remembered, and misremembered and invented, by its participants and eyewitnesses and recorded in the form of *akhbār* (sing. *khabar*), which were essentially short stories and anecdotes. These in turn were gathered together and edited by a later generation, at the beginning of the eighth century or earlier, into collections of accounts which over time became elaborated written accounts. In the form in which we have them today, they date from the mid-ninth century to the first half of the tenth, thus being a century and a half, or even two centuries, older than the events they describe. This apparent time gap has provoked considerable, and largely unhelpful, anguish among modern historians. The contradictions and discrepancies have been used to argue that this material is so unreliable as to be useless for reconstructing 'what really happened' or so partisan as to be actively misleading. But all historical writing is like that. The great historians of the early medieval Christian world, Procopius, Gregory of Tours, Bede and all their contemporaries and followers, used historical narrative to make points and arguments and selected those incidents and characters which would sustain the ideas they were presenting. So it was with the early Muslim recorders and compilers.

There are two important things we should remember

about the compilation of these early histories and the use we make of them. The first is that they present a wide variety of detail and interpretation within a broadly similar framework. Almost without exception, they tell us that there were four caliphs who followed the death of the Prophet, Abū Bakr (632–4), Umar (632–44), Uthmān (644–56) and Alī (656–61). That said, there are different opinions about these four characters. For some, probably the majority, they were venerable figures whose utterances and conduct should be studied and admired by all Muslims. Others, however, felt that the first two, Abū Bakr and Umar, were indeed great, but that things had started to go wrong in the reign of the third caliph, Uthmān, largely because of his personal failings, and that the proper order of things was only restored with the accession of Alī. Still others argued that Abū Bakr has usurped the rights of Alī, the true heir of the Prophet, and that Umar and Uthmān were also evil-doers whose rule was illegitimate and whose conduct was flawed. True caliphate always belonged to Alī and was only restored, if only briefly, during his reign. And so these differences of opinion continued under the Umayyads (661–750) and the Abbasids (750–1258) and under other dynasties with caliphal pretensions. Far from being unreliable or, even worse, deliberately dishonest, accounts of such differences are profoundly revealing of the attitudes and debates of the time. But the modern reader must always be aware that there are many elements in the sources which can be seized on and developed for later polemic.

And this is the second point about the early historical narratives. They are fundamental to all discussions of the nature of caliphate; they are the building blocks of political debate.

To determine the true nature and function of the office of caliph, most Muslim thinkers have turned, not to abstract theories or principles of political institutions, in the manner of Hobbes and Rousseau for example, but to the records of the ancient caliphs, especially the first four. These records are not just, as Wordsworth put it, of 'old, unhappy, far off-things, and battles long ago', but events which determine how people should behave and act in their own time, how they should reconcile the demands of living together with their fellow human beings with absolute obedience to the will of Almighty God. If this book seems burdened by historical narrative and discussion, this is because it is the way the debate about caliphate has always taken place and the way it is taking place now. If we are to understand this debate, Muslim and non-Muslim alike, we must understand the historical language in which it is conducted.

The following chapters, then, will set out to examine these three fundamental questions – how a caliph should be chosen, the nature and extent of his powers, and the way in which they were recorded and used – in the light of the different historical periods of the caliphate, and to show how men in different times and places have used, and perhaps abused, the basic concepts which have informed the idea of caliphate throughout the ages.

Transliterations and Dates

I have made every effort in this book not to intimidate, or indeed bore, the reader with huge numbers of Arabic names and terms. Some Arabic vocabulary, including of course the word caliph itself, is necessary because many of the concepts involved in the discussion have no direct English equivalent. Such words will be briefly explained on their first occurrence in the text and further explained in the Glossary. All dates will be given in the Common Era (AD) format to avoid confusion, although of course the Arabic writers who inform us about these issues use *hijrī* dates, based on the number of lunar years (eleven days shorter than solar years) which have passed since the Prophet's Hijra (emigration) from Mecca to Medina in 622.

History, particularly the history of periods so removed from our own, can occasionally seem like dull and dreary stuff, just 'one damn thing after another', as the Duke of Wellington described it. It is not surprising if Muslims and non-Muslims alike are put off by records of battles and conquests, not to speak by the unpronounceable and unmemorable names which litter so many books on Islamic history. So, at the risk of oversimplification, I have made a decision to keep the number of personal names to a minimum and make them more accessible by missing out the initial definite article (al-).

There is now a generally accepted system of transliteration of Arabic names and terms into Latin characters. This is important because it allows the English to convey with precision exactly which Arabic letters are used. I shall, however, use a simplified version of this to avoid the proliferation of dots under and lines over letters. It is not especially useful to the non-Arabist to know which of the different letters transliterated into Latin as d, s, t, z, are indicated. The only exception is the letter, unique to Arabic, known as *'ayn*, and transliterated as ' (as in *bay'a*), which indicates a guttural consonant but which can be sounded, by non-Arabic speakers, as an elongated vowel. Arabic also uses a glottal stop, called the *ḥamza*, which will be indicated as ' (as in Qā'im). On the other hand there is, it seems to me, a purpose in distinguishing long and short vowels because these determine the emphasis. Thus it helps to know that the name of the famous Abbasid caliph is pronounced Rasheed not Raashid, and to this end it is written as Rashīd. The two other long vowels, the extended ī (as in Alī) and the extended ū (as in Mansūr) will also be indicated, showing where the emphasis should lie.

The Arabic word *ibn* meaning 'son', a component of many Arabic names, I have simply rendered as 'b.' in full names (as in Abbās b. Firnās).

The Caliphate in the Umayyad
and Early Abbasid Period c.750

VOLGA
BULGARS

KHAZARS

Black Sea

GHUZZ

Aral
Sea

TURKS

Jaxartes

Caspian Sea

KHWĀRAZM
Gurganj •

TRANSOXANIA

FARGHĀNA
Bukhārā • Samarqand

SOGHDIA

USHRŪSANA

Araxes
Tiblisi •

ARRĀN

ARMENIA
Ardabīl •

JURJĀN

• Jurjān

Marw
• Tūs

Balkh •

BALKH

Hindu Kush Mountains

BADAKHSHĀN

Tarsus •

AL-AWASIM   AL-JAZĪRA

AZERBAIJAN

GĪLĀN

TABARISTĀN

KHURĀSĀN

• Bāmyān

• Antioch   Mosul •

Tigris

Euphrates

AL-JIBĀL

Rayy •

QŪHISTĀN

• Nīshāpūr

Cyprus

AL-SHĀM
• Damascus

Sāmarrā •

GHUR

Baghdad •

• Isfahān

SĪSTĀN

• PALESTINE

IRAQ

KHŪZISTĀN

Zaranj •

• Jerusalem

Kūfa •

Basra •

FĀRS

• Shīrāz

• Kirmān

BAHRAYN

Persian Gulf

• Sīrāf

KIRMĀN

Jīruft •

MAKRĀN

SIND

Nile

Red Sea

• Medina

HIJĀZ

NAJD

OMAN

Arabian
Sea

• Mecca

HADRAMAWT

YEMEN

Gulf of Aden

0   500   1000 km

0   500   1000 miles

The Lands of the Western Caliphates
from the 10th to the 12th Centuries

Tunis

CHAPTER 1

The First Caliphs

Adam was the first caliph. We know that because we are told so in the Qur'ān (2.28) where God says, in reference to Adam, 'I am placing a caliph on earth'. The Qur'ān refers to one other caliph by name (38.25) and that is when God tells the biblical King David, 'We have made you a caliph on earth.'

The office, or perhaps role would be more accurate, has scriptural authority and any ruler might be pleased to follow in succession to these two. But what does the word actually mean? The Arabic root *khalafa*, from which the Arabic term *khalīfa* (the origin of the English word caliph) comes, is well known, but like many Arabic words it has a variety of English equivalents. Basically it means to succeed or deputize for a person or, in this case, for Allah. It is used in ordinary administrative and secular contexts with these meanings. But, like many passages in the Qur'ān, its precise meaning here is difficult to determine. It clearly cannot mean successor, since God is eternal and therefore, by definition, cannot have a successor, so it must mean deputy or representative of God on earth. But how were Adam and King David chosen as caliphs when other much revered figures, Moses, Joseph and Jesus for example, were not? And what was their function supposed to be? The Holy Book is completely silent about this. All we can deduce from the Qur'anic references is that God did appoint caliphs on at least two occasions. It was therefore logical that He might appoint others as and when it seemed appropriate.

The term appears to have been used in the time of the Prophet Muhammad. When he left Medina on a military expedition or for any other reason, he would appoint a deputy (khalīfa) for the duration of his absence. We know the names of at least some of these and, curiously, most of them were obscure men who played no part in the later history of the institution and their powers were very limited. Only Uthmān, the third caliph, was among their number, and neither Abū Bakr nor Umar, the first two caliphs, were appointed. Nevertheless, it was perhaps because of this use of the term that the Muslims naturally adopted it at the moment of the Prophet's (permanent) absence.[1]

The beginnings of the office can be traced back to the swift-moving events which followed the Prophet's death in 632. According to the majority (Sunni) opinion, Muhammad had left no explicitly acknowledged successor, although he had asked his old friend and colleague Abū Bakr to lead the prayers in his final days, when he was too ill to do so in person. Muhammad had declared that he was the last of the Prophets, that great line of reformers and preachers which stretched back to Adam and who had all tried, with varying degrees of success, to bring mankind back to the worship of the one true God. After Muhammad, no one could claim the title of Prophet of God without proposing an existential challenge to Muhammad and his community.

Another possibility for succession was ruled out by family

considerations. Although Muhammad had had a number of wives and children, only one survived into adulthood, his daughter Fātima. There was therefore no question of direct hereditary succession in the male line, even if Muhammad and his community had wished that (and there is no evidence that they did).

What happened in the hours and days following Muhammad's death is not entirely clear, but the basic outlines seem to be generally accepted and the events had a profound and lasting influence on the whole later history of the caliphate. To understand them, and how they were remembered, it is necessary to look at the composition of the Muslim community as it existed in Medina at the time. Muhammad was not himself from Medina but was born and brought up in Mecca, some 200 miles to the south. Although tradition insists that his family was not rich, they were important socially as members of Quraysh, the powerful merchant tribe which dominated the city, and they had a prominent role in providing for the pilgrims who, from before the coming of Islam, came to pay their respects to the Ka'ba, the cube-shaped building at the centre of the city with the black stone inserted into one of its corners, which had been a place of devotion in pre-Islamic times and still forms the focus of the *hajj*, or Muslim pilgrimage. To be a member of Quraysh was to be part of a leading class which organized the political affairs of the town and the trading caravans which brought much wealth to the city in its barren and desolate environment. Within the Quraysh, Muhammad was a member of the extended family of the Banū Hāshim. This group included his uncle Abū Tālib, whose son Alī later became Muhammad's son-in-law when he married his daughter Fātima. It did not, however, include the rich and powerful Umayyad family, also from Quraysh, who dominated much of the trade and political life of the settlement.

When Muhammad's position in Mecca had become increasingly threatened because of hostile reactions to his preaching, especially from other groups in Quraysh like the Umayyads, he was saved by being invited to the city of Medina, then known as Yathrib, by a group of the inhabitants who wanted an outsider to come and try to judge and reconcile the feuds which had plagued the community. It was in these circumstances that he made his famous journey, his Hijra, to the city which was to be his home, and increasingly his power-base, for the rest of his life. He did not make the journey alone. He was joined by a number of members of Quraysh who were committed enough to follow him into exile. They included Abū Bakr, Umar, Uthmān and Alī. Together with their fellow exiles they were known as the *muhājirūn*, those who had made the Hijra with the Prophet. They came to form an elite within the nascent Muslim community and the epithet *muhājirūn*, with its connotations of selfless devotion to the Prophet, is one frequently used by jihadi groups today.

The newcomers settled in Medina alongside the existing inhabitants of the oasis, increasingly known as *ansār*, or helpers of the Prophet. Again, this is a title which has been accepted with honour by modern militant groups. In general the two groups shared the space and resources of the oasis city with remarkably little open friction, perhaps because of the Prophet's role as mediator. But the differences still existed, based ultimately on kinship, for the *ansār* of Medina were certainly not of Qurashi origin. There were perhaps social tensions too. The Quraysh were a widely respected group in Arabia, great merchants who organized caravans of camels to Syria and, less often, to Iraq and Yemen. They were men of the world with wide horizons, accustomed to leadership. The *ansār* were, by contrast, peasants who made their living from tilling the soil and harvesting dates and whose horizons were limited to their own small community. There can be no doubt that many of the Qurashi *muhājirūn* believed that power and authority naturally belonged to them.

When news spread through the town that Muhammad had died, both parties took action to secure their positions. The *ansār* gathered together under the portico of one of their houses, which was known as the Saqīfa (Portico) of the Banū Sā'ida, which was the name of the family who owned the house. Here some of them argued that, with Muhammad gone, his unique authority should be divided, and they should choose one leader while the *muhājirūn* should choose one of their own. At a crucial moment, a group of *muhājirūn* burst in on this meeting and demanded that everyone, *muhājirūn* and *ansār* alike, should swear allegiance to one of their number, the veteran Abū Bakr, an old man generally venerated by all for his wisdom and his close association with Muhammad. They all took an oath of loyalty to the new leader, an oath known in Arabic as a *bay'a* and symbolized by a stroking or laying on of hands.

There was one small group, however, who did not participate in this agreement. The immediate family of Muhammad was busy, as custom demanded, in washing the body prior to burial. Among them was of course his cousin and son-in-law Alī. He was excluded from the agreement, and though most sources insist that he later accepted it his followers, and perhaps Alī himself, saw this as a *coup d'état* which had essentially deprived him of his natural rights.

We can never know exactly what happened at the Saqīfa of the Banū Sa'ada, but it had momentous consequences for future leadership in the Muslim community in a way that none of those present can possibly have imagined. What had begun as an ad hoc response to a temporary crisis became a deciding point whose nature and import were hotly debated for the next fourteen centuries.

Two fundamental issues were at stake here. The first was that the principle was established that the leader of the community, let us call him caliph though the title itself may not have been decided at this early stage, was to be a member of Quraysh. Not everyone agreed, as we shall see when discussing the Kharijites, but most Muslims did and it remains a key doctrine shared by Sunnis and Shi'is alike. The other outcome was much more contentious: Alī and the Family of the Prophet more generally had been excluded from the process, denied any opportunity of claiming their rights to succession or expressing their opinions. Furthermore, the *ansār*, despite all their loyalty to the Prophet, a loyalty which had enabled him to establish his community in Medina and defended him against the onslaughts of the Quraysh of Mecca, were relegated to a second-class status. In the long history of the caliphate, no claimant has ever emerged to demand the title on the grounds of his descent from the *ansār*. It is impossible to understand the divisions within the Muslim community about the nature of caliphate without understanding what happened, or much more importantly, what was believed to have happened in the Saqīfa of the Banū Saʿada.

According to the later historical narrative, Abū Bakr was accepted by the Muslim community with the title of caliph and this has been the view generally held ever since. In fact, as we have seen, this is not certain and there is some suggestion that Umar was the first man to take the title.[2] Whatever the true position, the title was well recognized as that borne by the leader of the Muslim community within a decade of the Prophet's death.

But what did the early Muslims understand by it? None of the sources spell this out. No one at this early stage explained exactly what they had in mind in writing. Instead we have to deduce and infer from the evidence presented in the reports we find in later chronicles, records of public discussions, always polemical, letters and poetry. Of these, the poetry is in some ways the most valuable. This is because it probably adheres most closely to the usages of the time. While it is possible to edit both narratives and letters to reflect later language, it is hard to do so within the strict and formal metres of classical Arabic poetry without doing obvious violence to the text. Even so, most of the poetry on which we rely dates from the later Umayyad period rather than the very early years.

There was an important uncertainty in the use of the term caliph. *Khalīfa*, as has already been pointed out, can mean either deputy or successor: but which was it? And whom was the caliph deputy or successor of? Two views emerge in early Muslim debates on this issue. One is that it means the deputy of God – we often find the phrase 'deputy of God on his earth' (*khalīfat Allah fi ardihī*). There is no ambiguity here because, as we have seen, God cannot have a successor. Some people, however, disagreed, arguing that the full title was always, and should be, 'successor of the Messenger of God' (*khalīfat rasūl Allah*), which must mean successor of Muhammad. This difference mattered, and still does. If the caliph was deputy of God he had a quasi-divine status and authority which all Muslims should support and respect. If, on the other hand, he was simply the successor to Muhammad, that carried much less weight. He could not be a prophet, since Muhammad had been the last of those, so he must be an ordinary man who fulfilled some of the secular and administrative functions that the Messenger of God had performed in his lifetime.

Among both Muslims and western scholars the general assumption was that the real title was, and always had been, successor of the Prophet of God. In 1986, however, two scholars of the Islamic Middle East at Cambridge, Patricia Crone and Martin Hinds, published a short but very important book in which they convincingly demonstrated, from a whole variety of textual and numismatic evidence, that the title meant deputy of God from the beginning. The idea that it meant successor, they argue, was introduced by ninth-century *ulama* (religious scholars) as an attempt to downgrade the office in the great struggle between caliphs and scholars of that time to control the making of law and the establishment of Islamic norms.[3]

Caliph was not the only title used for the first leaders. From very early on we have references to the caliph as *Amīr al-Mu'minīn*, usually translated as Commander of the Faithful. *Amīr* (often emir in English) means commander or prince. It was a title often given to military leaders and local rulers in the years which followed the break-up of the Abbasid caliphate at the beginning of the tenth century and is still used as a royal title today in the Gulf States. The *Mu'minīn* element is more problematic: would it not have been much more logical and appropriate to use the word Muslims and describe the leader as *Amīr al-Muslimīn*? *Mu'minīn*, however, could be used to describe not just Muslims but also non-Muslims who had entered into a binding peace agreement with them. Unlike the word caliph, the title of Commander of the Faithful does not appear in the Qur'ān so we can find no guidance there, but the use of the term in later texts suggests that it was used very early on and dates from a time when the Muslims fought alongside non-Muslim allies. Whatever its origins and original implications, the title became inextricably linked to that of caliph: not just Umayyads and Abbasids but Fatimids and Almohads and many other rulers who claimed the caliphal title also described themselves as Commanders of the Faithful.

We also find the use of the title imam. Imam means essentially anyone who stands in front or leads. It often describes the prayer leader in a mosque. It is also used, especially among the Shi'a, to describe the ruler of the whole Muslim community and, as such, is often a synonym for caliph.

The Reigns of Abū Bakr and Umar, the First Caliphs

The first four caliphs, Abū Bakr (632–4), Umar b. al-Khattāb (634–44), Uthmān b. Affān (644–56) and Alī b. Abī Tālib (656–61), are described in the Arabic sources as *Rāshidūn*, usually translated into English as 'Orthodox'. This is a usage dating from the time when most Sunni Muslims could agree that these four were righteous and God-guided rulers, even if things had started to go wrong under their Umayyad and later successors. The term serves as a convenient and widely accepted way of designating the four unrelated and very different rulers.

The historical sources provide a huge variety of information about the four men because the events of these early years had significant and lasting consequences for the development of the Islamic community: crucially, they laid the basis of the division between Sunni and Shi'ite Muslims, which was to grow in the next four centuries. In the Sunni tradition, they emerge as very distinctive personalities: Abū Bakr the dignified and affable old man, Umar the organizer and stern moralist, Uthmān a good man fatally flawed by his predilection for his own family, and Alī a true ruler but vacillating and overwhelmed by events. These characteristics probably do reflect their real personalities, but they also serve to make points about the nature of caliphal government and later ages looked back to the first caliphs' reigns as examples of both good government and how things could go wrong. The Orthodox caliphs figure prominently in modern discussions about the caliphate.

All four had important issues to tackle. The first was to secure the continued existence of the Islamic community after the death of its founder and establish the position of its ruler. In the time of Umar, the most obvious priority was managing the great Arab conquests of the Middle East initiated under Abū Bakr and continued through Umar's reign. By the time of his death in 644, Muslims armies had conquered Syria, Iraq and Egypt, and in the first half of Uthmān's reign most of Iran and large swathes of North Africa had been added to the list. It was the caliphs, from their capital in the Prophet's city of Medina, who organized and dispatched the armies which brought down the great East Roman and Persian empires, though none of the caliphs led the Muslim armies in person.

Conquest did not mean that all the peoples of these areas became Muslim: it simply meant that they were forced to accept the political authority of the new Arab-Muslim ruling class. The conversion of the majority of populations to Islam was a much slower and more peaceful process, which probably took four or five centuries. It was a great achievement, which completely reshaped the ancient world and whose consequences are still very much with us today. Organizing the armies was, in a sense, the easy bit. More problematic was the administration of these rich and varied areas once they had come under Arab-Muslim control. And the most complex task was managing the Muslim elite and trying to keep the fierce rivalries which developed from splitting the Muslim world apart.

As soon as he became leader in 632, Abū Bakr was confronted with a major challenge. In the last two years of his life, the Prophet had attracted followers from all over the Arabian Peninsula. They came in delegations to pledge allegiance to him as the Messenger of God and as leader of an increasingly powerful tribal federation with whom it was important to keep on good terms. They often agreed to pay an alms tax (*sadaqa* or *zakat*). With the Prophet's death many of them repudiated the agreements made, arguing that they had pledged allegiance to Muhammad in person, not to his successors or the community in Medina. Others said that they wanted to continue to be Muslims but not to pay the tax. Yet others chose prophets of their own, like Musaylima in eastern Arabia, arguing that if Quraysh had a prophet, then it was only fair that they should have one too. In the Muslim tradition this movement was known as the *ridda*, or rejection.

Such a moment could have seen the break-up of the *umma* and a return to the fragmentation and anarchy which had characterized Arabia before the coming of Islam. However, Abū Bakr, ably supported by Umar, decided that this was not to be and initiated a series of military campaigns, often led by Khālid b. al-Walīd, a member of the old aristocracy of Quraysh and later venerated in history and legend as the 'Sword of Islam'. The campaigns were pursued without mercy and were swiftly successful. By the end of Abū Bakr's short reign in 634, the tribes of Arabia were effectively brought back under the control of Medina. In doing so, Abū Bakr and Umar had established a new principle: there was no going back on acceptance of Islam. The rejectionist, or apostate (Arabic *murtadd*), could and should be killed by any righteous Muslim. The *ridda* also led to the emergence of a new class of Muslims. If the *muhājirūn* and Quraysh more generally were the elite of the community, with the *ansār* in a subordinate but still important position, the rejectionists who had been brought back to the community in the wars were third-class citizens. This became significant later with the division of assets and spoils which followed the great Arab conquests.

Abū Bakr died peacefully in his old age. In his two-year reign he had accomplished a great deal. There is no explicit evidence that he ever held the title of caliph, but early Muslims certainly believed he had and his achievements and reputation meant that the office became established among them. He also acquired among writers and poets of the Umayyad period and later the informal title of Siddīq, the Truthful or Trustworthy, reflecting the respect in which his memory was held by most Muslims.

The great Arab conquests were essentially a continuation of the wars against the rejectionists. This is not the place to rehearse the details of the various campaigns and battles, but a few aspects should be noted. Initially, from around 634, there were two main fronts, Syria and Iraq. Syria had been the object of the first tentative expeditions at the end of the Prophet's life. This was pursued after his death and the conquest of Syria was achieved by comparatively small numbers of members of the Muslim elite and tribes from the Hijaz in western Arabia, sometimes in alliance with other tribes already established in Syria, some of whom were, and continued to be, Christians. It was they who defeated the Byzantine armies at the Battle of Yarmuk in 636 and brought to an end 1,000 years of rule by Greek-speaking elites in Syria and Palestine. In contrast, Iraq was conquered in the main by larger numbers of tribesmen from northern and eastern Arabia and as far south as Oman. The leadership of the campaigns was mostly entrusted to members of Quraysh such as Saʿd b. Abī Waqqās, who commanded the army which defeated the Persians at the decisive Battle of Qādisiyya, also in 636, and drove them out of Iraq. But most of the rank and file of the army came from non-elite groups and, in some cases, from those who had originally joined the rejectionists. This was to lead to continuous and sustained conflict between Iraqi and Syrian Arab Muslims, a conflict which ultimately led to the end of the Orthodox caliphate.

Another significant aspect of these conquests is that they were organized military expeditions. They were not a mass migration of barbarian tribesmen into a rich and civilized Middle East but armies recruited from volunteers who came to Medina and were assigned to various commanders and sent off in different directions. The overall management of this enterprise fell to the caliphs, above all Umar, who in the ten years of his rule masterminded the most important military operations.

The expeditions of conquest succeeded on a scale which must have been beyond the expectations of even the most optimistic of the early Muslims. In a few short years they had come to control large areas of territory and a numerous population in towns and villages, hamlets and farms, a desirable but unfamiliar resource base. How then were these lands to be administered and how were Muslims to be justly rewarded for their part in the victorious campaigns? At first, especially in Iraq, there was something of a free-for-all as individual commanders tried to seize estates and lands themselves. Umar, however soon put a stop to this and it is a measure of the authority and prestige already enjoyed by the caliph that he was able to do so.

Instead, he instituted a system in Iraq in which the conquered lands and the revenues which could be collected from them were kept as an undivided resource (*fay* is the Arabic word), the proceeds of which should be used to support the Arab tribesmen. These were not to be allowed to spread out throughout the conquered territory but were settled in specially founded new towns (Ar. *misr*, pl. *amsār*). The first of them were Kufa in central Iraq, south of modern Baghdad, and Basra at the head of the Gulf. They were followed by Fustat (Old Cairo) and Qayrawan in Tunisia, Mosul in northern Iraq and Shiraz in south-western Iran. Their names and the payments to which they were entitled were written in lists called *dīwāns*. None of these have survived in their original form, but their existence shows that firm government control had been established over the movements and settlements of the Arabs.

The new arrangements instituted by Umar had a profound and lasting effect on Muslim society. Much of this was positive. The presence of large numbers of soldiers, dependent on salaries paid by the government, was a major factor in the emergence of that vibrant market economy characteristic of the early Islamic world. It also meant that the government had to use coins and maintain a bureaucracy which was both literate and numerate. This in turn led to the development of a class educated in Arabic with the opportunity and knowledge to invest in writing and other intellectual activities.

At the same time, however, the arrangements gave rise to continuous conflicts over the distribution of resources. These arose at different levels. Within communities, they developed between early converts to Islam, who enjoyed precedence (*sābiqa*) and hence higher salaries, and later joiners and former rejectionists, who were on very low levels of reward. Then there were conflicts between those who believed that all the money raised in a province, say Kufa for example, should be spent in that province and those who argued that the surplus after paying salaries should be forwarded to the government of the caliph in Medina or, under the Umayyads, Damascus. The fact that the system had been inaugurated by the caliph Umar, as was later confirmed by Alī, gave it a quasi-religious authority. Those who believed that they had a right to all the tax revenues of the province, which should be distributed in the ways laid down by Umar, saw this not just as their earthly rights (*dunya*) but as part and parcel of their religious faith (*dīn*), and when the Umayyads tried to change the arrangements in the interests of more efficient government they were seen not only as mean and grasping but as impious and anti-Islamic.

Another lasting legacy for which the caliph is remembered is the so-called 'pact of Umar'. This is not so much a written document drawn up and signed by the caliph as a series of rules and guidelines which emerged concerning the status of his non-Muslim subjects, Jews, Christians, Zoroastrians and others. The basic outline of these agreements was that non-Muslims would be able to retain their faith, their worship and their places of worship, along with their personal property and their family possessions. There were, however, restrictions whose exact nature varied from one version of the pact to another. These mostly involved the prohibition of the building of new churches (and sometimes the repair of the old), of public religious processions, of expressing criticism of Islam and of bearing weapons. At times non-Muslims were also obliged to wear distinctive dress and forbidden to ride horses. Most importantly, the pact imposed the payment of a poll tax (*jizya*). Non-Muslims were referred to as protected peoples (*dhimmi*) and their security and freedom of worship were assured. At the same time they were definitely second-class citizens. Members of the minority communities were particularly keen to ascribe the arrangements to Umar because they were in a sense guaranteed by the authority and pious reputation of the great caliph.

Umar died in 644 at the hands of an assassin, a Persian slave, who killed him for personal reasons. In many ways he can be seen as the founding father of the caliphate. Although, as with Abū Bakr, there is no direct contemporary evidence that he bore the title, Arabic sources are virtually unanimous in saying that he did. He was certainly a well-known figure. When an Arab wanted to date a graffito bearing his name carved on a rock in western Arabia, he said simply that it was the year when Umar died, as if he were a personality who could be referred to without formality or explanation.[4] Umar's reputation survives in the Sunni Islamic tradition as the great law-giver, incorruptible and stern, quick to condemn extravagance or pretension among his governors and generals. His memory survives in anecdotes of his own rejection of the pomp and circumstance of rulership, describing how he slept in the corner of a mosque wrapped in his cloak, approachable to all. We also hear how Persians came as envoys or prisoners and, accustomed as they were to the formality and ostentatious display of the Persian court, were amazed, even incredulous, at the simplicity of his dress and style of living. These stories must reflect a historical reality, the personality of the real Umar, but they were also preserved and no doubt elaborated as a paradigm of Islamic monarchy and a clear rebuke to the extravagance and grandeur of later rulers.

Umar is admired not just in the Muslim tradition but in completely different cultures. Edward Gibbon, in eighteenth-century Britain, writes of him:

The abstinence and humility of Omar were not inferior to the virtues of Abubeker [Abū Bakr]: his food consisted of barley-bread or dates; his drink was water; he preached in a gown that was torn or tattered in twelve places; and a Persian satrap, who paid his homage as to the conqueror, found him asleep among the beggars on the steps of the mosch of Medina. Oeconomy is the source of liberality, and the increase of the revenue enabled Omar to establish a just and perpetual reward for the past and present services of the faithful. Careless of his own emolument, he assigned to Abbas, the uncle of the prophet, the first and most ample allowance of twenty-five thousand drachms or pieces of silver. Five thousand were allotted to each of the aged warriors, the relics of the field of Beder [Battle of Badr, 624, the first of Muhammad's military victories], and the last and the meanest of the companions of Mahomet was distinguished by the annual reward of three thousand pieces . . . Under his reign, and that of his predecessor, the conquerors of the East were the trusty servants of God and the people; the mass of public treasure was consecrated to the expenses of peace and war; a prudent mixture of justice and bounty maintained the discipline of the Saracens, and they united, by a rare felicity, the dispatch and execution of despotism, with the equal and frugal maxims of a republican government.[5]

Gibbon's perspective, steeped as he was in the writings of classical historians, may ring strangely in our ears and the reference to republican government is improbable, but it is striking how the views of an Enlightenment savant mirror, in his own language, the views of Muslims through the ages.

There was yet another side to this image, a more religious, even messianic aspect, which is difficult to understand after all these centuries. Like Abū Bakr before him and Uthmān after, Umar decided to spend his reign in the Hijaz, almost always in the Prophet's city of Medina. He did, however, make one exception. The city of Jerusalem played an import- ant part in early Islamic lore. It is said that the first Muslims prayed in this holy city before Muhammad changed the dir- ection of Muslim prayer, the *qibla*, to Mecca. It was from Jerusalem, not Mecca, that the Prophet is said to have begun his miraculous journey through the heavens in order to be shown the full glory of God's creation, from the site on the Temple Mount later covered by the Dome of the Rock. When in 638 it was apparent that the Muslim forces, having con- quered Damascus and most of the rest of Syria and Palestine (only the coastal city of Caesarea still held out against them), were on the verge of taking Jerusalem, then a city under Byzantine rule, Umar set out for the north. When he reached Jerusalem he accepted the surrender of the city from the venerable Christian Patriarch Sophronius.

A version of the treaty he made at this time still survives in the Arabic texts, allowing the *Rūm* (Romans, that is, Byzantines) to leave peacefully with their possessions and guaranteeing the population who remained their *dhimmi* status. He prayed on the Temple Mount, the site of the old Jewish temple. This seems to have been covered with ruins at the time and Umar ordered it to be cleared and cleaned. According to an ancient Jewish tradition, he also allowed Jews, who had been rigorously excluded from the city by the Byzantines, to return. He refused, however, to accept the invitation of the Patriarch to pray in the Church of the Holy Sepulchre, arguing that if he did, the Muslims would take possession of it and make it into a mosque. Instead he prayed outside at a site which is now marked by the much later mosque still called the Mosque of Umar. Much of this, perhaps legendary, detail survives in Arabic Christian narratives, which stress that the greatest caliph of them all had accepted the holiness of the church and the rights of the Christians.

It was probably as a result of this expedition that Umar acquired the title of Fārūq, by which he was sometimes known. This is an Aramaic, not an Arabic term, which means the Redeemer. Exactly what the early Muslims understood by Redeemer is not clear, but it has been suggested that it was part of an eschatological discourse which saw the Muslim conquest of Jerusalem as marking the end of days and the beginning of the Last Judgement. The exact significance of the word is lost beyond recovery, and the Muslim tradition does not discuss it in any detail, but it is evidence that the caliph had made a deep impression on Muslim and non-Muslim alike.

Uthmān and the First Crisis of the Caliphate

As Umar lay dying, he turned his attention to the arrangements for the choosing of his successor. The choices of Abū Bakr and Umar himself had been, to say the least, informal. Essentially Abū Bakr had been chosen by Umar and others of the *muhājirūn* while Umar in turn seems to have been nominated by Abū Bakr. There were no precedents here to which the community could turn. Umar, however, determined that there should be a *shūra*, an advisory council, which should select the next leader. He nominated six men: all of them were from Quraysh. The *ansār* of Medina and the rest of the Muslims were excluded, but Alī, who had not been able to participate in the choice of Abū Bakr, was among their number. After some deliberation the *shūra* settled on the old and distinguished merchant Uthmān, a Qurashi, of course, and one of Muhammad's first followers. He was duly offered allegiance by the leaders of the Muslim community.

The establishment of the *shūra* as a way of choosing the caliphs has had profound resonances in Muslim political thought ever since. Here was a system which seemed to offer legitimacy to what had previously been an ad hoc process. At the same time, the concept was very flexible and could be subject to a wide range of interpretations. The root Arabic *shawara*, from which the word *shūra* derives, is not about election in the sense of democratic choice but about advice and consultation. The *shūra* which chose Uthmān was the only open and properly constituted body in the history of the caliphate. The idea, however, remained alive and a source of inspiration to many through the ages who felt that some element of community engagement would give legitimacy to a process which often seemed obscure and arbitrary. The term was also used as a legitimizing discourse for processes of choice which were very far from open. After all, there was no law to lay down how many people should make up a *shūra*, that they should be in any sense representative of the wider Muslim community or that they should meet in open deliberation. It could be argued that a *shūra* of one, meeting in haste and secret, was, following the model laid down by Umar, a valid and acceptable way of choosing a new leader. The whole idea of *shūra* was, in turn, complete anathema to the Shi'a, for whom choosing the leader of the Muslims was usurping a function properly belonging to God alone.

Uthmān has a very varied reputation among Muslim historians and commentators. The events of his reign are not generally disputed. The traditional narrative says that he enjoyed six successful years, but at the end of these he dropped the Prophet's signet ring down a well and this meant the end of both his good fortune and his good governance. This period also saw the expansion of Muslim armies into Iran and the death of the last Sasanian shah, Yazdgard III, in 651. After that, military expansion largely came to a halt (though it was to resume again in the early eighth century) and the revenue from booty must have dried up. It was at this time too that resentment against Uthmān's rule began to grow among groups who felt that the elite in the community were becoming too rich and arrogant. This culminated in 656 when there were active revolts in both Iraq and Egypt. Armed groups set out from both these areas for Medina to make their demands forcefully. Arriving at the capital, they found the old man effectively defenceless, having been abandoned by all the leading members of the Muslim elite, including, crucially, Alī. He was murdered as he sat alone in his house reading the Qur'ān and his blood dripped on the open pages of the Holy Book.

The murder of Uthmān was a major trauma for the early Islamic community and continues to reverberate down to the twenty-first century. We can see the events which led to his assassination in strictly historical terms. Uthmān was trying to manage a huge and recently created empire. The conquests had stalled and resources were under pressure and many of the Muslims felt excluded and impoverished while they observed others living in the lap of luxury. Most conspicuous of these were the group of Qurashis who surrounded the caliph, many of them young men with no experience of the hard struggles of the early days of Islam. It was said, bitterly, that the rich lands of Iraq had become the 'Garden of Quraysh'. Uthmān, of course, would have seen it differently. Faced with the task of administering a vast and increasingly chaotic caliphate, he turned to the people he could most rely on, his family and kinsmen from Quraysh and the Umayyad clan.

The murder gave rise to an anguished debate. It was

deeply shocking. The caliph chosen by the community, a man who had known and supported the Prophet of God from the beginnings of his ministry and who put his ample resources in the service of Islam, a man whose piety and conduct could hardly be impugned, had been killed by his fellow Muslims. What had gone wrong?

The answer depended on your point of view. For the supporters of Uthmān, who belonged to what comes in later centuries to be the Sunni tradition, the rights and wrongs were crystal clear: the caliph of God had been murdered by people who claimed to be Muslims. It was a crime against God and man alike. Even if Uthmān had not been the most perfect ruler, perhaps not up to the standards of Abū Bakr and Umar before him, Muslims had no right to rebel against him, still less to take his life. His blood should be avenged and his murderers punished.

Other people were not so sure. Supposing Uthmān had not behaved like God's caliph but rather as a tyrannical pharaoh seizing the wealth that rightly belonged to pious and humble Muslims and giving it to his friends and family, how should pious Muslims respond? There were two approaches here. One could simply accept that things were problematic but agree too that Muslims should not rebel against a properly constituted authority. It was not always easy to determine God's will and perhaps Uthmān was, for all his sins, serving God's purpose and it was up to God to remove him or punish him if He saw proper. Yet others were clear that Uthmān was not fit to rule the community. He was so bad and had strayed so far from the ways of piety and justice that he could longer be considered an appropriate imam for Muslims:

it was the duty of pious and God-fearing men to remove and punish him and, hopefully, replace him with someone who could lead the community in the correct fashion.

The discussion of tyrannicide is as lively a theme in Islam as it is in western political thought. There is a widespread belief that the killing of a leader, however bad or inadequate he is seen to be, is always wrong, for it will lead to something worse, to *fitna*, that violence, division and destruction which imperils the lives of Muslims and makes the proper performance of true religion impossible.

Then there was the issue of the Qur'ān. The Muslim tradition describes how the Qur'ān was revealed by the Angel Gabriel to Muhammad, who in turn passed it on by word of mouth, for he himself was illiterate, to the Muslims. As it was revealed, it was written down on any materials which lay to hand: papyrus, leather, palm-leaves and even the flat shoulder bones of sheep. It was Uthmān who decided to edit and arrange this material into a book, the book we now know as the Qur'ān. It seems that versions were already in circulation, but the caliph ordered that they should all be destroyed in favour of his authorized version. Not everyone was happy with this. Some objected to the destruction of other versions that might have preserved elements of divine revelation which were now lost. Others objected that the caliph was exceeding his power and had no authority to do this. Yet others argued that only the members of the Family of the Prophet, with their unique understanding of the divine will and purpose, were able to undertake this successfully. History has been kind to Uthmān's edition of the Holy Book. It is generally accepted by Sunnis and, with some reservations, by

Shi'is as the authentic record of the revelation, but at the time it seems to have provoked an opposition which fed into the general dissatisfaction with Uthmān's rule.

It was symbolic, then, that he was killed reading the Holy Book. The Qur'ān of Uthmān became a sacred object, sealed with the martyred caliph's blood, the nearest thing the Islamic tradition would allow as a legitimizing relic. The Abbasid caliphs would later display the 'Qur'ān of Uthmān' on ceremonial occasions. We hear of 'Qur'āns of Uthmān' that were used by the Umayyads of Córdoba and later by their Almohad successors, there are such Qur'āns in libraries in Cairo and in the collections of the Ottoman sultans (and caliphs) in the Topkapi palace in Istanbul. A magnificent and undoubtedly very ancient one can still be seen, copiously spattered with what are alleged to be drops of caliphal blood, displayed with all due pomp in Tashkent, where it serves the present rulers of Uzbekistan as evidence of their real or feigned piety and commitment to Islam.

Alī and the End of the Orthodox Caliphate

The murder of Uthmān unleashed a complex series of events which revealed the many and varied views of what the caliphate should be and how the new caliph should be chosen. At first, authority passed to Alī. He and many others may have thought that his time had come, but there seems to have been no formal arrangement for the succession, and certainly no *shūra*. This lack of a clear mandate was one of the factors which undermined his rule from the beginning.

The first challenge came from within the elite of Quraysh. Alī was, of course, himself a member of the tribe, but he had been slow to accept Abū Bakr. He also had a considerable following among the *ansār* and perhaps his political loyalties were to them. He had converted to Islam early and had been close to the Prophet, but he was not the only one. Although it was a quarter of a century since Muhammad's death, there were other men who felt that their status within the tribe and early commitment to Islam entitled them to a leading role in the community. Among them was Zubayr b. al-Awwām. A prominent Qurashi, he had been one of a small group of Muslims who had emigrated to Ethiopia to escape the persecution that Muhammad and his followers had endured in Mecca before the Hijra to Medina in 622. He had returned and joined the Muslim community in Medina and had been one of the six prominent Muslims who had been chosen by Umar to make up the *shūra* which chose Uthmān. He and a companion of his from a very similar background, Talha b. Ubayd Allah, objected to the appointment of Alī and decided to challenge it. They were joined by a third person, the Prophet's wife Aisha, who some said was his favourite wife. Aisha was probably motivated by a long-standing personal antipathy to Alī, but she was also the daughter of Abū Bakr; she knew Zubayr and Talha well and would naturally be attracted to the Qurashi cause.

Alī faced a much bigger challenge to his credibility as caliph: his role, or rather his lack of role, in Uthmān's murder. There is no evidence that he had participated in the old man's death, or even that he had encouraged the attackers, but, on the other hand, he does not seem to have offered him any protection or support at a time of need despite being in Medina and having a substantial following among the inhabitants. Uthmān was dead, but his large and powerful family, the Umayyads, demanded, as was their right, that the murderers of their kinsman should be punished. Many of the Umayyads left Medina and took refuge with one of their number, Mu'āwiya b. Abī Sufyān. Mu'āwiya, like many of his family, seems to have been a fairly late convert to Islam but he had served as one of the Prophet's secretaries so had known him well. He had taken part in the conquest of Syria and when the country was conquered he had been appointed as governor. He had made Syria his powerbase, marrying into one of the most important local tribes, the Banū Kalb of the Palmyrene desert. He had come to represent the Syrian interest and command the loyalties of Syrians, both Muslims and others, like the chiefs of Kalb, who remained Christians. No other figure in the community could attract this degree of military and financial support. If Alī failed to avenge his murdered kinsman he would prove himself incapable of being a true caliph and until he fulfilled his duty Mu'āwiya would refuse to take the oath of allegiance.

The first military challenge to Alī's rule began almost immediately. Zubayr, along with Aisha and Talha, left Medina, whose inhabitants mostly supported Alī, and went to the Muslim new town of Basra in southern Iraq where they hoped to attract the support of members of the tribe of Thaqīf, old allies of Quraysh from pre-Islamic times, who had settled there. Alī, in turn, realized that he would have to find allies outside the capital and travelled to Iraq to appeal to the Muslims of Kufa. The connection between Alī and the Kufans may have begun because of his support of Kufan grievances against the rule of Uthmān. He certainly had many followers at this juncture and the connection between the Family of the Prophet, Alī and his descendants with the inhabitants of this large and turbulent Iraqi city was to be a continuing feature of the political landscape of the Muslim community for the next two centuries and of fundamental importance in the early development of Shi'ism.

The armies of Zubayr and Alī met in December 656 near Basra in a confrontation known to history as the Battle of the Camel. Zubayr and his allies do not seem to have attracted as much support as they had hoped and his army was defeated by the more numerous troops of Alī. Zubayr and Talha were both killed and Aisha, who had played a conspicuous part in directing the battle from the howdah on her camel, was forced to retire to the Hijaz where she passed her final days in political obscurity.

The Battle of the Camel had settled the immediate challenge to Alī's caliphate. It also meant that the idea of a Quraysh-dominated caliphate based in the Hijaz had been defeated for a generation, though it was to be revived with renewed vigour by Zubayr's son after the death of Mu'āwiya in 680. The Battle of the Camel was also the first open civil war within the Muslim community. The issue of the caliphate had been decided not by discussion in a *shūra* or designation by a previous ruler, but by hard military power and by the ability of one party to attract more military support than another. It set a pattern for much of the future development of the office.

It also marked an important change in another way.

Medina had been the residence of the Prophet and under Abū
Bakr and Umar was, in a real sense, the capital of the caliphate. Umar made his visit to Palestine to accept the surrender
of Jerusalem but he directed operations in the great wars of
conquest from Medina and Uthmān continued to use it as
the seat of government and it was here that he died. But
Medina was isolated in western Arabia and, as the population
grew, it became increasingly dependent on food supplies
imported from Egypt and elsewhere. There were now many
more Muslims living in Iraq and Syria than in Medina and no
one could hope to establish himself as caliph without their
support. When Alī had defeated Zubayr, he did not return to
Medina but stayed to base himself in Kufa as the centre of his
government. The dream of establishing a caliphate based in
the city of the Prophet lingered on, but when Muhammad the
Pure Soul, himself a direct descendant of Muhammad, tried
to make it a reality in the early Abbasid period in 762, it was
clear that the dream was just that, and not the basis for a
revived and renewed caliphate.

Zubayr was dead, his party defeated, but Mu'āwiya posed
a much bigger challenge to Alī's authority. Whatever his long-
term ambitions, he made no effort at this stage to claim the
caliphate. He simply demanded that Alī, if he wanted to
be caliph, should punish his kinsman's murderers. He must
have known that he was making an impossible demand, for
those who attacked Uthmān, and their relatives and friends
in Kufa, were the very people on whom Alī had now come to
depend for establishing his power. Kufa was not an easy town
to govern and had a wild, lawless atmosphere. The new town
boasted a mosque at its centre and the main *sūq*s surrounded

it, but it was mainly a network of dusty streets and mud-brick or wooden houses, often makeshift affairs erected by newcomers from the Arabian desert and non-Arabs from the conquered areas of Iraq and Iran who wanted to throw in their lots with the Muslims and benefit from some of the privileges and opportunities which they enjoyed. It was a city riven with social tensions.

At the top of the social pyramid were the leaders of the most powerful tribes in the city, men like Ash'ath b. Qays al-Kindī, who enjoyed both wealth and social respect because of their family background. But many of these, like Ash'ath himself, had joined the Muslim cause late. This group were known as *sharīf* (pl. *ashrāf*), or nobles. They had hardly known the Prophet, if indeed they had met him at all, and some of them had joined the *ridda* against the rule of Abū Bakr. Pitted against them, and also claiming leadership and power, were those who had joined the Islamic cause early and who had borne the brunt of the heat and dust of the early battles against the Persians. These were men like Mālik al-Ashtar, who had been one of the leaders of the anti-Uthmān movement in Iraq and who now became one of Alī's closest advisers. They were often from modest social backgrounds in the pre-Islamic tribal scheme of things, but they had *sābiqa*, precedence in Islam. Under the system set up by Umar, they had been awarded the highest ranks of payment and pensions, assets they were determined to preserve. There was plenty of reason for antagonism between these two elite groups.

Below them in the social scale were a host of ordinary tribesmen with no particular claim to elite status on either ground. These included men who, although they were now Muslims, had joined the cause late or who had failed to play a significant role in the armies of the conquests. Despite their membership of the community, their rewards were small and they had every reason to feel excluded from the benefits others enjoyed. This resentment was real among the first generation but must have become even more strongly felt in the generations which followed, when the elite enjoyed their high status not because of what they themselves had done but because of what their fathers and grandfathers before them had achieved.

At the bottom of the heap were the non-Arab converts to Islam. Many of these were Iranians of some social standing whose lives had been turned upside down by war and conquest and, in many cases, capture and slavery as well. In order to become Muslims, they attached themselves to an Arab-Muslim tribe or prominent individual and became their *mawālī* (sing. *mawlā*). This is a word which has no exact English translation. It can mean that they became clients of the tribe, accepting its leadership and supporting its political activities. It can also refer to freedmen, people who had been slaves but had been freed by their masters and converted to Islam. (To add to the confusion the term *mawlā* is used in later Arabic to mean lord or master but it is the earlier sense with which we are concerned here.) These *mawālī* felt that they too were Muslims equal to any others and entitled to their tax advantages, especially not paying the *jizya* or poll tax, a privilege which was the right of all Muslims.

It was a heady brew of rivalries and conflicts, fuelled by strong feelings of injustice. Islam promised so much in terms of equality in religion and membership of the community. It was easy to feel resentful and angry at the failure of the new order to deliver. The fundamental problem was one of resources. Iraq was the richest area of the Middle East and the revenues the Islamic government could extract were huge, but they were never enough to satisfy the demands of all these various constituencies. Inevitably there would be winners and losers; the question was whom they would be.

Alī set about trying to mobilize the military energies of these people to enforce his caliphal authority over the recalcitrant Mu'āwiya in Syria. It was not easy to persuade men of such different backgrounds and outlooks as the tribal aristocrat Ash'ath b. Qays and the pious early Muslim Mālik al-Ashtar to march in the same army and accept his leadership. He did, however, have two planks to his platform which won over many. The first was the hostility of Iraqi Muslims towards the Syrians and their fear that Syrian domination would lead to their exclusion from positions of power. Modern discussions of the conflict which developed between the supporters of Alī and Mu'āwiya have tended to concentrate on the religio-political issues which divided them from each other, proto-Sunnis supporting Mu'āwiya and proto-Shi'is supporting Alī. The early Arabic sources which describe these events lay just as much stress on the regional nature of the conflict: it was the *ahl* (people) of Iraq against the people of Syria. Of course, this did not mean all the people of Iraq and all the people of Syria, but the Arab Muslims of Iraq and the Arab Muslims of Syria with, perhaps, some of their *mawālī*. The rest, the Christian, Jews and Zoroastrians who formed the majority of the population, were neither consulted nor asked to participate in what was an inter-Muslim conflict.

Most of the people of Iraq could relate to this appeal, but Alī and his advisers tried to attract more support, and perhaps more committed support, in ways which were ultimately more divisive of Iraqi opinion. Alī's policy was a bold attempt to cut across the social divisions which so disturbed the Muslims of Iraq in general and Kufa in particular. He stressed the role of the caliph as imam, that is, religious leader of the community. As caliph, he was not to be a tyrannical tax-gatherer or a guardian of existing vested interests but a charismatic figure who would inspire and guide the believers in the formation of a truly Islamic community and bring justice to all Muslims. It was a powerful vision which staked new ground for the function and importance of the caliphate.

Alī's policies at this moment were, no doubt, a combination of idealism and practical considerations – he needed to recruit for his army – but they had enormous long-term implications. The first was that Alī, the Family of the Prophet, and after them the Shi'ite leaderships of later years, were firmly identified with Iraqi interests and particularly the interests of the Muslim inhabitants of the southern Iraqi towns of Kufa and Basra, areas in fact which are still Shi'ite today, 1,200 years later. The second, and even more important, implication was that the Family of the Prophet and later Shi'ite leaders became firmly identified with the interests of the deprived and excluded in Muslim society, those who felt that their rights had been ignored and trampled on by dominant elites. Of course, this has not always been the case.

There were times, for example in Fatimid Egypt in the eleventh century, when the Shi'ite leadership was firmly in support of the Shi'ite caliph. But this theme of concern for the poor and marginalized in Muslim society is a thread which has runs through much Shi'ite preaching from the proto-Shi'is of late seventh-century Iraq to Ayatollah Khomeini in late twentieth-century Iran and Ayatollah Sistani in Iraq even as I write these words.

In the spring and summer of 657 Alī led his Iraqi forces up the Euphrates valley to invade Syria. At the same time Mu'āwiya mobilized his Syrian supporters and came to meet them. The two armies faced each other at a place called Siffin, just up the river from Raqqa. They did not immediately engage in an all-out battle. Despite all the issues which divided them, there was a profound reluctance among many to fight their fellow Muslims if it could be avoided. There were a number of bloody skirmishes, notably over access to water in the burning heat of the Syrian summer, and there were contests of poetry as the propagandists on both sides tried to inspire their fellows and denigrate their enemies, but there were also negotiations. In July or August a real battle seemed to be developing, but the Syrian troops attached copies of the Qur'ān to their lances, demanding that there be an arbitration according to the book of God, and Alī felt that he had no option but to accept. An arbitration date was set for the next year and it was agreed that the two arbitrators, one from each side, should meet in the small town of Udhruh, now a ruined archaeological site in southern Jordan. So far so clear.

What was much less clear was the question of what exactly was going to be arbitrated. Was it a debate about whether Alī or Muʿāwiya was going to be caliph, a sort of two-man *shūra*, or was the issue simply that of the punishment of Uthmān's killers and the circumstances under which Muʿāwiya might accept Alī as caliph? By the time the two arbitrators did meet, events had moved on so quickly that any discussions they may have had were rendered irrelevant.

The Kharijite Alternative

Many of Alī's supporters were dismayed by what had happened, seeing their leader as a victim of a Syrian trick or, even worse, as having agreed to put his God-given authority to the judgement of two men. When he returned to Iraq, his uneasy coalition began to break up. Some of the tribal nobles began to enter into negotiations with the Syrian leader. Much more threatening than that, at the other end of the political spectrum, many of his more radical supporters abandoned him and went out to camp in a separate place, announcing that arbitration belonged only to God and implying that the issue should have been decided on the battlefield.

These dissenters became known as Kharijites (Ar. *khawārij*). They have survived as a sect down to the present day, notably in Oman and parts of southern Algeria. How the name originates is quite unclear. The word *khārijī* means literally one who goes out, but the often quoted explanation that they went out from Alī's camp seems feeble. More attractive is the historian Andrew Marsham's suggestion that it related to the verses in the Qurʾān which urge Muslims to 'go out' (on the *jihād*) rather than stay at home.[6] Kharijites were associating with the militant activists among the earliest Muslims. They have never constituted more than a small percentage of the Muslim population. but they are important in the history of the caliphate because they developed theories of the office, how the caliph or imam (they used both terms to describe their leaders) should be chosen and what they should do, which were radically different from the concepts of both Sunni and Shi'i.

The Kharijites split from the emerging consensus over two main issues. The first was that they believed the caliph should be chosen from all the Muslims as the most pious and meritorious of them. Quraysh descent was absolutely not required and any Muslim, no matter how humble his social origins, could be considered for office. Some said that even a slave could be chosen, and it is alleged that a few even argued that women were eligible, though this point of view never seems to have been widely accepted. They generally agreed that Abū Bakr and Umar were lawful caliphs, but only because they were the best men of their time, not because of any Qurashi descent, and they completely rejected Uthmān and all subsequent claimants. When others had their doubts, the Kharijites were proudly unrepentant of the role some of them played in the murder of Uthmān, seeing it as entirely justified, even necessary, because of his deviation from proper Islamic behaviour. Quite how the choosing of the new leader was going to take place was not really specified: certainly there was no discussion of the practicalities of either election or *shūra*. It was sort of taken for granted that the most meritorious would emerge and be accepted by the community. If the caliph they chose went astray or proved to be corrupt and tyrannical then he should be corrected, first by being warned that his conduct was unacceptable and, if this failed, by being deposed or killed. Patricia Crone shows how this could be pushed to its logical conclusion and beyond:

> When Najda b. Āmir, founder of the Najdiya group of Kharijites, did various things of which his followers disapproved they demanded that he repent, which he did. But then a group of them regretted having asked him to repent and told him: 'We were wrong to ask you to repent for you are an imam. We have repented of it so now you should repent of your repentance and demand that those who asked you to repent should repent of having done so. If you don't, we will separate from you.' So he went out and announced to the people that he repented of his repentance. His followers then began to quarrel among themselves.[7]

So there you have it: the caliph/imam being held to account in a lively exchange of views but nonetheless respected for his position. In one sense it was a conditional and contractual vision of monarchy, rare in Islamic political thought, though the rules and mechanisms by which conditionality might be put into practice are left unclear and the issue was not whether the caliph/imam did what was beneficial for the community but whether he was acting in agreement with God's law.

According to the Kharijites, the caliph/imam had the authority to decide matters of law and religious practice, but he should do so in consultation with the scholars in the community and it was the community which could judge whether he had acted in accordance with God's law. The caliph, in fact, was to lead by consent to command and he had no God-given authority.

The other main idea in Kharijite ideology was that those who sinned grievously should no longer be considered as Muslims, no matter what they said, but were rather heathens, *kuffār* (sing. *kāfir*). All true believers should hunt these *kuffār* down and kill them, and sell their women and children into slavery. Among the sins which could mean that you were treated as a *kāfir* was, of course, refusal to accept the authority of the Kharijite community and its views of the caliphate. This ideology of *takfīr*, considering those you disagreed with to be non-Muslim, even if they claimed to be good Muslims, seems to have originated with the Kharijites at this time, but has been adopted by other groups right down to the present and is the basis of the attitude of Islamic State towards Muslims who disagree with them.

Kharijite views were no mere debating point: these people meant action. Their defection from Alī's camp led to a collapse of his military effort against Muʿāwiya and it was a Kharijite who assassinated Alī in 661 (they had intended to assassinate Muʿāwiya too, for they hated both of them equally, but the attempt failed).

The Kharijite movement also had a strong social basis to it, although this was never spelt out in their ideology. It gained its recruits among those who rejected not just the caliphates of Uthmān and Alī but the whole norms and behaviour of settled life which most Muslims had adopted after the great conquests and the migrations which followed. Many of their followers left the newly established garrison cities and led a wandering life, half nomads, half brigands, in the deserts of Arabia and southern Iran. To some they were romantic figures, harking back to the days of freedom when there were no taxes and no law-enforcement agencies, and their poetry, of which a great deal survives, was full of the spirit of the Jābiliyya, or pre-Islamic times, glorifying the Bedouin warrior and the life of travel and camp, raid and battle, albeit within a Muslim framework.

The movement divided into a number of groups. Two of these, known after their first leaders as the Azāriqa and Najdiya, abandoned the urban life entirely and went out to terrorize their opponents and to raid settled communities. Unsurprisingly they came into conflict with the Umayyad authorities and both of them were violently suppressed, the Najdiya in Arabia in 693 and the Azāriqa in Iran in 699. The Ibādiya, by contrast, developed a position that enabled them to live together with their non-Kharijite neighbours and accept a secular authority while waiting and hoping for the arrival of a truly Kharijite imam. This quietist attitude enabled them to survive in parts of Algeria and Oman right down to the present day.

The assassination of Alī in 661, followed as it was by the assumption of power of Mu'āwiya, the first Umayyad caliph, marked the end of an era marked by violence and division; but the thirty years since the death of the Prophet Muhammad had also been a period of astonishing achievements. Arab Muslims had conquered almost all of what we might describe as the central Middle East, from the eastern borders of Iran to southern Tunisia. The governments of the caliphs had also set up systems which ensured that Arab-Muslim government lasted after the initial conquests were over. The caliphs and the idea of caliphate played a key role in this achievement. The nature of the office was still undefined and the method of choosing the leader hardly explored. But this uncertainty encouraged flexibility.

Many different groups had their own ideas about who the caliph should be and what he could do, but no one, apart possibly from some small groups of Kharijites, argued that the caliphate was unnecessary and could be abolished. The concept offered the opportunity for diverse groups to develop it as they saw fit, but fundamentally presented an ideal of rulership which combined political and military leadership with spiritual guidance. It could also offer a leadership which was responsive to the needs of Muslims but was also, and crucially, respectful of what were seen to be God's decrees. The history of the caliphate of the Orthodox period raised almost all the main issues about powers and personalities which have dominated the discussions of the nature and potential of the office ever since.

CHAPTER 2

The Executive Caliphate

THE RULE OF THE UMAYYADS

Mu'āwiya and the Establishment of the Umayyad Caliphate

The first of the Umayyad caliphs, Mu'āwiya b. Abī Sufyān, came to the caliphate in 661 almost by default. The death of Alī at the hands of a Kharijite assassin and his own lucky survival meant that he was in a much stronger position than any of his potential rivals. He was fully in charge in Syria and led a powerful and effective army. His enemies were demoralized, defeated and divided. Soon after Alī's death he led his forces to Iraq where he made agreements with many of the prominent figures, including the most important tribal leaders, and with Hasan, Alī's son, who might have been a catalyst for opposition. Hasan was paid considerable sums of money and withdrew to the Hijaz where he lived a life of comfortable retirement. His younger brother Husayn seems to have been less reconciled to Mu'āwiya's rule but bided his time as long as the Umayyad leader lived.

These events inaugurated the Umayyad caliphate, which was to last until 750. By any normal standards of historical judgement, it was a period of huge success. The boundaries of the Islamic world were vastly extended: in the west with the conquest of modern Morocco and then, from 711 to 716, most of modern Spain and Portugal, and in the east with the conquests of Central Asia between 705 and 715 and Sind (southern

Pakistan) in 712. Not only did Umayyad armies conquer these areas, but they governed them effectively. In the distant Iberian Peninsula, known to Muslims as Andalus, governors were appointed and dismissed on the orders of the caliphs in Damascus and Syrian armies were sent to quell disturbances. At the same time a regular administration and tax system, building on the foundations laid by Umar, was developed, coins were minted using the Arabic language and Muslim religious formulae. The first great Islamic buildings, including the Dome of the Rock and the Umayyad Mosque in Damascus, buildings we can still see and enjoy, were erected. The Umayyads led the Muslim *jihād* against the Byzantine Empire and they enabled and secured the *hajj* to Mecca, either leading it in person or sending members of their family to do so.

Despite all these successes, however, they had a very mixed reputation in the later Islamic tradition. From the start the Umayyads faced a series of challenges, from the Quraysh of the Hijaz and the supporters of the Family of the Prophet in Iraq and numerous groups of Kharijites among others. They were later held to have been impious, and not true Muslim rulers. They were described as 'kings' (*mulūk*, sing. *malik*), that is, secular rulers, as opposed to the truly Muslim Abbasids who followed them. Looking at the historical record, it is difficult to account for this verdict. Some of the Umayyad caliphs, such as Walīd II (743–4), led wayward lives, much publicized both by admiring poets and pious opponents, but he was very much the exception. Most of them seem to have lived lives of at least conventional piety and one, Abd al-Malik (685–705), enjoyed a considerable reputation as a religious scholar.

To understand this hostility we must look at the people

who held and publicized such negative attitudes. The great chroniclers of the Umayyad caliphate, Balādhuri (d. 892) and Tabarī (d. 923), record the deeds of the caliphs of the dynasty objectively and usually without moral judgements. It is with the *ulama*, the religious scholars, and later historians that these prejudices become apparent. This is partly because they wrote under the rule of the Abbasids, who would have a natural interest in denigrating the achievements of the dynasty they had overthrown. *Ulama* also overwhelmingly came from Iraq and the Iraqis remembered the Syrian-based regime of the Umayyads and how the Syrian army had been sent to occupy and cow their country from their newly established garrison city at Wasit in central Iraq. But much of this hostility derives from the fact that the *ulama* of later years used the Umayyads as examples of how not to be caliphs in their veiled criticisms. The Umayyads, in fact, were made to pay for the sins of rulers much nearer their own time. The reality is that most Umayyad caliphs were strong, effective rulers and pious, believing Muslims.

During the Umayyad period, many features of the caliphate became established and in time traditional in ways which continued long after the dynasty itself had been swept away. Among the most obvious of these were the rituals of inauguration. Caliphs were not crowned. A crown of the Byzantine or Persian sort would have represented an acceptance of all the traditions of ancient monarchy, with its pomp and hierarchy, which the early Muslims rejected and sought to replace. There was absolutely no religious figure to take the role of the popes and archbishops of the western tradition and place a crown on a ruler's head.

Instead of these ancient and discredited rituals, caliphs were inaugurated through the performance of the *bay'a*, the public oath of allegiance signifying acceptance of an individual as ruler. A ceremony usually involving hand-to-hand contact – stroking or pressing rather than shaking – in this respect at least it resembled the swearing of homage by knights to their lords in medieval western Europe. In Umayyad and early Abbasid periods such ceremonies could be grand public occasions, a very visible sign that the public accepted their new ruler, and marked the inauguration of a new reign. In later times the *bay'a* lost its public role and ordinary people no longer participated. It was confined to the military, who expected and demanded a bonus payment for taking part, and to members of the court. From the beginning too the *bay'a* was sometimes offered by proxy on behalf of people who were too distant from the centre of power to be able to attend. It was a ritual through which rebels who wished to claim the caliphate for themselves could attach their supporters firmly to their cause. Despite the varied and apparently informal nature of the ceremonies, the *bay'a* was usually taken very seriously. To break it was a bad thing to do, unless the caliph was so obviously wicked or useless as to justify it, and could have the most dreadful consequences.

The fact that the *bay'a* became the primary ritual of inauguration in the caliphate was important. It was a fundamentally Arab idea expressed in Arabic words and Arab gestures. It made it clear that this Islamic leadership was quite unlike the ancient empires with their lavish and extravagant ceremonies. It was also a symbol of a relationship between free men, the subjects voluntarily accepting the authority of the new ruler. At the same time it had no divine approval or sanction. Of course, to break a solemn oath went against the law of God as it did the law of man, and most people accepted that the new ruler was in power because, in some way, God willed it thus, but the ritual itself was essentially a contract between men and that was all that was necessary to confirm a new caliph in power.

The idea of *bay'a* is an old one used among the pre-Islamic tribes of Arabia to seal alliances and agreement. Some sources say that a *bay'a* was taken to Muhammad by the people of Mecca in 630 when he gained control over the city. It is assumed by later sources that a *bay'a* was taken to Abū Bakr, Umar and Uthmān in turn as caliphs, but there are no detailed descriptions of how this was done and we may be simply looking at a back-projection of later Islamic practice to the era of the Orthodox caliphs.

Mu'āwiya's assumption of the caliphate is the first case in which we have a clear contemporary description of how the oath of allegiance was given and taken. It comes from a rather unexpected source. This is the so-called Maronite Chronicle, written in Syriac, the ancient liturgical language of the eastern churches in Syria, by a Christian author probably between 664 and 681, during the reign of Mu'āwiya, in fact. This makes it extremely valuable evidence for early practice. Not only is it earlier than any surviving Arabic-Muslim account, but it is not in any way influenced by later Muslim ideas. Its author may even have been an eye-witness. Among accounts of earthquakes and quarrels between different groups of Christians he writes of Mu'āwiya's assumption of power:

In . . . Constans' 18th year [the Christian chronicler dates events to the regnal year of the Byzantine emperor in distant Constantinople] many nomads gathered at Jerusalem and made Muʿāwiya king and he went up and sat down on Golgotha [the site of the crucifixion of Christ]: he prayed there, and went to Gethsemane and went down to the tomb of the blessed Mary to pray in it.

Later he records how, in July 660,

the emirs and many nomads gathered and pledged allegiance [lit. 'proffered their right hand'] to Muʿāwiya. Then an order went out that he should be proclaimed king in all the villages and cities of his dominion and that they should make acclamations and invocations to him. He also minted gold and silver, but it was not accepted, because it had no cross on it [the Byzantine coins in normal use all carried images of the cross as well as those of the reigning emperors]. Furthermore, he did not wear a crown like other kings in the world. He placed his throne in Damascus and refused to go to Muḥammad's throne [that is to Medina].[1]

Earlier the chronicler describes how Muʿāwiya had gone to Ḥīra, by which he means Kufa in Iraq, where all the Arabs pledged allegiance to him.

These short accounts make many interesting points. The pledging of allegiance by stretching out the right hand is a key feature. It is done by the people described as nomads and Arabs: non-Arabs are not involved. However, the new caliph visits the site of the crucifixion of Christ and the tomb of his mother Mary to pray. No mosque is mentioned. There is no suggestion that Mu'āwiya was a crypto-Christian, but both Jesus and his mother are, of course, highly respected in the Muslim tradition. This account may simply be wishful thinking on the part of our author, anxious to show how the new ruler respected the Christian holy places, but it may reflect a gesture by the new caliph to acknowledge his Christian subjects, who were, at this time, much more numerous in Syria than the Muslims. He is confident enough in his religion not to put crosses on his coins, showing that he is not a Christian ruler, but it does not work and he has no power to force the new money on his subjects. It was not until the reign of his successor Abd al-Malik, a generation later, that a Muslim ruler could issue an Islamic currency which would be generally accepted. Finally, the new ruler is different. He may be called a king, but he does not wear a crown as kings usually do. On the other hand, he makes it clear that Syria is to be his base and Damascus his capital when he refuses to go to Medina.

Mu'āwiya was a forceful and effective ruler, but he was no dictator. Much of the success of his long and largely peaceful reign was that he negotiated and made agreements with local elites in Iraq and Egypt while he largely confined his activities to Syria. His right to rule rested partly on his membership of Quraysh, though his settlement in Damascus represented a rejection of the Qurashi legacy in the Hijaz, and, no doubt, partly of his kinship with the murdered Uthmān, but above all it was based on his ability to attract the *bay'a* of the Arab Muslim leaders, not only in Syria but in hostile Iraq as well.

He was clearly a Muslim leader: 'The earth belongs to God and I am God's deputy [*khalīfat Allah*],' he proclaimed.[2] You could not be much clearer than that. He showed his religious authority not by forcing people to accept his beliefs but by leading the Muslim people in *jihād* against the Byzantines and he devoted massive resources to naval expeditions against the city of Constantinople itself. He also promoted the *hajj*, so showing deference to the Arabian origins of the new religion of Islam. These two policies, leading the Muslims against the Byzantines and safeguarding the *hajj*, were to be key elements in the public role of any man who wished to be considered a proper caliph right down through the ages.

Civil War and the Rise of Abd al-Malik

Mu'āwiya died, full of years and achievement, in 680. Before that, however, he had made a move which aroused bitter opposition and overshadowed his later years. He had his son Yazīd proclaimed as his heir, his successor as caliph. He seems to have known that the adoption of hereditary succession to decide the caliphate would be controversial and to have taken all the precautions he could to ensure that the *bay'a* to his son aroused as little controversy as was possible. The young prince was put in charge of a summer expedition against the Byzantines to establish his Islamic bona fides with military Arabs of the frontier region. Mu'āwiya and Yazīd seem to have led the *hajj* one after another, again making the point about father and son as leaders of the

Muslim community. In Mecca they solicited the *bay'a* from some senior members of Quraysh, among them Zubayr's son Abd Allah, but were rebuffed, at least according to local tradition. Ibn al-Zubayr is said to have called for a new *shūra* to choose a new caliph. There was also opposition from some Syrian Arab tribes, unhappy with the close family and political connections with the tribe of Kalb to the exclusion of others. Mu'āwiya could persuade, cajole and bribe, but he could not force the Muslims to accept his decision. In the end, however, his will prevailed: Syrians took the *bay'a* in person and delegations came from Iraq and other provinces to offer their allegiance. When the old caliph died, the succession initially passed smoothly: as one contemporary is said to have written to Yazīd, 'You have lost the Caliph of God and been given the Caliph of God', a curious parallel with the English formula, 'The King is dead, long live the King', on such occasions.

Ostensibly, and according to later tradition, the issue was whether caliphate should be hereditary, which would make it, the critics argued, like an old-fashioned kingship, exactly the sort of arrangement the Muslims had so clearly rejected. Mu'āwiya had been careful not to claim a hereditary right for his son to succeed but simply to assert that he was the best candidate. His opponents seem to have been unimpressed, which probably reflected their unhappiness about being excluded from the decision. By the time Abd al-Malik was making provision for the succession a quarter of a century later, such doubts seem to have disappeared and it was generally accepted that the caliph could arrange the succession among the members of his family as he saw fit. The Abbasids, their rivals the Alids, the Fatimids and the caliphs of the west all took it for granted that hereditary succession would be the norm and so did their subjects. Hereditary succession within a wider family circle was, however, different from primogeniture. It was by no means the case that the eldest son should automatically be preferred to his younger siblings. Perceived ability, paternal favouritism, maternal pressure and the views of the civil and military establishment all played their part. Only among the Shi'a did the ideal of primogeniture hold any sway, and that was because it was held to be a manifestation of God's choice, not of family custom.

The accession of Yazīd in 680 temporarily solved these problems. Except among the diehard supporters of the family of Alī, the new caliph was generally accepted and continued the policies of his father, but the apparent peace was soon to be disrupted by the second great trauma, after the murder of Uthmān, of early Islamic history, one that would end up splitting the Muslim community from top to bottom.

Until recently, when the Iranian government banned the practice, if you walked through the streets of Iranian towns or travelled along the old roads which link them at the time of Ashura, in the first month of the Muslim year, you would come across groups of men, sometimes just a dozen or so, sometimes many hundred in number, walking the dusty routes and flogging themselves over their shoulders with painful whips. Blood was often drawn. The reason for this was to remind themselves of the events of the death of Husayn fourteen centuries ago and to expiate the sins of their predecessors, who failed to come to the aid of the grandson of the Prophet in his hour of need. And in the centre of Iranian towns, small and large, you will see, played out by passionate and emotional actors, the events which surrounded this tragic incident. It is remarkably similar in spirit to a traditional Christian passion play. The heroes and villains are easy to identify: Husayn and his family on one side, the caliph Yazīd and his henchman Ubayd Allah b. Ziyād, the governor of Iraq, on the other. The events that unfold are both entirely predictable and deeply moving as Husayn and his family are surrounded by the forces of brutal oppression, deprived of water and shade and finally done to death by the soldiers of the Umayyad regime. These Iranian passion plays are remarkable as the only form of ancient indigenous theatre in the Islamic world, but perhaps even more so because they show how the events of that remote period still move people and define their thinking so many centuries later.

So what do we know of the historical events which inspired this devotion?

When Mu'āwiya took over Iraq after Alī's assassination and made his agreements with the tribal notables, Alī's eldest son Hasan had been effectively bought off and his younger brother Husayn had remained in Medina, probably looking for an opportunity to seize his father's inheritance. With the death of the old caliph he saw his opportunity to claim the caliphate for himself and the Family of Muhammad. He must already have been in touch with Alī's old supporters in Kufa where devotion to the descendants of the Prophet was lively and widespread. Husayn and a small group of family and followers crossed the desert to Iraq, expecting and hoping that

the people of Kufa, so enthusiastic in their letters and prom-
ises, would come out to meet them and bring them in triumph to the city. Instead they were met by soldiers of the
Umayyad governor, forewarned and well prepared. The conflict was short and violent. On 10 October 680, the grandson
of the Prophet, whom the old man had fondly played with as
a boy, was killed by the forces of godless repression as he
tried to claim his father's caliphate and bring the rule of justice and true Islam to the Muslims.

The killing of Husayn put an end to this first and most
famous attempt to establish an Alid caliphate, but the memory
of what was attempted and what happened stayed alive. In
the immediate aftermath, a large group of Kufans, ashamed
of their failure to come to Husayn's aid, set out from the city
to avenge his death. Calling themselves the Repenters, they
were enthusiastic but not militarily experienced and were
soon defeated by the Umayyad troops. Yet, all these centuries later, modern Iranians remember them and scourge
themselves to atone for their shortcomings.

If Yazīd had lived to be as old as his father, he might have
established the custom of hereditary succession beyond challenge, but he did not and he died in November 683 in his
favourite residence at Hawwarin on the road from Damascus
to Palmyra. He left a young son who died after only a few
weeks. The hereditary idea, such as it was, had died as a
result of obvious natural causes.

Once more the whole future of the caliphate was cast into
doubt. For more than five years the Islamic world was divided by bitter rivalries and civil wars. The events were complex, but in the end three main parties emerged to claim the

caliphate, each with very different ideas as to what sort of caliphate they wished and where it should be based.

One of these parties was the Umayyad family, but with Yazīd gone none of Mu'āwiya's immediate relatives inspired much confidence. However, another branch of the Umayyads came from Medina to take refuge in Syria. They were led by Marwān b. al-Hakam. He was now an old man, having been born around the time of Muhammad's Hijra, and was one of the last major figures in Islamic politics to have known the Prophet personally. He had served Uthmān well and had remained in Medina after the caliph's death. He died in 685 soon after his arrival, and his son Abd al-Malik took over the leadership of the Umayyad party. He was an energetic young man who was to become one of the most important figures in the creation of the Islamic world. But at the time of his father's death it was all he could do to maintain the Umayyad position in Syria where he had to contend with numerous enemies.

The second party was led by Abd Allah b. al-Zubayr, the son of that Zubayr who had been killed at the Battle of the Camel. His political platform was, in the literal sense of the word, reactionary. He reacted against the policies of the Umayyads. He wanted the new caliph to be chosen not just from the Umayyads but from all Quraysh, and he is said to have called for a new *shūra* to achieve this. He wanted the caliph to be based in the Hijaz and specifically in Mecca, the original stronghold of Quraysh. This Ibn al-Zubayr was a charismatic figure, at least in the accounts we have of him, a stern and modest Muslim who rejected any form of royal display, and his personal courage in battle and in the face of death was indisputable. He was perhaps the first of many Muslims through the ages who advocated a return to what they thought to be the simple certainties of that time and follow the ways of the *salaf*, the pious first generation. He was also probably the man who rebuilt the Ka'ba in the form in which we have it today. He was ably supported by his brother Mus'ab, perhaps more worldly and politically savvy, whom he sent to Iraq to drum up support against the Umayyads.

Unfortunately for the Zubayrid cause, Kufa had already been taken over by another pretender, Mukhtār b. Abī Ubayd. Mukhtār came from the Hijazi tribe of Thaqīf, but he was not a Qurashi and never seems to have considered claiming the caliphate in his own right. He was also now an old man, having been born around the time of the Hijra. His father had been the commander of an early, and unsuccessful, Arab raid on Iraq at the very beginning of the conquests and he had deep roots in Iraq. He now proclaimed that the caliphate should belong to the Family of the Prophet. This cause was sure to arouse support in Kufa, where many still remembered the sad fate of Husayn barely five years before and were anxious to avenge his killing and restore their prestige.

The problem for Mukhtār was that he needed to find a member of the Family who would take up the leadership and claim the caliphate. After what had happened to his father, Alī b. al-Husayn, who was living a quiet and modestly prosperous life in Medina, understandably turned him down. He did however get a more favourable response from Muhammad b. al-Hanafiya who did not come to Kufa but allowed his name to be used as a candidate for the caliphate.

He was an interesting choice because, although he was a son of Alī, he was not the child of Fātima but, as his name suggests, of a woman of the Hanafi tribe. This meant that the blood of the Prophet did not flow through his veins and his acceptance was a sign that the memory of Alī himself was increasingly revered in Iraq and descent from him alone could justify a claim to the caliphate. Mukhtār proclaimed Ibn al-Hanafiya not just as caliph but as Mahdī, the first time that this title was used by a would-be leader of the community. *Mahdī* meant God-guided, and implied a leader who could begin a new era and make radical changes to bring in a truly Islamic government. This term was to be used frequently throughout Islamic history, usually in Shi'ite circles, as a symbol of hope and messianic expectation. Some later caliphs claimed to be Mahdīs, notably the Shi'ite Fatimid caliphs of Egypt (969–1171), but most did not and the title retained its revolutionary, even apocalyptic overtones.

Mukhtār appealed to and based his support on the 'weak', the have-nots in Kufan society, those Arab Muslims who struggled along on low or non-existent incomes, and especially the non-Arab converts, the *mawālī*, at least 500 of whom joined his army, and he appointed one of their number to the important role of chief of police. The *mawālī* had plenty of grievances. Although believing Muslims, they were still treated as inferiors by the Arab leaders and in many cases were still forced to pay the *jizya*. They formed an important part of Mukhtār's military forces and he came increasingly to rely on them. This alarmed and angered the noble Arabs, the *ashrāf,* who complained that the *mawālī* had been given horses, paid salaries and generally favoured.

A brief conflict broke out in the city, and the nobles and their allies were driven out. Ten thousand of them promptly marched south to Basra to join the forces being assembled by Mus'ab, Ibn al-Zubayr's brother. From here they returned with their new allies to reconquer their home town of Kufa, which they did in April 687, Mukhtār himself being killed in the battle. His radical social experiment had been crushed by the forces of conservatism, but the memory lingered on among the marginalized and dispossessed, many of whom continued to believe that a Mahdī from the Family of the Prophet would come to usher in a more just and equal Islamic society. These people were often labelled *ghulāt*, or extremists, because of their radical views, both social and religious, and they made an important contribution to the Shi'ite ideology which was to emerge in the ninth and tenth centuries.

With the death of Mukhtār and the dispersal of his followers there were now only two main protagonists, the forces of Ibn al-Zubayr in the Hijaz and Iraq and those of Abd al-Malik the Umayyad in Syria. On the fringes, raiding and killing but with no real possibility of taking over the major centres of power, were the Kharijites, hated by Umayyads and Zubayrids alike.

By 691, six years after he had been proclaimed caliph, Abd al-Malik had reasserted Umayyad control over all Syria and the Syrians. He led his army in person to confront Mus'ab and at a battle near Kufa the Syrians completely defeated the Iraqis, divided and weakened as they were by the bitter rifts which remained as a result of Mus'ab's killing of Mukhtār and the suppression of his movement. Only Ibn al-Zubayr himself now remained, establishing himself not in the Prophet's city of Medina but in Mecca, the only centre of Qurashi power. A force was sent to crush him, led by a figure who was to become Abd al-Malik's right-hand man in Iraq and a lasting symbol of strong, no-nonsense government in the Muslim tradition, Hajjāj b. Yūsuf. He pursued his campaign with ruthless efficiency, having no qualms about directing his siege engines on the Ka'ba. Ibn Zubayr's forces were no match for this and he was killed, fighting bravely, in October 692. Finally the unity of the Muslim world had been restored.

The events of this seven-year civil war are, to say the least, complex, but they are also revealing about the nature of caliphate and the different expectations different groups had of the office. The long years of fighting were essentially about who was to be caliph. None of the participants proposed to abolish the office or divide the caliphate into separate areas. Their disagreements were not about personalities or personal rivalries or, in general, about tribal differences and factionalism. They rather reflected profound and lasting social and regional differences among the Muslims. At the regional level the conflict was about where the caliphate was to be based, the Hijaz, Iraq or Syria. The location was significant because wherever the caliph was based would be the centre of power and wealth.

Then there were the social divisions. Both Umayyads and Zubayrids were socially conservative, believing in rule through the tribal elites, whereas Mukhtār proposed a radically new social order where these distinctions would cease to matter. While Zubayrids and Umayyads stood for a caliphate which would maintain the existing social structures with security and justice for all, essentially a governmental role, many of the followers of Mukhtār hoped for a revolutionary caliph who would use his office and his status as a member of the Family of the Prophet to transform society. All these different groups were Muslim and many of the participants personally, no doubt, very devout: non-Muslims played no part in these discussions and struggles. Yet they had very different visions of what an Islamic society should look like and especially of the role and function of the caliph. Finally it should be noted that these differences were not solved and ended by discussion and compromise but by military power and strength. The Umayyads did not win because they had the most persuasive and popular arguments, but because they had the most effective military machine and military leadership.

Abd al-Malik was now the undisputed ruler of the Muslim world, but experience of the long years of civil war and the challenge this had meant to Umayyad rule seems to have made him determined to develop a strong state structure which would prevent such problems occurring again. He abandoned Muʿāwiya's tradition of exerting power through a network of alliances and informal agreements and created a more autocratic, top-down caliphate. Much of what we might call the infrastructure of Muslim government as it existed down to modern times was developed by this forceful and imaginative ruler. He began the minting of a specifically Muslim coinage, usually bearing the caliph's name; he standardized the system of taxation and the paying of the military and the appointment of governors to provinces by investing them with banners. His right-hand man Hajjāj and a small group of trusted men, composed mostly of *mawālī*, formed a sort of inner cabinet. Some of these *mawālī* may have been Greek converts with experience of Byzantine administration and techniques, but the structures which Abd al-Malik developed were thoroughly Islamic in presentation and intention.

The foundations of his power lay in the Syrian army. Recruited from the Arab tribesmen of greater Syria, they were organized and paid to maintain Islamic rule throughout the Muslim world. The first priority was Iraq, rich and populous and, in many cases, resistant to Syrian control. Hajjāj developed a new city called Wasit because it was between the old established garrison towns of Basra and Kufa. He ruled here as governor and the Syrian army enforced his orders. What was even more galling for the Iraqis was that they were paid from the revenues of Iraq or, as people at the time put it, 'they ate the *fay*, the income from taxation, of Iraq', which most Iraqis believed should rightly be paid to them. Needless to say, there was discontent which sometimes flared into open rebellion, but the Umayyad forces were always powerful enough to defeat the rebels and maintain the caliph's authority.

This Syrian army, backbone of the state, needed to be paid and the caliph made an effort to standardize the different systems throughout the caliphate. In around the year 700 Abd al-Malik decreed that all government departments should use Arabic as their working language and that all records should be kept in Arabic. Until this time Greek in the west and Pahlavi (middle Persian) in the east had remained the language of much administrative activity. Now all that was swept away and so was much of the culture that went with it. No one learned Greek or Pahlavi any more because there were no longer any jobs which required them. Even the Melkite (Greek Orthodox) church was using Arabic as a liturgical language in much of the Middle East by the eighth century.

We can be sure about the spread of Arabic because we have surviving documents from two very different areas of the Muslim world. The most numerous are from Egypt. Here government records were written on papyrus (woven reeds), which has survived in the very dry climate. Administrative documents started to be written in Arabic within a year of the initial Muslim conquest in 641, but for many years Greek was still used as well. By the eighth century, however, Arabic was clearly the only language used in the central administration in Old Cairo, though Greek sometimes still appeared in documents for local consumption. From the 750s, at the other end of the caliphate, we have a small collection of tax and legal records written in Arabic on leather. They come from a small town called Rob now in north-eastern Afghanistan, still today a remote and inaccessible area, which was conquered by Muslim armies in the first decades of the eighth century. The Arabic language and figures used in these documents would have been instantly comprehensible to scribes working at the same time in the Egyptian bureaucracy. Such was the reach of caliphal power.

One of Abd al-Malik's major projects was the establishment of an Islamic coinage. We have already seen how Mu'āwiya had attempted to introduce a new coinage without the Christian symbol of the cross and how this had been rejected by the people. Abd al-Malik, with greater resources and more determination, tackled this again. He first experimented with coins with portrait images of himself: we have surviving examples of 'standing caliph' coins with images of a figure standing in long robes, a straight sword buckled around his waist, with long hair, flowing beard and sporting a recognizably Arab headdress. For reasons which are unclear, this imagery was soon abandoned in favour of a purely epigraphic coinage, that is, one using only Arabic inscriptions. These varied from time to time and according to the types of coins, but they were essentially quotes from the Qur'ān or religious slogans, names of the caliphs, the place of minting and the date. The new coins came in three main types. The most valuable of these was the gold *dīnār*, based on the Byzantine *solidus*, about the size of a modern British 5-pence or 2-euro cents piece. Then there was the silver *dirham*, based on the old Sasanian *drachm*, slightly larger and thinner than a 10-pence or 2-euro piece. Finally there were copper coins, called *fals* (pl. *fulūs*), which were minted locally in different areas to much cruder designs. The gold dinars, mostly minted in Damascus, were predominantly used in the former Byzantine territories of the western half of the caliphate and the dirhams, usually minted in Wasit, in the formerly Sasanian lands of the east. Both types of coins, however, circulated throughout the caliphate. A coin minted in Damascus would be accepted without question in Bukhara or Samarqand.

This monetary reform is interesting for all sorts of reasons. Purely epigraphic coinages continued to be used, with few exceptions, in the Islamic world down to the nineteenth century when images of rulers, on the European model, began to reappear. The memory of these ancient coins survives in modern currency, in the dinars of Jordan, Iraq, the Gulf States and Tunisia and the dirhams of Morocco. Money in general is still referred to as *fulūs* in modern Levantine Arabic.

The currency was witness to the caliph's authority. All minting of gold and silver was done by the government. The *sikka*, the right to have coins minted and to inscribe the ruler's name on them, became one of the key indicators of sovereignty in the Muslim world. There were none of those private coinages minted by nobles and bishops which were so prevalent in much of western Europe in this era. The inscriptions made clear to all who could read who the ruler was. From Portugal to Central Asia, people used coins which proclaimed an Islamic state. Just as importantly, they carried the Arabic language to the remotest corners of the Muslim world, confirming its status as the language of power and rule.

The caliph had other ways of making his presence known. Abd al-Malik erected a series of milestones along the main roads he travelled in Syria and Palestine – tall, conical pillars about two metres high with Arabic inscriptions giving both distances on the road and the name of the caliph who had commissioned them. Here again he was in some ways following the tradition of Roman milestones, many of which must have still been visible along the main roads, but he was proclaiming that this was now an Arab Muslim empire and that what had been the responsibility of the Roman imperial authorities had now been taken over by the Muslim caliph.

The most conspicuous and lasting of Abd al-Malik's

achievements was in architecture, and here we must include the works of his son and successor Walīd I (705–15), who followed closely in his father's footsteps. The Orthodox caliphs seem to have built nothing, certainly nothing that has survived in physical shape or written record apart from a small structure on the Temple platform in Jerusalem, which Umar is said to have ordered to be built when he cleaned the site up. We are told that mosques were erected in the garrison towns of Kufa and Basra, but we have no detailed descriptions and no surviving evidence. This was not, all in all, a very impressive record.

Abd al-Malik changed all that with the building of the Dome of the Rock in Jerusalem. Now 1,400 years old, this astonishing building still exists in more or less its original form and it preserves much of the original decoration. This is not the place for a detailed architectural description, but something must be said about the caliph's role in its construction. Two explanations for the building can be put forward. The first is that construction work began when Ibn al-Zubayr was ruling Mecca and that the Dome was constructed as an alternative focus for *hajj*. Certainly the form of the building, which is centred on the eponymous rock and surrounded by circular and octagonal aisles, seems designed for the circumambulation (*tawwāf*) which lay at the heart of the *hajj* ritual. This is not to argue that Abd al-Malik wished to replace Mecca and the Ka'ba, but rather to provide an alternative while Mecca lay in the power of his enemy; and who knew how long that would be?

The second and complementary explanation is that it was built to assert the Islamic presence in Jerusalem. It looks across the valley which lies at the heart of the old city to the Church of the Holy Sepulchre, whose dome, constructed on the orders of the emperor Constantine at the beginning of the fourth century, was the grandest and most conspicuous monument in the city. The Dome of the Rock is higher, looking down on the church, and it is slightly larger. Further support is given to this idea by the gold mosaic inscription which runs around the inside of the dome. This is the earliest monumental inscription in Arabic. It is not a text from the Qur'ān but rather uses Qur'anic quotations to emphasize the oneness of God, a clear critique of the Christian doctrine of the Trinity, which Muslims often attacked for assigning partners to God (*shirk*). And the inscription announces for all to see and read that the building was the work of Caliph Abd al-Malik – or rather it used to: when the Abbasid caliph Ma'mūn visited the city in 832, he insisted that his own name be put up in the place of Abd al-Malik's, a crude substitution which deceived no one). With its conspicuous position and its lavish decoration of marble and gold-leaf mosaic, the Dome of the Rock clearly echoed Byzantine imperial style (though of course without the images of Christ and his saints which would have adorned a Byzantine building). It was a very public proclamation of the glory and triumph of Islam and an equally public proclamation of the caliph as the builder and creator of this triumph.

Walīd followed his father's example. In Medina he rebuilt the Mosque of the Prophet, though nothing of his work survives there, and in Damascus be demolished the cathedral, after arranging the payment of compensation to the Christian community. Then, sometimes working, we are told, with his own hands, he set about building the magnificent mosque which is still the great architectural glory of the ancient city. A marble inscription, now lost, proclaimed his role as the builder.

In most complex human societies, one of the ruler's most important functions is the making of law and the passing of judgement. In the Roman Empire law was created by the emperor: 'Whatever pleases the prince [*princeps*, that is, emperor] is law' runs the maxim. In the Byzantine Empire it was the emperor himself, from Justinian on, who issued and revised laws. In Britain law is created, at least in theory, by the Queen in Parliament. It is interesting to consider, then, whether the caliph had a similar role. Here we are confronted by a problem. The sources on which we depend date from the ninth century and after. In the ninth century it was the case that the caliph was almost completely excluded both from law-making and from judgement. Law-making, or rather law-finding, had become the preserve of the *ulama*, those who knew the Qur'ān and the Traditions of the Prophet, by this time accepted as the only valid sources of law. But did this apply to the Umayyads in the first half of the eighth century and did the Umayyads function as law-makers and judges?

To begin with we must be clear what sort of law we are talking about. The caliph or his representatives (governors, or emirs) had effective control over what we might call criminal and political offences. Highway robbers, violent criminals and, above all, those who rebelled against the caliph and his government were all summarily punished by the ruler and his officers. This was, however, only a small part of the law. All those issues that can be described as part of *sharī'a*, family law, laws of contract, laws regulating slavery and the complex rules of inheritance were typical of the issues in which law was found by the *ulama* and cases decided by the *qādī*, or judge, in his court. This meant that there were whole areas of deciding and enforcing law which lay outside the caliph's authority, potentially weakening his overall power.

The evidence of the pre-ninth century, such as it is, suggests that the caliph did, at that stage, have the position of ultimate and supreme judge and did have the power in certain circumstances to make and decide law. It comes from letters and poems of the period. The role of the caliph as judge was supported in the Qur'ān where God tells David: 'We have appointed you caliph on earth so judge among the people with truth' (38.25). The poets of the Umayyad court took it for granted that the caliph was a judge. In the words of the great Umayyad poet Farazdaq (d. *c.*729), the caliphs were 'imams of guidance and beaters of skulls'. Another poet, Ahwas, said of the caliph Sulaymān that he had been appointed by God 'so judge and be just'; and Jarīr, the great rival of Farazdaq as court poet, said, 'He is the caliph, so accept what he judges for you in truth'.

Abd al-Malik held formal courts acting as *qādī* and a page would recite poetry on legal justice before business got underway.[3] In a complex and well-reported case we are told how different caliphs responded to the legal problems which arose from the ownership of churches in Damascus and of the attempts of successive caliphs to resolve the issues. Enough evidence exists to show that Umayyad caliphs acted as judges, but it is also clear that they could decide laws. Abd al-Malik wrote instructions to his governors about how to deal with cases of slave girls in whom a defect had been discovered after purchase and Caliph Hishām wrote to his *qāḍī* in Egypt to clear up complex points about dowries. Above all, Umar II made a complex decree about the taxing of non-Muslims and converts which has been preserved in full. He did not ask the *ulama* or consult the Traditions of the Prophet, he made a decision according to his understanding of law and of the equity of the situation and wrote to his governors ordering them to enforce it. Nobody objected that he was acting beyond his powers. Provincial governors and private individuals would write to caliphs like Abd al-Malik seeking their rulings on difficult questions: what to do with a slave who slanders a freeman; is it permissible to revoke a will in which a slave has been manumitted? All these are complex points of law and the caliph was expected to resolve them. His decisions were remembered, perhaps to be used as precedents for future cases.

The caliph could also be credited with almost miraculous powers: for the poet Akhtal (d. *c.*710), he was 'the caliph of God through whom rain was sought', while for Farazdaq he was simply 'the shepherd of God on earth'. Hajjāj, Abd al-Malik's right-hand man, considered that the caliph was superior to the Prophet himself and Khālid al-Qasri, Hajjāj's successor in Iraq, expressed much the same sentiments about Walīd I, sentiments which would certainly have seemed blasphemous to many later and modern Muslims, but which seem to have been unchallenged at the time.

In many ways the caliphates of Abd al-Malik and his son Walīd I represent the high-water mark of caliphal power and prestige. He was deputy of God on earth, commander of the army, leader of the Muslims in *jihād* and *hajj*, minter of coins, chief judge and law-maker. Only his obligations to God and his deference to the stipulations of the Qur'ān meant that his powers were more restricted than those of the most absolute Roman emperor.

The Later Umayyad Caliphs and the Fall of the Dynasty

The death of Walīd I in 715 was followed by the short reigns of one of Abd al-Malik's other sons, Sulaymān (715–17), and of his nephew Umar II (717–20), both of whom died young of natural causes. Abd al-Malik had made elaborate arrangements for his succession and no less than four of his sons and one nephew became caliph without any overt opposition. The legality of the caliph designating his heirs was accepted as part of the natural order of things.

Sulaymān, named of course after the great biblical King Solomon, has a reputation in the Arabic sources for luxurious living and generous expenditure, but no one seems to have thought that this made him unworthy of the caliphate.

He was followed by the most enigmatic of the Umayyad caliphs, Umar II. Umar was not the son of Abd al-Malik but of his brother, Abd al-Azīz, the long-time governor of Egypt. He spent much of his youth in the Hijaz where he had the reputation of being something of a playboy. As caliph, however, he adopted a puritanical and pious persona, perhaps in imitation of his namesake, Umar I. He has a reputation in later sources of being 'the good Umayyad' and of rejecting the oppressive policies of his dynasty, and of ruling according to God's book and His *sunna* (ordinances as laid out in the practice of the Prophet and his words).

There was certainly some truth in this. He attempted to break away from the factionalism which increasingly divided the Umayyad ruling class and to make appointments from many different groups across the whole spectrum of the Muslim elite. The important city of Kufa, for example, was governed by a descendant of Umar I in an attempt to win over its resentful and recalcitrant population. He also made a bold move to solve one of the major social problems which had emerged in the caliphate: the tax status of the *mawālī* converts. Under the rule of Hajjāj in Iraq, converts continued to be taxed as if they were non-Muslims, Hajjāj being concerned about the damage that would be done to state revenues if they escaped paying the *kharāj*, the land tax which non-Muslims paid on their property, and were required to pay only the alms tax obligatory on all Muslims. In order to reduce the damage done to the treasury, he also decreed that, on conversion, their lands should become the property of their communities, and so still liable for the land tax. It was an ingenious attempt to reconcile the fiscal demands of the state with the teachings of Islamic law. It also shows Umar II as legislator, deciding major issues of policy on the basis of his own judgement.

Umar II also seems to have been the only Umayyad caliph to make an effort to safeguard the rights of his non-Muslim subjects. It was this most pious of caliphs who ruled that churches in Damascus which had been taken over by Muslims should be returned to Christians because they had been taken unjustly according to the original surrender agreements which had been made at the time of the Muslim conquests – a ruling which aroused considerable anger among Muslims who hated to see Christian worship restored in what had been mosques. For Umar, the rule of law and the adherence to solemn agreements was more important. According to a tradition after his death in 720 he was buried near the shrine of St Simeon Stylites, the greatest Christian holy place in Syria. This was not because he was a secret Christian, but probably because he saw Christian holy men of the pre-Islamic period as servants of God in the monotheistic tradition which united Christians and Muslims.

With Umar's premature death his reforms were undone or allowed to lapse and strong authoritarian government was re-established under the last great Umayyad caliph, Hishām (724–43). Hishām had a reputation for running a puritanical, even miserly, court from his new base at Rusafa in northern Syria, but he also spent very substantial sums of money on public works like the irrigation canal he ordered to be dug to improve the water supply of the expanding city of Mosul in northern Iraq.

Among the Arabic historical sources of the period reflecting on different aspects of caliphal power is a story dating from the reign of the short-lived caliph Yazīd II (720–24), which says much about the prestige and power of his position.[4] At this time the Muslim settlers in the frontier province of Cilicia (now in southern Turkey), which bordered the Byzantine Empire, were having problems with the lions which made travelling between the Muslim outposts hazardous (wild lions, smaller than African lions but still dangerous, were found in the Middle East as late as the fifteenth century) and they wrote about this to Yazīd. Now it happened that, shortly before this, Muslim armies had conquered much of the province of Sind. There they had encountered numerous water buffaloes, which seem to have been unknown in the Middle East before then. The conquering Arab general had sent some 4,000 of the beasts to Iraq where they throve in the marshes of the south of the country. The caliph ordered that the buffaloes, with their Sindi keepers, be transferred to Cilicia, a hot and well-watered area where, apparently, they frightened the lions away. In other words, if you had a problem with lions you turned to the caliph and asked him to do something about it. And he did, mobilizing the resources of the vast Muslim empire to resolve the problem – or at least that is what we are told.

On Caliph Hishām's death in 743 the Umayyad caliphate entered a seven-year crisis of assassination and civil war from which it was unable to recover. A detailed history of this crisis is beyond the scope of this volume, but some salient points can be noted.

Hishām was succeeded, in accordance with family arrangements made long before, by his nephew Walīd II. If Umar II was the 'good Umayyad' in later memory, Walīd II was definitely the bad one. Before becoming caliph, he had lived the life of a hedonistic hell-raiser well away from the court of his severe uncle. The two did not get on well and Hishām was, rightfully, anxious about the fate of the caliphate when his wayward nephew succeeded.

Walīd II built a series of palaces in the steppe lands bordering the Syrian desert, which are some of the most

conspicuous and memorable legacies of the Umayyad caliphate. The Umayyad caliphs did not in general live in towns
and visited their 'capital' in Damascus only on occasions. Abd
al-Malik, like Mu'āwiya before him, lived what was essentially
a transhumant life. The summer was spent in the high plains
of the Biqa valley around Baalbek, in what is now Lebanon.
In the autumn they passed through Damascus but preferred
to stay at a Christian monastery, Dayr Murrān, on the hills
overlooking the city rather than at the Palace of the Green
Dome Mu'āwiya had built in the city centre. The winter was
spent in the milder climate of the Jordan valley, often at
Sinnabra at the south end of the Sea of Galilee. Later caliphs
chose different bases. Sulaymān founded a new royal city at
Ramla in Palestine while Hishām established his court in the
northern Palmyrena.

The ruins of many of their palaces still survive. They
resemble in many ways Roman villas in their scale and architecture, a series of courtyards surrounded by colonnades,
and often a reception hall where the caliph or prince would
sit on a throne in an apse to receive and impress guests.
There would always be a bath-house and a court mosque.
Many were decorated with paintings and mosaics and
there was no inhibition in these private environments
about the portrayal of human beings and animals. A number
of the palaces were also the centres of agricultural estates
and game parks and elaborate irrigation schemes were constructed to keep the gardens green and the water flowing in
the baths.

The Umayyads were exceptional in their living arrangements and no later rulers of Syria emulated their example.

The Abbasids built huge palaces in the centres of towns. Why, then, did the Umayyads adopt this style? An idea which was prevalent in much western scholarship in the twentieth century was that this represented a sort of nostalgia for the Bedouin life of their ancestors. In this romantic vision they were free sons of the desert, in contrast to their Abbasid successors, oriental despots lurking in their gigantic palaces along the Tigris. Perhaps again they wished to keep their hedonistic lifestyles of wine, hunting and dancing girls, what Robert Hillenbrand memorably described as their '*dolce vita*', away from the censorious eyes of their disapproving subjects.[5]

Other explanations are more down to earth. The Umayyad caliphs were able to keep hold of power because they enjoyed the support of the leaders of the Syrian Bedouin tribes. Some at least of these palaces were used to maintain these links, the ruler or prince going to the desert margins in those wonderful weeks of spring which the Arabs called *rabīʿ*, when the steppe is green with grass and bright with flowers. Here he could entertain them with parties, poetry and the luxuries of the bath-house while hearing their grievances and encouraging them to support his plans. Other historians have pointed out the financial advantages of these developments. Islamic taxation law offers tax breaks to those who bring new lands under cultivation. Even for princes of the blood, it was more profitable to bring new lands under the spade and plough than to acquire properties in already cultivated areas. There is no doubt an element of truth in all these explanations and the life of the 'desert castles' has given a stylish romantic gloss to the Umayyad caliphs which later monarchs have lacked.

None of the caliphs cultivated this lifestyle more assiduously than Walīd II. It is to him that we owe the building of Qusayr (little castle) Amra in the Jordanian desert east of Amman. It is a small building which consists of an audience hall with a bath-house attached. The scale is intimate, with no sleeping accommodation or other living areas. Presumably the people who came to enjoy the facilities pitched their tents around it. What distinguishes Qusayr Amra from other more or less similar complexes is the survival of a whole programme of fresco wall-paintings. These are executed with fluent, confident brushwork which suggests that they were part of a developed art form rather than a one-off. The subjects depicted are various and not all understood. There is a serious element which shows us the prince in his alcove and the portraits of kings whom the Islamic armies had defeated, including naturally the Byzantine emperor and the Sasanian king, but also Roderick, king of the Visigoths in distant Spain. Another series in the ceiling vaults shows us the building of the palace and the preparation of materials. Most of the rest consists of vigorous and lively depictions of the pleasures of bath and hunt. The prince as mighty hunter is shown dispatching the onagers (wild asses) which have been driven towards him for slaughter, while on the opposite walls scantily clad girls dance and sing. These paintings have long been attributed to the patronage of Walīd, but recently, in one of those moments which archaeologists dream of but seldom experience, an inscription has been uncovered which says plainly that it was built by Walīd b. Yazīd, that is, Walīd before he became caliph.

The stories about Walīd were numerous. He was an

accomplished Arabic poet in his own right and attracted poets and singers to his court. He is said to have behaved in a brazen and scandalous way. When he went on the *hajj*, he brought his singing girls with him and, they said, had wine-drinking parties in the Kaʻba itself. At the same time the caliph held a very definite view of his office. We have a letter in which he announces to the governors of the provinces of the empire that he has appointed his two sons, Hakam and Uthmān, as his heirs. It was clearly composed by a chancery scribe, but it is one of the few documents in which we can see how an Umayyad caliph himself viewed his office.

The letter amounts to some eight pages of closely printed text in the translation provided by Crone and Hinds.[6] It is written in an elaborate and repetitive style which cannot have made easy reading then or now, but the message that it is the duty of all Muslims to obey the caliph is clear and repeatedly rammed home. He begins by describing how God sent prophets to mankind until prophethood eventually reached Muhammad. When Muhammad himself passed away, God appointed caliphs to implement His decrees, establish His practice (*sunna*), administer justice and keep men away from forbidden things. The caliphate was 'part of the completion of Islam and the perfection of those mighty favours by which God makes His people obliged to him'. At no point does the writer contemplate the possibility that the caliph may commit an error, or that resistance to his authority could possibly be justified; this would be to challenge God. The caliph was, in fact, both judge and interpreter of God's law and it was God, not any gathering or consensus of men, which had established him in this position. The function and duty of his subjects was absolute obedience and, if they strayed from this path, bad things, very bad things, would happen to them in this world and the next.

This is a theory of rulership which seems very similar the divine right of kings familiar from western European political practice. The letter finishes by explaining how the caliph, in order to avoid any doubt or uncertainty, has decided to appoint his two sons as heirs, Uthmān to succeed his elder brother Hakam in due course of time. Here again there is no question of the caliph taking advice or consulting. He alone has decided this and it will be done.

Not everyone was as impressed by his God-given authority as the caliph himself. Many within the Umayyad elite in Syria were shocked by Walīd's flagrant behaviour, while his political enemies used it as a pretext to garner support for themselves. They mobilized and found the caliph in one of his desert residences at Bakhra, just south-west of Palmyra: the ruins, abandoned and neglected, can still be seen. He was virtually unprotected and they stormed the building, killing him as he was reading the Qur'ān, like Uthmān before him. The caliph may have been unpopular, and his conduct outrageous, but inevitably the assassination solved nothing and the Umayyad caliphate soon began to disintegrate into rancour and civil war.

Something of the criticism which was directed at the Umayyads can be seen in an angry polemical sermon delivered by a Kharijite leader, Abū Hamza, in the Hijaz around the year 747. In this he gives a potted history of the caliphate, beginning with Abū Bakr, who fought the *ridda* and acted according to the Qur'ān and *sunna*. Next came Umar, whose achievements included paying the stipends of the Muslims, establishing the garrison cities and the *dīwāns*, organizing the night-time prayers during Ramadan and decreeing eighty lashes as the penalty for drinking wine. But things then began to go wrong. Uthmān never measured up to the standards set by Abū Bakr and Umar and got worse as time went on; Alī acted well until he agreed to the arbitration (at Siffin), after which he achieved nothing. Mu'āwiya was cursed by Muhammad and made the servants of God slaves and his *dīn* (religion) was a cause of corruption. Yazīd was no better, following his bad example and 'a sinner in his belly and his private parts'. Things only got worse with Abd al-Malik, who made Hajjāj his imam, leading him to hell-fire; Walīd was a stupid fool; Sulaymān, like Yazīd I, was concerned only with food and sex. Umar II provided a brief interlude in this catalogue of depravity: he had good intentions but was unable to act upon them. Yazīd II was back to the old Umayyad model with picturesque detail added. He dressed up in expensive clothes and

> sat Habāba on his right and Sallāma on his left and said, 'Sing to me Habāba: give me drink Sallāma.' Then when he had become drunk and the wine had taken hold of him, he rent the garments which had been acquired for a thousand dinars, dinars for which skins had been flayed, hair shaved off and veils torn away [that is, the money had been collected by violence against the ordinary Muslims]. Then he turned to one of the girls and said, 'Surely I will fly', and indeed he will fly to hell-fire!

The squint-eyed Hishām misused the funds of Muslims; Walīd II 'drank wine openly and deliberately made manifest what is abominable'; and Marwān II, the last Umayyad caliph, was distinguished by his cruelty. Abū Hamza ends up with a general diatribe against the whole dynasty:

> the Umayyads are parties of waywardness. Their might is self-magnification. They arrest on suspicion, make decrees capriciously, kill in anger, and judge by passing over crimes without punishment. They take the alms tax from the incorrect source and make it over to the wrong people . . . These people [the Umayyads] have acted as unbelievers, by God, in the most blatant fashion. So curse them, may God curse them![7]

The rhetoric is impassioned, but the charges against the Umayyads are fairly predictable – cruelty and oppression, misusing the wealth of Muslims, drink and sex. What makes this speech so intriguing is the fact that, unlike so much of our evidence, it dates from the time of the last Umayyad caliph and reflects not the prejudices of the Abbasid period but the perceptions of people at the time. It can also stand as an epitaph for the dynasty, showing why many Muslims were prepared to reject the Umayyads' authority and rise against them.

CHAPTER 3

The Early Abbasid Caliphate

While the Abbasid dynasty lasted until 1258, when it was finally defeated by the Mongols, the early period from 750 to 945 marks in many ways the apogee of the power and prestige of the caliphate. When modern commentators look for a classic caliphate to demonstrate what caliphate has been and could be, they frequently look to the Abbasids in their period of greatest power and glory. For the conservative scholar and jurist Ibn Kathīr (d. 1373) for instance, writing in Damascus more than a century after the last Abbasid caliph of Baghdad had been killed by the Mongols, the Abbasids were still the caliphs *par excellence*, the only true embodiment of the office. The legacy and memory persist to the present day. To give just one example, the choice of the colour black as a symbol and sort of uniform by the present ISIS caliphate in the Jazira province is a clear and direct reference to the Abbasids, who adopted black as the official colour for court dress, an attempt in fact to position this new caliphate as inheriting the role and prestige of their predecessors.

In this chapter I will investigate how the Abbasids came to represent the caliphate, how they eventually succeeded and what powers they claimed. Finally we must consider the nature of and reasons for the break-up of the caliphate in the tenth century and what this meant for both the past and the future of the institution.

The Abbasid Revolution and Its Aftermath

The Abbasid family, perhaps fifty in number by this time, were descendants of the Prophet's paternal uncle, Abbās b. Abd al-Muttalib, and therefore members of the Family of the Prophet. This was a very important relationship, all the more so because Muhammad's own father died young and Abbās was in many ways his guardian and protector. At the same time they were not Muhammad's biological descendants. Since his blood did not flow in their veins, they constantly had to counter the claim that they were, in a sense, imposters.

Abbās' son Abd Allah figures frequently as a much respected authority of the Traditions of the Prophet, a reputation which may, of course, owe much to the political success of his descendants. He was not, however, one of the six members of the *shūra* chosen by Umar to elect the caliph after his death and he does not seem to have played a notable role in the Muslim conquests. The family enjoyed a quiet prosperity under the Umayyad caliphs and the remains of their palace have been uncovered by archaeologists at Humayma, in southern Jordan. Compared with the residences of the ruling dynasty, it is a modest structure, with rooms built around a single courtyard. And there is a small mosque outside, clearly identified by its orientation and its *mihrab* (prayer niche), Ornamental ivories, probably originally attached to pieces of furniture, suggest a degree of wealth and comfort but not extravagant opulence. Along with its agricultural possibilities – the family cultivated olives – the property at Humayma had one other advantage: it lay on the main route from Syria to the Hijaz and the Holy Cities. Plenty of people passed by and the Abbasids must have been well informed about what was going on.

Until around 720 they seem to have played no active political role and attracted no followers, but at this time Muhammad b. Alī, then the leading member of the family, began to make contact with disillusioned Muslims in the distant north-eastern province of Khurasan. He argued that the Abbasids were members of the Family of the Prophet and had a good claim to lead the Muslim people.

The Abbasid claim to the caliphate, as it was articulated after they had come to power, was based on three arguments: The first was, of course, their membership of the Family of the Prophet. This carried some weight, but many Muslims who wanted the rule of the Family to bring about change thought that the ruler should be a descendant of Alī and Fātima themselves. The second idea was that of *nass*, designation by a previous caliph or claimant. Mukhtār, the rebel in Kufa, had tried to establish an Alid caliphate in the name of Muhammad b. al-Hanafiya, a descendant, as already noted, of Alī but not of Fātima. The attempt had failed and Muhammad died in obscurity, but he left a son called Abū Hāshim, who inherited a claim of sorts to the caliphate. He was himself childless and the story goes that, perhaps travelling through Humayma, he designated Muhammad b. Alī as his successor. It was, to say the least, a flimsy claim, even if the chain of events was true, but, put together with other arguments, it could carry some weight.

The third point, put forward after the Abbasids had achieved power, was essentially an argument based on action rather than inheritance. It was they who had dealt with the impious Umayyads and, above all, they who had avenged the blood of the martyred Husayn: it was therefore the Abbasids, rather than the direct descendants of Alī, who could rightfully claim the caliphate. They laid considerable emphasis on themselves as the 'Hāshimiya'. This term may in part be a reference to their supposed designation by Abū Hāshim, but it had a wider significance as well. An earlier Hāshim, who died before the coming of Islam, was the ancestor of the Alids and the Abbasids, but not, and this was the crucial factor, of the Umayyads. By claiming to be the Hāshimiya they were staking their claim to be part of the same kin as their Alid cousins.

None of these arguments would have been of much use if they had not been backed by the prospect of military force, and this is where the Khurasanis came into the picture. Khurasan was the name given to the vast north-eastern province of the Muslim world. In modern political geography it includes north-east Iran, Afghanistan and the Muslim areas of the Central Asian republics, including Bukhara, Samarqand and the Farghana valley. This huge and diverse province was ruled by Umayyad governors from the great ancient city of Merv, now in modern Turkmenistan. Although it was remote from the centres of Muslim power, a substantial number of Arabs lived there, almost all of them Iraqis sent or encouraged to settle in the frontier cities of the province. This meant that, in contrast with western and central Iran, there was by now a large Muslim population, which included Arabs but also a substantial number of *mawālī*, non-Arab converts to Islam. As this was a frontier province, many of the Muslims were used to bearing arms and experienced in warfare.

Quite how the Abbasid connection with Khurasan began is not clear, but from 720 onwards there were increasing contacts between the family based in Humayma and disaffected Muslims, Arab and *mawālī* alike, in the province, more than a thousand miles away. The leadership in Khurasan was taken by a mysterious and charismatic man known as Abū Muslim. His origins are uncertain, but it seems most likely that he was a former slave from Iraq who was sent to Khurasan by the Abbasids. The point, made by the simplicity of his name, was that he was neither clearly Arab nor clearly non-Arab and he had no tribal or family links. He was simply a Muslim everyman to whom all sections of Khurasani society could relate. This was a fundamental part of the Abbasid appeal.

The movement in favour of an Abbasid caliphate was fortunate in its timing. In 743 Hishām, the last of the great Umayyad caliphs, died and the next year his successor Walīd II was murdered. The regime began to disintegrate, plagued by infighting between different factions. Meanwhile Abū Muslim was managing to persuade large numbers of men to rally to the cause of a campaign to replace the Umayyads as caliphs, not openly naming the Abbasids at this stage but calling for a 'chosen one from the Family of the Prophet'. No doubt many imagined that this meant a descendant of Alī and Fātima, and Abū Muslim did not disabuse them.

The movement tapped into a whole spectrum of grievances against the Umayyads. It appealed to Arabs who felt that their interests had been disregarded by the powerful governor Nasr b. Sayyār, *mawālī* who resented being treated as second-class Muslims, Khurasanis of all backgrounds who no longer wanted to be ruled by a distant government in Syria which collected taxes but seemed to give nothing in return, and pious Muslims who hoped that the coming of the rule of the Family of the Prophet would begin a new era of truly Islamic rule by God-guided caliphs. Abū Muslim marshalled the disparate forces and in 747 was powerful enough to attack and take possession of Merv, the capital of the province. Nasr b. Sayyār was driven out and the new Abbasid army began to march through Iran to take over the rest of the Muslim world. This was no mere provincial rebellion, it was a revolutionary movement which intended to bring radical change to the whole Muslim community.

The last Umayyad caliph, Marwān II (744–50), was a tough and experienced soldier, but the Umayyad armies were exhausted by many years of fighting; their leaders were divided and Syria itself had recently been ravaged by a terrible earthquake which had left many of its cities in ruins. In a series of battles the Umayyad armies were defeated and Marwān was pursued through Syria to Egypt where he was cornered and killed in a skirmish on the edge of the Nile delta.

Now the real political manoeuvring began. It was centred on Kufa where an Abbasid agent called Abū Salama, who had acted as a link between the Abbasids in Humayma and Abū Muslim in Khurasan, attempted to hold the ring. Even at this stage, the movement was still calling for an unnamed 'Chosen One'. Meanwhile members of the Abbasid family travelled to Kufa. Abū Salama prevaricated: it is possible that he intended a new *shūra* to choose who the new caliph would be. But Abū Muslim, who had remained in Khurasan, was having none of it. He ordered men he trusted in the army to kill Abū Salama and arranged the public proclamation of an Abbasid as caliph.

Abū'l-Abbās, known as Saffāh, was proclaimed caliph in the great mosque in Kufa. A public *bay'a* was held and large numbers came and touched hands with the new caliph in person to accept him as their leader. He began to preach, but had to step down when the fever from which he was suffering overcame him.

What purports to be the text of this sermon has been preserved. Whether this is actually what was said we can never know, but it gives the fullest justification of caliphate which has come down to us from the early Islamic period, and serves as a real manifesto for the new dynasty. After praising God, Abū'l-Abbās explains that God has created the Abbasids, 'the leaders of Islam, its cave and its fortress, and made us to uphold it, protect it and support it'. The sermon goes on to establish that the Abbasids are indeed 'the kin of God's Messenger. He created us from the ancestors of the Prophet, causing us to grow from his tree', and follows with a number of quotations from the Qur'ān emphasizing the importance of the Family of the Prophet. Of course, the Abbasids could not claim, and never did claim, to be descended from Muhammad, but they argued that the Family of the Prophet was wider than his blood descendants. The sermon attacks the 'Sabā'iyyah', a derogatory term for those who claim that only the direct descendants of Alī and Fātima have any claim to the caliphate. Abū'l-Abbās then explains how, after the Prophet's death, his companions took authority and ruled by mutual agreement, leading the conquests and distributing the 'inheritance of the nations' (the profits of the conquests) justly. Then the Umayyads came and appropriated the resources of the Muslims, 'tyrannizing and oppressing those entitled to it'. God put up with them for some time, but then 'He took revenge on them at our hands . . . He vouchsafed our victory and established our authority in order to grant benefit to those who had grown feeble on the earth.' Finally Abū'l-Abbās goes on to praise the people of Kufa for their stead-fastness to the cause of the Family of the Prophet against the oppressors and he ends by promising them all a pay rise of a hundred dirhams. Then he stepped down because the fever made it impossible for him to go on.

The new caliph's place on the pulpit was taken by his uncle Dāwūd, who continues in a much more rhetorical vein:

> Now are the dark nights of this world put to flight, its covering lifted. Now light breaks in the earth and in the heavens, and the sun rises from the springs of the day while the moon ascends from its appointed place . . . Rule has come back to where it originated, among the people of the house of your Prophet.

He denies that the Abbasids are claiming the caliphate for reasons of financial gain: 'We did not rebel seeking this authority to grow rich in silver and in gold, nor to dig a canal nor build a castle', an implicit criticism here of Umayyad building and land-reclamation projects. He stresses that the Umayyads had taken the payments which rightly belonged to the Muslims of Iraq. But now things would be different:

> You are under the protection of God's Messenger . . . and the protection of Abbās. We will rule you according to what He has sent down and treat you in accordance with His book and act with the commoner and elite among you following the practice of God's Messenger.

He then attacks the Umayyads for their impiety and tyranny: 'God's punishment came upon them like a night raid when they were sleeping [a classic trope of Bedouin poetry]. They were torn all to tatters, and thus may an oppressive people perish!' After claiming again that he has restored the rights of the people of Kufa and Khurasan, he extolls this nephew the new caliph:

> He has made manifest among you a caliph of the house of Hāshim, brightening your faces and making you to prevail over the army of Syria, transferring the sovereignty and the glory of Islam to you. He has graced you with an imam [caliph] whose gift is justice and granted him good government . . . So know the authority is with us and will not depart from us until we surrender it to Jesus son of Mary [at the end of the world], God's blessing be upon him. Praise be to God, Lord of the universe, for that with which He has tried us and entrusted to us.[1]

The sermon, or rather political speech, is a tour de force of Arabic rhetoric which also makes important points. According to Dāwūd, the Abbasids have come to power by God's will and because they are of the Family of the Prophet (albeit not his direct descendants). They had avenged the wrongs done of the Family. He also stresses the fact that power has passed to the Kufan and Khurasani Muslims, away from the Syrians, and that they will now get their just rewards, including that hundred dirham pay rise. They will rule according to the will of God and the words of the Qur'ān: nothing more specific in terms of policy is mentioned.

The moment of triumph was followed by a period of consolidation. Members of the extensive Abbasid family were appointed to lead armies and to govern the provinces of Iraq, Syria and Egypt. Most of the remaining members of the Umayyad family were rounded up and massacred, except for one who fled to North Africa and eventually to Spain, where he set up an independent Umayyad state which eventually became the caliphate of Córdoba. By the time Saffāh died, four years later in 754, the Abbasids had established their control over the entire Muslim world apart from North Africa and the Iberian Peninsula.

The coming of the new regime left many questions unanswered. Would the caliphate be hereditary in the Abbasid family? What, if any, would be the role of the Alids? Would the new caliphate be a military state as the Umayyad one had been, and would the Khurasani army simply take over the role that the Syrians had played under the Umayyads? All this remained to be decided.

The new caliphate looked very different from that of the Umayyads. Black banners had been raised in the east to usher in the new era and two centuries later Muslim tourists in the city of Merv were still shown the house in which the first robes had been dyed black when the revolution first began. Black was to be the distinctive colour of Abbasid court dress for the next two centuries, and wearing it a sign of allegiance to the dynasty.

The Abbasids developed a very distinctive style of court dress, something which, as far as we know, was unknown under the Orthodox and Umayyad caliphs. Apart from black robes, one of the features was a hat called a *qalansuwa*. We have no clear or realistic depictions of this headgear, but it seems to have been a tall, conical hat, sometimes supported on the inside by sticks to prevent it collapsing. People remarked that it looked like a tall black jar. The *qalansuwa* was of Persian origin. It had been elite wear in the late Sasanian court and was adopted or revived by the Abbasids. Like court dress through the ages, the most important features of it were that it was impractical and expensive, therefore indicating high status. It was also uncomfortable: one story tells of a courtier returning from the palace to his house and throwing off court dress in relief only to have to put it on again when he was summoned back by the caliph. When the caliph Amīn dreamt that the wall on which he was sitting was attacked by one of his enemies, the fact that his black *qalansuwa* fell off was an indication of the disasters which were to follow. The *qalansuwa* appears to have been abandoned at the beginning of the tenth century, along with many other features of what had by then become traditional Abbasid court style. It is also at least possible that it is the ultimate origin of the camelaucum, the tall, conical papal tiara which seems to appear in the eighth and ninth centuries.

Another innovation of the new regime was the giving of

caliphal titles, called *laqab*. The Orthodox caliphs and the Umayyads had simply been known by their given names, Umar, Uthmān, etc. The first Abbasid caliph seems to have been given the title Saffāh, meaning either 'the Generous' or 'the Blood-shedder', though it is not clear that he bore the title in his own lifetime. His successor Mansūr certainly was known by his title rather than by his (very common) given name of Abd Allah. Every subsequent Abbasid caliph was given a title. These names usually meant 'Victorious', 'God-guided' or similar meanings. Among the thirty-seven Abbasid caliphs who reigned before 1258, no name was ever used twice. This led to the invention of more and more elaborate, and sometimes virtually unpronounceable, verbal forms to ring the changes.

This pattern was adopted by other dynasties which claimed the caliphal title. The Fatimids in Tunisia and later Egypt used titles from the beginning and the Fatimids have both a Mansūr and a Mahdī among their earliest caliphs. When the Umayyads proclaimed their caliphate in Córdoba in 929 they too chose such titles, as did the later Almohads in the west. Even if caliphs, like some of the later Abbasids, were virtually powerless and commanded little or no respect, they always had high-sounding official names.

The formality of court life was emphasized by its architectural setting. There had never been any question that the Abbasids would not base themselves in Iraq. Khurasan, the homeland of the troops who had brought them to power, was too remote to be an effective capital and clearly Syria was out of the question. Iraqis had always looked to the Family of the Prophet for political leadership, even if they usually understood these to be Alids rather than Abbasids. There were good economic reasons too for basing the caliphate in Iraq. Until the tenth century Iraq was the richest and most productive area of the Muslim world. The regime would be stronger and more secure for being able to take advantage of this prosperity.

The second Abbasid caliph, Mansūr, began the construction of the first royal city in Islam specifically designed for the performance of monarchy. Baghdad was founded in 762 as a deliberate act of policy by the caliph. In the twelve years which followed the change in regime the Abbasid court moved around from one site to another in central Iraq before settling on the site of the small village of Baghdad. Mansūr chose the site because of its position at the hub of the waterways of Iraq. The Tigris and Euphrates are closest together here and the two rivers were connected by a network of canals. Grain could come from the plains of the Jazira and dates from Basra, all by river. This access to river transport allowed the city to expand way beyond the resources of its immediate hinterland.

Mansūr created a striking setting for his caliphate in an impressive round city, surrounded by high walls pierced by four gates. At its centre was a great mosque and a palace surmounted by a tall dome. At the beginning this seems to have been a city with markets and tradesmen, but it soon became a court city, the residence of the ruler and his entourage and security services, the guard (*haras*) and police (*shurta*). Outside the walls, on both banks of the Tigris, a thriving metropolis grew as the people came from all over the caliphate to offer goods and services to the court and the well-paid soldiers and bureaucrats. The caliph allowed his favourite courtiers to make fortunes by developing land for the construction of markets and residential quarters. Mansūr's original city lay on the west bank of the Tigris, but he encouraged his son and heir, Mahdī, to build on the east bank and here too there were mosques and palaces. A masonry bridge over the swift-flowing river was out of the question so three bridges of boats were constructed. As well as these there were countless small boats on the river and the connecting canals. It must have seemed like a Middle Eastern Venice. By the middle of the ninth century Baghdad seems to have had a population of around 500,000, though of course no statistics were kept, and it may well have been the most populous city on the planet.

The Madinat al-Salam (City of Peace), as the capital was officially known, served as a model and inspiration for later caliphal capitals, notably Cairo. God's caliph should have a residence which reflected his power and wealth for all to see. It was essential for the caliphate to have strong economic as well as political and religious foundations. Only then could the caliph reward his faithful followers and pay an army to ward off the attacks of rivals and defend the frontiers as well as funding such annual public displays of piety as the *hajj* and the *kiswa* (the great cloth which covered the Ka'ba and which was renewed every year). Without a strong economy, the caliphate would lack the power and awe without which it would not be able to perform its functions of leadership and enforcement. The Abbasid caliphate and the city of Baghdad were closely linked: when the caliphate declined, the city did too.

Mansūr was not just the chief architect of the city, he was also the chief architect of the political structure of the state. Anyone who had supported the revolution imagining that it would begin a new era of government by pious and humble members of the Family and their advisers was in for a big disappointment. Mansūr constructed a state caliphate which was very similar to that of the Umayyads. The caliph was an autocrat who ruled through a powerful and well-paid military. The ruling family was given the most prestigious governorates and allowed to make vast fortunes. Mansūr even employed some of the army chiefs who had served the Umayyads before, although he was unwilling to tolerate any potential rivals. Abū Muslim, the great general and organizer of the revolution, was clearly one such potential rival. Persuaded to leave his Khurasani stronghold and come west to Iraq on his way to the *hajj*, he was lured to the caliph's camp (this was before the building of Baghdad) and separated from his loyal troops. Then, in the presence of the caliph, he was killed by the palace guards and his body rolled up in a carpet in a corner of the royal tent while his head was displayed to his followers. The man to whom the Abbasids owed so much was brutally slain when he seemed to be a challenge to the power of the regime, much as the first Fatimid caliph in Tunisia killed the missionary who had brought the Berber troops to support him. Abū Muslim's name went down in history as a victim of ungrateful tyrants, but Mansūr remained caliph, his authority strengthened.

Mansūr was also deeply suspicious of the Alids, knowing, as did everybody else, that they had a better claim to represent the Family of the Prophet, and he used his security forces to keep them under close surveillance. In 762, just as he was involved in the construction of Baghdad, one of them, Muhammad b. Abd Allah, known as 'the Pure Soul', a descendant of the Prophet seeking to rule in the city of the Prophet, launched a bid to establish a caliphate in Medina. Mansūr was having none of it and used his powerful army to crush the rebellion by force and kill its leader.

Mansūr was succeeded by his son and heir, Mahdī, who had been designated by his father. The Abbasids never adopted a formal policy of hereditary succession, but in fact this is what it amounted to. Not necessarily the eldest, but certainly one of the sons or brothers of the reigning caliph would be chosen and the *bay'a* would be arranged among the leading men of the state to confirm it. The right of the caliph to nominate his heir seems to have been generally accepted, though there were vigorous and sometime violent disputes about which of the sons should be selected. The choice of the name is significant. Mahdī had been used, especially in early Shi'ite circles, to denote the rightly guided, almost messianic figure whose role it would be to lead the faithful to salvation. The Abbasids here were trying to pre-empt the Shi'ite challenge by arguing that the Mahdī was the real ruler now, not some figure to be hoped and yearned for at some undetermined future date. Whereas Mansūr had seen his role as the enforcer of Abbasid rule, Mahdī seems to have tried to develop his claim to be a spiritual guide. In his personal life he did not drink alcohol, though he made no efforts at general prohibition. In his public life he played the Muslim ruler, taking measures against Christians and the Sabian pagans of northern Syria and building mosques.

He persecuted a group known as the Zindīqs, who seem to have been dualist heretics (who believed in two gods, one good and one evil). A number of them were executed, a rare example of the caliph defending Islamic orthodoxy with violence. He also tried to conciliate the Alids, inviting them to court and giving their supporters in Medina positions in the army. No doubt some were pleased, but these were hardly revolutionary measures and certainly not enough to win over the diehards for whom the Abbasids could never be the real leaders of the Family.

Mahdī was killed comparatively young, apparently in a hunting accident, in August 785. He had already nominated two of his sons as heirs, with the intention that they should succeed one after the other. The Umayyads had made similar provisions. Given the trouble that these complex arrangements gave rise to, it is curious that caliphs persisted in them. It was a classic recipe for family strife. No doubt part of the reason was the need for 'an heir and a spare'. At a time when men frequently died young and suddenly, it was important to have water-tight arrangements to secure a smooth transition of power within the dynasty, not allowing outsiders to make mischief. There also seems to have been a desire to accommodate different factions at court. Each son who was named heir would attract a constituency of supporters who would want to make sure that their man succeeded and the reigning caliph may have wanted to give many different groups a stake in the future of the dynasty. What history did show, however, was that such arrangements were, to say the least, problematic because, almost inevitably, the new caliph would wish to nominate his own son to succeed instead of his brother and would be urged to do so by his courtiers and army officers.

Mahdī nominated two of his sons and it was only the sudden and, some suggested, suspicious death of the eldest in September 786 after a reign of little more than a year which prevented violent strife. Even in this short period he had begun to make moves to nominate his own sons. In the event the younger brother, Hārūn, who would be called Hārūn al-Rashīd, was able to succeed without open opposition in 786.

Hārūn al-Rashīd and His Successors

Hārūn al-Rashīd could be described as the greatest caliph of them all. Certainly, in terms of popular imagination, he has a presence and name recognition that none of the others, even rulers like Mansūr who were arguably much greater leaders and politicians, have attained. He is, for example, the only one of the Abbasids who is generally known by his given name as well as his title. Any book on the caliphate has to investigate the man and his reputation.

Hārūn's reputation as a great and mighty ruler is to some extent a product of the disasters which followed his death – disasters that were largely, it must be said, of his making. The long civil war between his sons, and the catastrophic effect this had in Baghdad, meant that his reign was looked back on as a sort of golden age before things started to go wrong. It was a period and environment in which some of the greatest classical Arabic poets of all time, including Abū Nuwās (d. 813) and Abū'l-Atāhiya (d. 825), to name only two, were writing. It was also the time when the glittering and culti-vated Barmakid viziers (from Ar. *wazīr*, meaning chief adviser) held court, and when their power was brutally destroyed by caliphal decree, some said by caliphal whim, it became a proverbial example of the arbitrary power of rulers and the unavoidable workings of fate. This all feeds into the Arabian Nights image of Hārūn.

The Nights, as they have come down to us, date from the later Middle Ages, but they are a product of many centuries of evolution. One strand is a series of narratives about the Abbasid court and in particular the court of Hārūn. Though they are clearly not strictly historical, they give a lively and vivid image of how the Abbasid court at its height was imagined by subsequent generations. A typical story begins with the caliph summoning his vizier Ja'far the Barmakid one night and saying, 'I want to go down to the city to ask the common people about the governors who have charge of them, so as to depose any of them they complain about and promote those to whom they are grateful.'[2] And so the adven-ture begins with the two of them, accompanied by the gen-eral factotum and executioner Masrūr, meeting a poor old fisherman who recites a poem about his misfortunes, and one improbable event follows another. The caliph is often shown as the symbol of stern but fair justice, who can put anything right with his commands, but also as a man who enjoys jokes, disguise, wine-drinking, poetry and the com-pany of women, both his beloved wife Zubayda and a number of slave girls who strive to please him. He is accompanied by a small caste of actors, Ja'far and Masrūr, the crafty judge Abū Yūsuf and the outrageous poet Abū Nuwās, who were real historical people of the age, but we should not imagine that the events are historical. Instead this world of rich fabrics, chests of gold dinars, exquisite food and wine and beautiful women and boys testifies to the grip the Abbasid court held on the popular imagination, for, as the princess-storyteller Shahrazad says at the end of one such narrative, 'Where is such generosity to be found now, after the passing of the Abbasid caliphs, may Almighty God have mercy on them all?'[3] And not just in the Middle East. It was the nineteenth-century English poet Alfred Lord Tennyson who coined the phrase 'the golden prime of Harun al-Rashid' to describe this period. Many people nowadays who want to see the return of a caliphate must have, at least at the back of their minds, the image of Hārūn as a stern but just autocrat, ruling Muslims with a benign if sometimes heavy hand.

It is a hard image to live up to and the historical Hārūn al-Rashīd, as far as we can recover him, did not always succeed. He was an inexperienced youth when he succeeded his brother after the latter's unexpected death. In his first years he was guided by his mother Khayzurān (Slender Reed). Khayzurān was the first of a number of powerful women who exercised enormous power as queen mothers guiding their young sons, and Hārūn was her favourite son.

The rich and glamorous Barmakid family also attempted to guide the young Hārūn. Their literary and philosophical salons were home to much of the cultural and intellectual activity that made the Baghdad of Hārūn so famous. Their story also illustrates the diversity of the Abbasid court, which attracted intelligent and ambitious people from all over the Muslim world and did not discriminate against non-Arabs or people from the remotest provinces. Far from being Arabs, they came originally from the ancient city of Balkh, now in northern Afghanistan. The family were hereditary priests and guardians of a great Buddhist temple, whose remains can still be seen outside the ruined city walls. At the time of the Abbasid revolution they, like many other Khurasanis, joined the cause, converted to Islam and rapidly rose in the ranks of the Abbasid administration, not as soldiers but as accountants, perhaps making use of the newly imported Indian mathematical notation which was now being studied in the Muslim world and which we now know as Arabic numerals.

In the next generation Yahya the Barmakid became a major figure at court, acting as tutor and mentor to the young prince, while his son Ja'far became his close friend and constant companion. When Hārūn succeeded as caliph, the Barmakids came into their own, and their generous patronage of poets and thinkers often overshadowed that of the caliph himself. It was a magnificent but perilous position and, after some fifteen years of this tutelage, Hārūn seems to have tired of them. One day, apparently out of the blue, though many know-alls claimed that they had seen it coming, he ordered the arrest of the family, including the old and revered Yahya who had done so much for him, and, even more shocking, the immediate execution of Ja'far. We are given poignant accounts of how the young man, on confronting the executioner Masrūr, his former companion in adventure, assumes that there has been a mistake and then, when Masrūr persists, begs to be allowed to see Hārūn to plead for his life. The caliph was unrelenting, absolutely refusing to speak to his old friend, and the next day Ja'far's head and body were displayed for all to see on the main bridge of boats which united the two sides of the city, a spectacle for the common people to gawp at. It was a terrifying demonstration of arbitrary power: the court of the caliphs was a place of luxury and entertainment, and a potential source of vast wealth, but it could also be a place of danger and sudden death. For centuries after, moralists could point to the tragic events as perfect warning against 'putting your trust in princes'.

In two aspects Hārūn did fulfil the duties of the caliphal position more assiduously than any of his predecessors or successors: the leading of the summer expeditions against the Byzantines and that of the *hajj*. The expeditions against the Byzantines were the only campaigns in which the Abbasid caliphs participated. It was an opportunity for the caliph to show himself as the military leader of the Muslims. His army would be clearly visible in the frontier provinces of Syria and the Jazira and volunteers would come to join from all over the Islamic world. It was also the period when traditionalists like Ibn Mubārak (d. 797) were establishing the religious theory and legal basis of *jihād*. The caliph's actions were consistent with a growing body of opinion among ordinary Muslims. In June 806, for example, he is said to have assembled 135,000 men, regulars and volunteers, and though we should treat such large numbers with some scepticism, this was clearly a very significant expedition and triumphantly showed the caliph as the Commander of the Faithful. He wore a *qalansuwa* with the words 'Warrior for the Faith and Pilgrim' (*ghazi, hajj*) embroidered on it for all to see.[4]

He also sought to exert Muslim naval power in the

Mediterranean by organizing a large-scale attack on Cyprus, though in fact the military results were comparatively modest, and in southern Anatolia the little town of Heracleia was seized, its inhabitants imprisoned and taken back to Syria, but no attempts were made to expand Muslim territory north of the Taurus Mountains on a regular basis. The caliph did commemorate his triumph by starting work on a great public victory monument in a new settlement which he called Hiraqla after his conquests on the Euphrates in Syria. Only the rectangular foundations remain today and it is not clear that it was ever completed, but it was certainly intended to be a lasting and visible monument to Hārūn's military achievements on the main route from Baghdad and his second capital at Raqqa to the Byzantine frontier.

Hārūn was equally committed to the celebration of the *hajj*. He made the pilgrimage to Mecca no less than nine times in his twenty-three-year reign. This was more than any caliph before him. He was also the last reigning caliph, of any dynasty, who ever made the sacred journey. These pilgrimages were very grand affairs: much of the government and the political elite accompanied him, and he had the opportunity to demonstrate his leadership and his piety in front of Muslims from all over the Islamic world. It was superb publicity. One small but significant example of such display is found in an account of the *hajj* made by his father Mahdī. At this time the *hajj* was in high summer, and the heat in Mecca stifling, but one of his most wealthy courtiers, his cousin Muhammad b. Sulaymān, contrived to present the caliph with ice to cool his drinks. He had done this, we must presume, by ordering that ice be collected in the Zagros Mountains of western Iran in the winter, kept in underground ice-houses, and then wrapped in straw for insulation and put in boxes to be carried across the desert for the caliph's enjoyment. So the caliph appeared before his people not just as a sovereign enjoying the plenitude of power but virtually as a miracle worker who could defy the laws of nature.

The caliph and his family invested heavily in the *hajj* in other ways, notably the construction of the pilgrim route known as the Darb Zubayda, named after his favourite wife. In Umayyad times the main *hajj* route had been from Syria through the Hijaz and Umayyad caliphs had, from time to time, made efforts to clear it and make it easier for pilgrims. When the Abbasids moved the centre of power to Iraq, the *hajj* became much more difficult and the long route across the deserts of central Arabia was a real challenge. Hārūn and his mother spent large sums of money on clearing stones from the path (the results can still be seen in aerial photographs today) and building water cisterns and small forts and way-stations along the route. Not only was it the biggest civil-engineering project of the early Islamic period, but it is virtually the only example we have of the Abbasid government spending money on this sort of infrastructure. Inscriptions were put up to commemorate the pious benefactions of different members of the ruling family and the fact that the road is still referred to as the Darb Zubayda (Zubayda's Road) today shows how widely known the name was.

The 'golden prime' of Hārūn al-Rashīd came to an end with his death in 809. Despite the image sometimes projected of a stern and wise elder statesman, Hārūn was only in his late forties when he died. Of the great Abbasid caliphs, only Mansūr reached the age of sixty, and many of the others died in their thirties and forties, all still young men by our standards. Hārūn left behind him an arrangement for the succession which was to prove disastrous for the Abbasids and the caliphate in general. In a great gathering in Mecca at the *hajj* of 803 he had arranged that his (and Zubayda's) son Amīn should be caliph and in effective charge of Baghdad, Iraq and the western Islamic world, while another son, Ma'mūn, was to rule in Khurasan and eastern Iran, and, more problematically, was to be Amīn's heir.

It took only two years for war to break out between the brothers. Ma'mūn's forces, led by the brilliant commander Tāhir b. Husayn, swept westwards, defeated Amīn's much larger armies and were soon at the outskirts of Baghdad. From August 812 to September 813 the great city was besieged and much of it ruined by the fighting between rival militias claiming to support either Amīn or Ma'mūn but in many cases simply taking advantage of the chaos to enrich themselves. Especially damaging were the large swing-beam catapults, which both sides used and which killed and demolished indiscriminately. The conflict produced a remarkable literature of protest poetry, angry and sad in equal measures at the damage these armed groups caused to the ordinary people of the city. It is eerily reminiscent of the situation in the city 1,200 years later as different militias fought for control in 2006 and 2007.

At the heart of the storm was Caliph Amīn, finally holed up in his great-grandfather Mansūr's imposing round city with his enemies all about him. He knew he could not hold out, but the dilemma was choosing to whom he should give himself up with the best chance of saving his life. The account of what happened on the night of 25 September 813, when he made his decision, is one of the most dramatic and moving narratives in the whole of early Arabic historical writing. The doomed caliph wanted to hand himself over to an old family retainer, Harthama b. Ayan, who was serving with Ma'mūn's forces, but this was vigorously opposed by Tāhir, worried that there would be a reconciliation between the brothers and he would be deprived of the fruits of his victory. In the end a compromise was arranged: Amīn would surrender himself to Harthama, but the caliphal regalia, the staff, mantle and signet ring of the Prophet, should be surrendered to Tāhir 'for that', they argued, 'is the caliphate'. We hear little in sources about these relics. They were seldom referred to and never seem to have been displayed in public yet they had, it would seem, a very important symbolic value.

Events turned out very differently. Amīn rode down to the dark shore of the Tigris to meet Harthama's boat, but Tāhir had stationed men there to upset it, pitching Amīn and his rescuers into the water. He swam ashore but was soon captured by Tāhir's men and taken to a safe house where he was locked up in a bare room with only some rugs and cushions. What happened next is narrated in the voice of one of his courtiers who had been picked up at the same time. It is an interesting story, for in it our perspective on the caliph is radically altered. In accounts of Amīn when his father was alive and in the early days of his own reign he is depicted as idle, stupid and frivolous, constantly shown up by his wiser and more mature brother Ma'mūn. But in his final hours, like

Shakespeare's Richard II, he acquires a dignity he has never had before and, by the time he was murdered by a group of Persian soldiers from Ma'mūn's army in the small hours of the morning, he has become a martyr, trying to fend off the swords of his murderers with the cushions left in the room. 'I am the cousin of the Prophet of God!' he cries. 'May God avenge my blood.' The death of a caliph was always a terrible thing. Uthmān, Walīd II and Amīn all had their failings, but their murders were seen by most Muslims as horrible crimes and their deaths only unleashed more suffering.

After the death of Amīn it took some six years for Ma'mūn, with the aid of his eastern Iranian supporters, to establish control over the whole caliphate, though even then Tunisia was never recovered by the Baghdad government and independent rulers appeared in the Maghreb as they had in Spain fifty years before. Ma'mūn brought with him a whole new elite of eastern Iranian aristocrats and Turkish mercenary soldiers. Turks from Central Asia (modern Turkey was not settled by Turkish speakers until the end of the eleventh century) were renowned for their hardiness in warfare and their skill in horsemanship: they made formidable professional soldiers. Apart from the caliph himself, and some members of his immediate family, virtually no one who had served under Hārūn al-Rashīd was accepted into the new ruling class and their children and grandchildren mostly disappeared into the seething mass of the Baghdad population. The new elite brutally deposed their predecessors. In Egypt, for example, it was decreed that the Arabs of the old army of the province should be dropped from the payroll and replaced by Turkish soldiers, newly arrived from the east, with little knowledge of Islam or the Arabic language of the Egyptians over whom they ruled and whose taxes paid their salaries.

In the short run the policy was effective. The new army suppressed revolts efficiently and the power of the caliphs was largely unchallenged, but in the long run the changes were fatal to the caliphal office and the unity of the Muslim community it symbolized. There was now a huge gap between ordinary rulers and the caliph and his advisers, hidden behind the forbidding walls of the vast palaces they built along the banks of the Tigris. The caliph could no longer count on the support and allegiance of the wider Muslim community.

Along with a new ruling elite and army, the new regime brought new ideas. Ma'mūn, as we shall see in the next chapter, was a genuine intellectual with a keen interest in science and philosophy, but not all his ideas were popular with his subjects. The most contentious of his moves was to support the doctrine of the 'createdness' of the Qur'ān. Muslims accepted that the Qur'ān was indeed the word of God – no one disputed that – but some held that it had been created by God at a particular moment in time, that is when God revealed it to Muhammad through the mouth of the angel Gabriel. The opponents of this view were convinced that the Qur'ān had existed in all eternity, coeval with God, and that it had simply been presented to mankind at the time of Muhammad's revelation. At first sight this looks like an obscure difference over a point of doctrine which is intrinsically unknowable. Yet it provoked a storm of opposition which, in the end, did enormous damage to the reputation and power of the caliphs.

People objected to the doctrine because it could be argued that if the Qur'ān was created in time, it could be interpreted in view of changing conditions. Perhaps, even, new revelations would come to light. And it would fall to the caliph to judge on these matters. People also objected to the way in which Ma'mūn asserted the right of the caliph to make judgements and decisions on such questions of belief. Previous caliphs, Umayyads and Abbasids alike, had claimed the right to adjudicate on difficult points of Islamic law, but this was different. It was a bold move by the caliph to assert his right to define doctrine, very much as the popes of the high Middle Ages were to do in western Europe.

Many of the leaders of the opposition to the doctrine came from families which had been prominent in the army and bureaucracy of the early Abbasid regime but who had now lost their status and their salaries. Discontent had only increased when Ma'mūn's successor, the military caliph Mu'tasim, moved the capital from Baghdad to his newly founded city of Samarra, eighty miles north, where he established the centre of government. In part, the opposition to the new doctrine was based in Baghdad, at least in part a product of the resentment of its inhabitants with the moving of the capital and the losses that this entailed.

The new regime was determined to push through this new ideology. All employees of the government had to support it; prisoners taken by the Byzantines in frontier warfare and wanting to be ransomed had to agree that the Qur'ān was created before the authorities would pay for their freedom. For the only time in the long history of the office, a caliph had taken it upon himself to decide on a major theological issue and to enforce his opinion on anyone who wanted to play an important part in the military or civilian hierarchy. In order to do this an inquisition (*mihna*) was set up to examine and, if necessary, punish those who objected. Again, this was the first and last time such a body was set up by a caliph.

The policy aroused enormous opposition, especially in Baghdad. The most vocal advocate of opposition was Ahmad b. Hanbal. Ibn Hanbal was a jurist and polemicist who argued forcefully that any decisions about Islamic law and practice should be based on the Traditions of the Prophet and nothing else. The guardians and interpreters of the Traditions were the scholars who collected and studied them, the professionals in fact. No caliph or ruler could acquire the amount of information or memorize the number of Traditions required to make an intelligent judgement.

There was a minor popular rebellion in Baghdad, though it was easily suppressed by government forces. The more general opposition, fuelled by the writings and preaching of the Hanbalites, persisted stubbornly. In the end Caliph Mutawwakil (847–61) and his advisers decided to abandon the losing struggle and the doctrine of the createdness of the Qur'ān was quietly dropped while a raft of measures, including the stigmatization of religious minorities, was introduced to demonstrate the caliph's commitment to Islamic values. The whole incident shaped the political and above all the religious role of the caliph from then on. The powers of judgement which the Orthodox caliphs, the Umayyads and the early Abbasids had assumed as a matter of course were lost to the professional jurists. Their power and authority came not from the caliph or any government official but from the respect of their fellow jurists and the approbation of the public, who sought and valued their *fatwas* (legal opinions). The caliph had become a ruler without powers of legislation in many of the matters which affected his subjects most closely.

This ideological debacle was followed by political collapse. The caliphs had moved to Samarra and lived in great palaces surrounded by high fortress-like walls, seldom, as far as we know, appearing in public. They were surrounded by the Turkish troops who formed their guard. In 861 Mutawwakil was murdered in his palace during one of the wine-drinking sessions which were a conspicuous feature of his reign. The reasons lay in the jealousy of his son and heir, who feared that he was being replaced by his brother, and the Turkish guards, who equally felt that their status was being undermined by other groups in the army. As in the cases of Uthmān, Walīd II and Amīn, the killing of the caliph opened the door to tragedy and disaster. The new caliph had little time to enjoy his status, and in the claustrophobic and murderous world of Samarra caliphs succeeded each other with terrifying rapidity, killed in most cases by Turkish soldiers whose salaries they had been unable to pay.

From 861 to 870 the caliphs were largely isolated by the power struggles in Samarra. Meanwhile, in the rest of the Islamic world, people found that they could do without a ruling and effective caliph. In Egypt the local governor Ibn Tūlūn, himself of Turkish descent, simply took over the province, the first independent ruler of Egypt, it has been said, since Cleopatra, and ushered in a time of peace and prosperity which contrasted markedly with the mayhem in Iraq. Most of eastern Iran was taken over by a family of military adventurers called the Saffarids. They were Muslims, to be sure, but they were also Persians who knew no Arabic (they had to have panegyrics written in the New Persian language so that they could understand, and enjoy, the praises of the poets). Their allegiance was to Islam, not to the powerless caliph.

The anarchy came to an end in 870 with a new and largely powerless caliph in Samarra and, more importantly, his brother, who took the quasi-caliphal title of Muwaffaq (though he never became caliph himself). He succeeded because he had close relations with commanders of the Turkish military, but he ruled over a very diminished realm. Only central Iraq and some areas of Syria and western Iran remained to the caliphs. Muwaffaq began to regain the territory lost to the government The first task was to recover southern Iraq, which had been taken over by a group of rebels known as the Zanj. The Zanj were East African slaves who had been imported into southern Iraq by rich landowners to help clear the salt which had accumulated on the irrigated fields and was making agriculture impossible. It was terrible work in the baking hot, shadeless fields and it is not surprising that social revolt broke out – the only mass slave revolt in Middle Eastern history. It seems that their leader was an Arab who claimed to be a member of the Family of the Prophet and, ideologically, this was a Shi'ite rebellion, with the Family once more casting themselves as leaders of the oppressed. Muwaffaq, however, chose to portray it as an anti-Islamic, essentially pagan movement. This enabled him to claim that his men were fighting a *jihād*, led by the Abbasid family, to save Islam. The long-drawn-out campaign was described in detail in a long narrative account commissioned by Muwaffaq and his victories were widely publicized by letters and from the pulpits.

In the end the rebels were conquered and the revived Abbasid caliphate was established as an important regional power, ruling over Iraq and parts of Iran and Syria. In 905 they even reconquered Egypt for a short while. Furthermore, many of the other regional powers found it useful to have diplomas of investiture from the caliph to establish their legitimacy, even if the banner and the diploma which came from Baghdad (now again the capital) were simply recognizing a fait accompli.

The Disastrous Reign of Caliph Muqtadir

This modest revival, which might in turn have led to a more widespread acceptance of Abbasid rule in the Islamic world, came to a halt in the reign of Caliph Muqtadir (908–32). He succeeded his brother Muktafī as a result of a court intrigue. The problem was that he was a boy who had barely entered his teens, very much under the influence of his powerful and controlling mother, known to all as Sayyida (Lady). Many disapproved of the appointment of an inexperienced youth to this highest office, but, for a small and powerful clique led by the vizier Ibn al-Furāt, his young age was his chief attraction: he could be managed and manipulated. The reign was an almost unmitigated disaster. The administration was paralysed by repeated financial crises and frequent changes of vizier.

Meanwhile the Byzantines, taking advantage of the chaos, were beginning to capture Muslim-held towns on the frontier and, perhaps even worse, the pilgrimage caravans were attacked by a Bedouin group following a Shi'ite ideology known as the Qarāmita or Carmathians. Male pilgrims were massacred, their women and children sold into captivity. Even Mecca itself, under nominal Abbasid rule, was not safe: the city was sacked, the corpses of massacred inhabitants were thrown into the sacred well Zamzam and the Black Stone was wrenched from the fabric of the Ka'ba and stolen by the rebels. The Abbasid could do nothing to fulfil the most central obligation of the caliph: to protect the frontiers of Islam and ensure the safety of the *hajj*. The end came when Muqtadir, still a comparatively young man, was killed in battle fighting the chief of the army which was supposed to be protecting him. In the confused period which followed, power was assumed by a series of military adventurers who took the title of Emir of Emirs, a title which implied complete control over all aspects of the secular administration but which carried no religious implications. Not only did they take over the remains of the army, they took over all the civil bureaucracy as well, abolishing the vizierate and leaving the caliph a powerless figurehead in his vast palace beside the Tigris. The failure of the Abbasid caliphate was clear for every Muslim to see.

Despite, or perhaps because of, this political weakness, there seems to have been an attempt by the Abbasid administration to develop the role of the caliph as leader of the

Muslims in relation with the non-Muslim world. After the initial Arab conquests of the seventh and early eighth centuries which established the great caliphate, the caliphs conducted little foreign policy. Those who lived beyond the borders of the Dār al-Islam (House of Islam), in the unchartered and barbarous wastes of the Dār al-Harb (House of War), were too insignificant and too poor to be of much interest. The Byzantine Empire was the only power with which the caliphs could deal on anything like equal terms, but their sporadic negotiations over truces and exchanges of prisoners hardly amounted to diplomacy.

In the tenth century there were signs that this was changing. Whether this was a deliberate policy on the part of Caliph Muqtadir and his advisers to expand and publicize the caliph's role as a spokesman for the *umma*, or whether it was chance, is difficult to know. But sources preserve two narratives which show the ruler in this role and the very fact that these narratives were elaborated points to a measure of official interest if nothing more.

The first of these narratives gives the fullest description of Abbasid ceremonial during the reception of two ambassadors from the Byzantine Empire in June 917. They had come to ask for a truce on the frontier and an exchange of prisoners, fairly routine business, but the vizier Ibn al-Furāt decided to make a great show of it. The envoys were given lodgings and provided with all they required. When the day for audience came

> the vizier gave orders that the soldiers should line the
> streets the whole way from the palace of Sa'id [where they
> were staying] to his own palace and that his own retainers

and troops with the vice-chamberlains posted in the palace should form a line from the doorway of the palace to the reception room. A vast saloon with a gilt roof in a wing of the palace called the Garden Wing was splendidly furnished and hung with curtains resembling carpets. 30,000 dinars was spent on new furniture, carpets and curtains. No mode of beautifying the palace or increasing the magnificence of the occasion was neglected. The vizier himself sat on a splendid prayer carpet with a lofty throne behind him and serving men in front and behind and left and right while the saloon was filled with military and civil officials. The two envoys were then introduced, having seen on their way such troops and crowds as might fill them with awe.

When they entered the public apartments, they were told to sit down in the veranda, the apartment being filled with troops. They were then taken down a long passage which took them to the quadrangle of the Garden which led them to the room in which the vizier was seated. The magnificence of the room and of its furniture and the crowd of attendants formed an impressive spectacle. They were accompanied by an interpreter and the prefect of police and his whole force. They were made to stand before the vizier whom they saluted, their words being translated by the interpreter, and the vizier made a reply which was also interpreted. They made a request for the redemption of the captives and asked for the vizier's help in obtaining the agreement of Muqtadir. He informed them that he would have to interview the caliph on the subject, and would have to act according to the instructions he received . . . They were dismissed and led out by the same route they had come in, soldiers still lining the road in full dress and perfect equipment. The uniform consisted of royal satin tunics, with close-fitting caps over which were satin hoods pointed at the top.[5]

The interview with the caliph himself followed the same pattern. The envoys were led to the palace through streets lined with uniformed soldiers.

When they reached the palace they were taken into a corridor which led into one of the quadrangles, thence they turned into another corridor which led to a quadrangle wider than the first and the chamberlains kept leading them through corridors and quadrangles until they were weary with walking and quite bewildered. These corridors and quadrangles were all crowded with retainers and servants. Finally they approached the saloon in which Muqtadir was to be found, where all the officers of state were be found standing according to their different ranks, while Muqtadir was seated on his imperial throne, with the vizier Ibn al-Furāt standing near him and Mu'nis the eunuch [commander of the army] with his officers next to him stationed on his right and left. When they entered the saloon they kissed the ground and stationed themselves where they were told to stand by Nasr the Chamberlain. They then delivered their master's letter, proposing a ransoming of prisoners and asking for a favourable response. The vizier replied for the caliph that he accepted the proposal out of compassion for the Muslim prisoners and the desire to set them free and his zeal to obey God and deliver them . . . When the envoys left the imperial presence they were presented with precious cloaks adorned with gold and turbans of the same material and similar honours were bestowed on the interpreter, who rode home with them.

Each of the envoys was given a private present of 20,000 silver dirhams. The account then goes on to relate how Mu'nis was given the enormous sum of 170,000 gold dinars from the Baghdad treasury to effect the ransoming.

The account is interesting for the insight it gives into the role of the caliph and the manipulation of the caliphal image. A broadly similar one is repeated in several Arabic sources but not in any Byzantine ones. The great display of troops in Baghdad, the elaborate ceremonial in the palace and the publicity which followed were designed to impress the Muslim population with the splendour and power of the caliph and his concern for the welfare of Muslims. It was also the last hurrah of Abbasid power. Within only a few years Ibn al-Furāt and the caliph were dead and the huge palace had become the scene of murder and mayhem as different factions fought for control over the increasingly powerless caliphate.

The second narrative preserves the record of caliphal diplomacy outside the lands of Islam. It is also the earliest first-person travel narrative in Arabic literature.[6] It describes the travels of one Ibn Fadlān, an agent of the Baghdad government, who travelled to Central Asia and in the Volga region of what is now Russia on a diplomatic mission. Ibn Fadlān's account, discovered in a manuscript in Mashad, Iran, only in

1923, is now mostly read for his exceptional, even lurid, description of the customs of a people whom he refers to as the Rus, which seems to be the earliest eye-witness description of the ancestors of the Russians. However, the account is also revealing as a record of the travels and reactions of a caliphal official at a time when his master's power was visibly waning. We know almost nothing about the author except what he tells us incidentally in his narrative. He was clearly a bureaucrat of some standing and education but not important enough to appear in any of the general narrative sources of the period.

The mission set out in response to a letter which had been sent to the caliph by the king of the Volga Bulgars, who had converted to Islam. He professed his loyalty to the caliph and said that his name would be proclaimed in the Friday sermons in the Bulgar lands. He asked that the caliph send him men who could teach him and his followers about Islamic law and the correct performance of prayer and other rituals. He also asked for money to build a castle (*hisn*) to defend him against his enemies in this land of felt yurts and wooden huts. The connection between monotheism and masonry is one that we find in many places in Celtic, Slavic and Scandinavian Europe at the time. The king wanted proper religion and new technology, both important aspects of being modern in the early tenth century, and for him, at least, the caliph was the proper person to ask. In western Christendom it would probably have been the pope.

The court in Baghdad decided to send a mission and the expedition set out on 21 June 921. It was to be a long journey. The men eventually arrived at the court of the Bulgar king on the Volga river eleven months later, on 12 May 922, having travelled about 3,000 miles, meaning that they must have averaged about ten miles a day. Given the political uncertainties and the terrible winter weather they encountered, this was a pretty impressive record. Their route lay through the Zagros Mountains and along the northern edge of the central Iranian desert to Bukhara, where the Samanid emir held court in the name of the caliph but in reality as an independent ruler. From there they headed for the fertile province of Khwarazm (modern Khorezm) on the delta of the river Oxus at the south end of the Aral Sea. These were the last outposts of Muslim settlement and civilization and from here they had to strike out into the unknown.

The first stages of the journey were easy enough, through the cultivated lands of central Iraq and along the old Khurasan road, which led through the mountains to the Iranian plateau. As they approached the ancient city of Rayy (just south of modern Tehran), in the narrow gap between the great desert to the south and the mountains to the north, they became aware, if they were not already, of the limitations of the power of the caliph. Rayy and the other towns on the route were under the control of the Zaydi Shi'ite imams, based in Daylam at the south-west corner of the Caspian Sea. These Shi'ite rulers were not simply usurpers of caliphal power but men who rejected the legitimacy of the Abbasids and their right to be considered leaders of the *umma*. The members of the mission were obliged to hide their identity and mingle with the rest of the caravan.

It must have been with considerable relief that they reached Nishapur and the protection of the Samanid army.

They pushed on east to Merv, where they changed camels for the journey across the waterless desert to the Oxus. After crossing the river they passed through the trading town of Paykant and the well-watered villages of the Bukhara oasis until they reached the capital. Here they were on friendly territory. The Samanid vizier, a man called Jayhānī, was a cultivated bureaucrat and a man with a keen interest in geography. He made arrangements for a residence for the party and 'appointed someone to attend to our needs and concerns and made sure that we experienced no difficulty in getting what we wanted'. He also arranged for them to have an audience with the Samanid emir Nasr b. Ahmad in person. They discovered, apparently to Ibn Fadlān's surprise, that he was a beardless boy. Young though he may have been, he was well trained in diplomatic niceties. He greeted them and invited them to sit down. 'How was my master (mawlā) the Commander of the Faithful when you left him? May God give him long life and cherish him and his retinue and his spiritual companions.' 'He was well,' they replied. He said, 'May God increase his well-being!' That was the easy part: now they had to get down to business and it was here that the limitations of the authority of the caliph in this distant but important province became apparent.

The next stop was Khwarazm where the emir was a vassal of the Samanids. The welcome they received was mixed. They were greeted warmly and given a place to stay, but the governor was suspicious about their desire to meet the king of the Bulgars: if anyone should represent the Muslims to these infidels, it should be the Samanid emir in Bukhara, not the distant and virtually powerless caliph in Baghdad.

He argued that the mission was too dangerous and that he should write to the emir, who would in turn write to the caliph to consult him. It was clearly a delaying tactic, which would almost certainly have prevented the mission from continuing, but Ibn Fadlān and his companions persisted: 'We have the letter of the Commander of the Faithful,' they said. 'Why do you need to consult?' In the end they were allowed to proceed into the bitter cold of the steppe: our author paints a vivid picture of the cold and suffering they endured, so different from the heat of Baghdad.

When they finally approached the camp of the king of the Bulgars in May 922, they were met first by a guard of honour of the king's sons and then by the monarch himself, who dismounted and prostrated himself, giving thanks to God. They were led to the camp and assigned their own yurts while the king prepared to give them a ceremonial welcome. After four days they were granted an audience. They presented the king with two standards, symbolizing the conferment of office, a saddle and a black turban. Ibn Fadlān then read out the caliph's letter, insisting that all stood to hear it. 'Peace be upon you,' he read. 'On your behalf I praise God – there is no other god but Him.' And he then ordered them to return the greeting of the Commander of the Faithful, which they duly did. Next began the present-giving – perfumes, garments and pearls and a robe of honour for the queen who, in complete contrast to Muslim court protocol, was sitting by the king's side.

An hour later there was another audience in the royal yurt. On the king's right were seated vassal kings while the envoys were placed on his left. His sons sat before him while he himself sat at the centre on a throne covered with Byzantine silk. A ceremonial meal followed with the king cutting choice bits of meat, first for himself and then for his guests. Then the king drank a toast in mead speaking of his joy in his master (*mawlā*) the Commander of the Faithful, 'may God prolong his life'.

Ibn Fadlān also gave instruction in the performance of prayers. Before he came, blessings were called on the kings from the *minbar* at Friday prayers, but Ibn Fadlān advised that 'God is the king and he alone should be accorded that title from the *minbar*. Your master, the Commander of the Faithful, for example, is satisfied with the phrase, "Lord God, keep in piety your slave and caliph the imam Ja'far al-Muqtadir bi-llah, Commander of the Faithful," as this is proclaimed from all the *minbars* in east and west.' He also drew attention to the *hadīth* in which the Prophet says that Muslims should not exaggerate his importance in the way in which the Christians exaggerated the importance of Jesus son of Mary, and that He was simply the slave of God and his messenger.

Naturally the king then asked what should be proclaimed from the pulpit on Friday. 'Your name and the name of your father,' was the reply. 'But my father was an unbeliever,' he said, 'and I do not wish to have his name proclaimed from the *minbar*. Indeed I do not wish to have my own name mentioned, because it was given to me by an unbeliever. What is the name of my master (*mawlā*), the Commander of the Faithful?'

'Ja'far,' Ibn Fadlān replied.

'Am I permitted to take his name?'

'Yes.

'Then I take Ja'far as my name and Abd Allah as the name of my father. Tell this to the preacher.'

Ibn Fadlān did as instructed and the proclamation during the sermon on Friday became 'Lord God, keep in piety your slave Ja'far b. Abd Allah, the *amīr* of the Bulghars, whose master is the Commander of the Faithful.'

Many in the Muslim world held Muqtadir in contempt. Youthful and inexperienced, his failure to live up to the achievements of his Abbasid ancestors was coming close to making a mockery of the office of caliph. Yet for the king of the Bulgars the caliph represented the Muslim world in a very personal way. His master was not the *umma*, not the religious scholars, not Muslims in general, but the caliph in person.

The Break-up of the Abbasid Caliphate

The break-up of the caliphate was a long and complex business, but the reasons for it need to be explored. Any discussion of a future or revived caliphate at the present day must address why the Abbasid dynasty, despite its political power and its connections with the Family of the Prophet, disintegrated when it did. The problems of holding together a multicultural Muslim world becoming ever more diverse under a single leadership were never fully resolved and will form a major and intractable challenge to anyone wishing to revive the office in the future.

One reason has been touched on above: the growing alienation of the caliphs from the mass of the Muslim population. This was partly physical, as the caliphs increasingly isolated themselves within the walls of their palaces, but also ideological, as the governing elite initially tried to enforce belief in the createdness of the Qur'ān. Even though this policy had been abandoned, it had left a deep and lasting rift between the caliphs and the religious leaders who were respected and consulted by the mass of Muslims. This alienation was compounded by the failure of the Abbasid caliphs in the first half of the tenth century to perform the most obvious public duties of the office, to defend the frontiers of the Muslim world, especially against the Byzantines, and to protect and lead the *hajj*.

But there were other more long-term problems. The first was the economic collapse of Iraq and especially of Iraqi agriculture. At the time of the Muslim conquests Iraq had been the richest province of the caliphate in terms of tax revenue (the only figures we have). It yielded four times as much as Egypt, the next richest area, and five times as much as Syria and Palestine together. During the early Islamic period this situation changed, partly due to environmental factors like the increasing salinization and exhaustion of the soil, and partly because repeated civil wars and disturbances damaged the complex irrigation systems which carried water to the fields. This culminated in 935, when the greatest of the canals, the Nahrawan, which dated to pre-Islamic times, was breached by a military adventurer for short-term tactical gains and never subsequently repaired.

The tax revenues of Iraq were what enabled the Abbasids to pay the armies which enforced their authority and the bureaucrats who collected the revenues. As revenues declined inexorably, there were repeated army mutinies until the armies of the caliphs spent most of their energies fighting rival military groups and trying to extort money from the caliphs themselves.

There was another factor which was, in a way, more positive, and that was the conversion of an increasingly large proportion of the population of the caliphate to Islam. It can be argued that the break-up of the caliphate was the inevitable result of the success of Islam as a popular religion. This is a very difficult process to measure. We can be certain that there were no Muslims in these areas before the Arab conquests. Conversion was slow in the seventh and early eighth centuries but after that gathered pace, especially in the tenth century. By the year 1100, and before in some places, it is likely that 50 per cent of the population were Muslims of one group or another.

These new Muslims were not, in the main, Arabs. They probably never went to Baghdad (except if they passed through on the road from Iran to the Holy Cities) and they had no contact with the caliphs. As has already been mentioned, groups like the Saffarid rulers of much of Iran in the late ninth century were Muslims but not Arabs. Their loyalties lay with fellow Muslims in the provinces where they originated and the caliphate was for them at best an irrelevance and at worst a source of vexatious tax demands. New Muslims had no reason to support an institution which had little or nothing to offer them.

This did not mean that the Muslim world divided into separate political units with no contact between them. Arabic was widely used as the language of religious and philosophical discussion. Merchants traded across borders with little or no interference from government, administrators wandered from one court to another looking for lucrative employment. In many ways the *umma* was a united commonwealth: it was just that the caliphs had no significant role in this.

CHAPTER 4

The Culture of the Abbasid Caliphate

In the year 932 the new caliph, Qāhir, asked one of his courtiers, Muhammad b. Alī al-Abdī, to chronicle the achievements of his Abbasid predecessors. It was a difficult time for the caliphate. Muqtadir had just been killed fighting his own army and enemies pressed in on every side. It was a far cry from the glory days of Hārūn al-Rashīd. The courtier, who was a specialist in history, responded with a short but fascinating series of portraits of the caliphs of the dynasty, and gives some guidance as to what the people remembered about them. This was then recorded by the leading historian of the day, Mas‘ūdī, in his 'Meadows of Gold' (*Murūj al-dhahab*), which is why it comes down to us.[1]

Caliph Qāhir was a genuinely frightening man, given to violent and unpredictable outbursts, which, combined with his heavy drinking, soon led to him being deposed and blinded. With a spear in his hand, he had the historian stand before him, and demanded the truth on pain of death.

Abdī began with the first Abbasid caliph Saffāh (750–54), who was 'quick to spill blood . . . but atoned for this defect by considerable nobility of spirit and great generosity. He gave constantly and scattered gold with an open hand.' His successor Mansūr (754–75) was the first to sow discord between the family of Abbās and the family of Alī, who until then had made common cause. He was the first of the caliphs to bring astrologers to his court and make decisions according to the stars . . . He was also the first caliph to have foreign works of literature translated into Arabic, for example, *Kalīla wa Dimna* [celebrated animal fables translated from the Persian], the *Sindhind* [presumably a book about India], Aristotle's treatises on logic and other subjects, Ptolemy's *Almagest*, the book of Euclid, the 'treatise on arithmetic', and all the other ancient works, Greek, Byzantine, Pahlavi [Middle Persian] and Syriac. Once in possession of these books, the public read and studied them avidly.

According to Abdī, Mansūr was also the first ruler to distribute public offices among his freedmen and pages. He employed them in matters of importance and advanced them over the Arabs. This practice was followed after his time by the caliphs who were his heirs and it was thus that the Arabs lost the high command, the supremacy and the honours they had enjoyed until then.

From the time of his accession to the throne, Mansūr devoted himself to learning. He applied himself to the study of religious and philosophical ideas and acquired a profound knowledge of the different Muslim sects as well as of the Muslim Tradition. During his reign, the schools of the Traditionists (that is, those who studied the *hadīth* of Muhammad) increased in number and widened the scope of their studies.

Abdī's account continued:

Mahdī [775–85] was good and generous and his character was noble and liberal . . . This caliph had the habit, when appearing in public, of having purses filled with gold and silver carried before him. No one solicited his charity in vain and the steward who walked ahead had orders to give alms to those who did not dare to ask, anticipating their need . . . He was merciless in exterminating heretics.

Here Abdī lists the dualists and other sect who appeared during Mahdī's reign, adding that Mahdī

was the first to order the polemicists of the theological schools to refute them. They produced convincing proofs against their wrong-headed adversaries and overthrew the weak arguments of the heretics and made the truth shine forth to all who doubted. He rebuilt the mosque in Mecca and that of the Prophet in Medina in the form they stand today and he rebuilt Jerusalem, which had been damaged by earthquakes.

Of Hārūn al-Rashīd (786–809), Abdī said that he was

scrupulous in fulfilling his role as a pilgrim and in waging holy war. He undertook public works, wells, cisterns, forts on the road to Mecca, and also in that city at Mina and Arafat [both important sites in the *hajj* rituals], and in Medina. He scattered both wealth and the treasure of his justice on all his subjects. He strengthened the frontiers against the Byzantine Empire, built cities, fortified several towns such as Tarsus and Adana, revived the prosperity of Massissa and Marash [all now in southern Turkey but then part of the network of Muslim settlements along the frontier] and carried out innumerable works of military architecture, as well as building caravanserais. His officials followed his example. The people imitated his behaviour and followed the direction he pointed out. Error was repressed, the truth reappeared and Islam, shining with new splendour, eclipsed all other nations.

The very type of generosity and charity in this reign was manifested in the person of Umm Ja'far Zubayda, the daughter of Ja'far and the granddaughter of [the caliph] Mansūr. This princess had numerous caravanserais built at Mecca and she filled this city, and the pilgrim road which bears her name, with cisterns, wells and buildings which survive to this day. She also built several hospices for travellers along the Syrian frontier and at Tarsus and endowed them.

The Barmakids then get a mention for their generosity before the author returns to Hārūn as the first caliph to popularize the game of polo, shooting arrows at the *birjās* (quintain, a movable target on a pole) and playing with balls and rackets. He rewarded those who distinguished them-selves in these various exercises and these games spread among the people. He was also the first among the Abbasid caliphs to play chess and backgammon. He favoured players who distinguished themselves and paid them salaries. Such was the splendour, wealth and prosperity of his reign that they called this period the Days of Marriage and Feast.

The narrator was then interrupted by the caliph, who demanded that he say more about Zubayda. 'I obey,' he said. 'The nobility and magnificence of this princess, in serious

THE CULTURE OF THE ABBASID CALIPHATE

matters as well as frivolous, have led her to be placed in the
very first rank.' As regards the more serious matters, he gives
more details of her pious building works and especially the
water supply of Mecca. He then moves on to the more frivolous expenses:

> those of which kings are most vain . . . She was the first to
> be served on dishes of gold and silver enriched with
> precious stones. For her the finest clothes were made of the
> multicoloured silk known as *washī*, a single length of which,
> designed for her, cost 50,000 dinars. She was the first to
> organize an escort of eunuchs (who, of course, could serve
> her in a personal capacity) and slave girls who rode by her
> side, fulfilled her orders and delivered her messages. She
> was the first to make use of tents of silver, ebony and
> sandalwood, decorated with clasps of gold and silver and
> hung with embroidered silk, sable, brocade and red, yellow,
> green and blue silk. She was the first to introduce the
> fashion for slippers embroidered with precious stones and
> for candles made of ambergris, fashions which spread to
> the public. Then, O Commander of the Faithful, when the
> caliphate passed to her son [Amīn 809–13], he favoured his
> eunuchs and showed his preference by bestowing on them
> the highest honours. Zubayda, noticing her son's marked
> taste for these eunuchs and the influence they were having
> over him, chose young girls remarkable for the elegance of
> their figures and the charm of their faces. She had them
> wear turbans, and gave them clothes woven and
> embroidered in the royal factories, and had them fix their
> hair with fringes and lovelocks and draw it back to the nape

of the neck after the fashion of young men. She dressed them in the close-fitting, wide-sleeved robes called *qaba* and wide belts which showed off their waists and their curves. Then she sent them to her son Amin and as they filed into his presence he was enchanted. He was captivated by their looks and appeared with them in public. It was then that the fashion for having young slave girls with short hair, wearing *qaba* and belts, became established at all levels of society. They were called 'page girls'.

Here the caliph interrupted again. 'Page,' he cried out, 'a cup of wine in honour of the slave girls!' Immediately a swarm of young girls appeared, all the same height and all looking like young men. They were all wearing tight-fitting jackets, *qaba* and all had fringes. They wore their hair in lovelocks and had belts of gold and silver. While the caliph was raising his cup, I admired the purity of its jewels, the sparkle of the wine which gilded it with its rays, and I went into raptures about the beauty of these young girls.

But Qāhir was still holding his frightening lance. He drank the cup straight off and said to me, 'Go on!'

The historian went on, diplomatically avoiding discussion of the deposed and murdered Amīn, and moving on to his brother, Ma'mūn (813–33):

At the beginning of his reign this caliph was under the influence of Fadl b. Sahl [his Persian vizier] and other courtiers. He devoted himself to the study of astrology and its rulings. He modelled his conduct on the Sasanian kings like Ardashir son of Babak [224–41] and others. He had a passion for old books and studied them constantly, pursuing his researches until he succeeded in understanding them and getting to their very heart . . . On his arrival in Iraq, Ma'mūn gave up his favourite studies and professed the doctrine of Unity and the Promise and the Threat,[2] that is, the doctrines of the Mu'tazilites. He presided over conferences of theologians and attracted to his court polemicists famous in debate. His meetings were always attended by learned jurists and literary men whom he brought from many different cities and to whom he gave salaries. The populace acquired a taste for philosophical speculation, the study of dialectic became fashionable and each school wrote works in support of their arguments and the doctrines they professed.

As for Ma'mūn himself:

He was the most clement and patient of men. No one has made better use of their power, been more open-handed, more general in their gifts or less inclined to regret them. Ministers and courtiers all imitated him carefully; all followed his example and walked in his footsteps.

The historian finishes with brief accounts of Mu'tasim (833–42), 'fond of horses and wishing to imitate Persian kings in his table service'; Wāthiq (842–7), strict in his religious beliefs and a great gourmet; and Mutawwakil (847–61), 'who forbade the study of different religious opinions and re-established belief in authority and the teaching of the Traditions. His reign was happy and his government stable and well founded.' None of the later caliphs is mentioned.

Mas'ūdi's account is interesting for all sorts of reasons.

Perhaps the most striking is that the leading role is played by a woman, Zubayda, who is admired for her pious works but also as the epitome of court style. He also makes some political judgements, for example about Mansūr's promotion of freedmen and the consequent loss of status for the Arabs. It is surprising to see Mansūr, who comes across in other sources as the ultimate hard-headed politician, depicted as a patron of astrology and the translation of philosophical literature. We know of Ma'mūn's interest in ancient literature and old books from other sources but he, like Mansūr, is also credited here with the encouragement of the religious sciences like the study of the Qur'ān and the Traditions of the Prophet. Mahdī's active protection of the faith against heresy and Mutawwakil's return to strict orthodoxy after the more speculative intellectual atmosphere of the court of his predecessors both demonstrate the important influence individual caliphs could exert as leaders of the Muslim community.

The Knowledge Economy under the Abbasids

The period of the greatness of the Abbasid caliphate, from 750 to 945, saw an extraordinary explosion of cultural activity. It was a time of intellectual openness and diversity which has few parallels in human history. What caused this tremendous cultural efflorescence?

Let us begin by looking at the infrastructure of knowledge. It has already been pointed out that the administrative systems developed by Umar I after the great Arab conquests, and subsequently elaborated by both Umayyad and Abbasid governments, led to the emergence of very large towns, first in Iraq in Kufa and Basra, later in Egypt at Fustat, in Tunisia at Qayrawan and in Khurasan at Merv. To these centres were added, from the middle of the eighth century, the two greatest Muslim cities of the early Middle Ages, Baghdad and Córdoba. In all these cities, there were bureaucrats and soldiers who were paid salaries on a regular basis. These salaries meant that they could spend money on the necessities of everyday life, food and clothing and so on, but many of them also had money to spend on discretionary purchases, which might include fine textiles, ceramics and exotic foods but also books and intangible but very important cultural productions like poetry, song and the Traditions of the Prophet. All these items bore cultural capital and social prestige.

The administrative arrangements led to the development of an infrastructure of skilled people who could manage it. It is well known that the Umayyad caliph Abd al-Malik made Arabic the language of administration throughout the caliphate. The effect of this was to produce a class of secular bureaucrats who could read and write. It also generated a demand for education in mathematics, not only accounting skills to deal with tax receipts but also the geometrical skills required for assessing areas of land for taxation purposes. If skills had not been essential for the needs of government, it is unlikely that either Arabic literacy or mathematical knowledge would have developed in the way they did.

The rise of the importance of the bureaucracy coincided with the emergence of a wide reading public. Levels of literacy are impossible to assess in the absence of any statistical data, but it appears from accounts of literary activity in, say, Baghdad in the ninth century, that the ability to read and write was regarded as normal and taken for granted, not just among an intellectual elite but in a wide cross-section of society. Of course, this was encouraged by the need to read and understand the text of the Qur'ān for the proper practice of the Muslim faith. All the Umayyad and Abbasid caliphs were literate, although the warrior caliph Mu'tasim is said to have had difficulty with his letters, whereas it is worth remembering that the first English king who is known to have been able to read and write, with the exception perhaps of Alfred, was Edward I in the late thirteenth century.

A substantial reading population was of course essential to the growth of what literary historian Shawkat Toorawa has called a 'writerly culture' in ninth-century Baghdad,[3] but other developments were important for the infrastructure of culture as well. One of these was the introduction of paper. Paper had been invented and used in China for many centuries, but the arrival of this technology in the Islamic Middle East can be dated fairly precisely. There was a story current in the eleventh century that the art of paper-making was brought by Chinese prisoners of war captured by the Abbasid armies at the Battle of Talas (now in Kazakhstan) in 751, the only occasion on which Muslim and Chinese imperial armies came into direct conflict. Of course, historians have treated such simple explanatory narratives with some scepticism, but this may be unjustified. We know that Chinese prisoners of war were active in Iraq in the decades after the battle because one of them wrote an account of Iraq, in Chinese, after his return to his homeland. He does not mention paper, but the story provides a plausible context for this important transfer of technological know-how.

Just as important is the fact that there was a ready demand for new and more efficient writing materials in the society of the early Abbasid period: without this demand the introduction of paper would have been no more than a diverting curiosity. This paper, like almost all paper before the nineteenth century, was rag-paper, that is to say it was made of old textiles: wood-pulp paper was effectively unknown at this time. This was fortunate: there was probably not much timber to harvest in Abbasid Iraq in lands that had been intensively cultivated for millennia, but there were plenty of old clothes.

Jonathan Bloom, the historian of Islamic art, has shown how important the advent of paper was in cultural development, for, in a very fundamental way, paper democratized writing. It was both cheaper than parchment (animal skins) and more efficient than papyrus, the most widely used writing surfaces before this time. Paper meant that books could be produced cheaply and economically. Bloom points out that the invention transformed book production in a way which is perhaps comparable with the coming of printing in early modern Europe.[4]

There was another innovation at this time, again generated by the demand for easier and quicker production of reading materials, and that was the development of new forms of writing. We have a number of manuscripts, mostly but not entirely Qur'anic, which show Arabic hands of the seventh and early eighth century in a style of writing known as Kufic. It is formal, careful and often very elegant, but at the same time it was slow to write, each letter being carefully formed individually. In the early tenth century, if not before, a new hand emerged. It is said to have been first developed by Ibn Muqla, vizier to the caliph Muqtadir, but it is probable that his achievement was the culmination of some decades of experimentation. The new script, known as *naskhi*, or copyists' hand, was much faster and easier to write, almost a sort of shorthand, and while grand Qur'āns may still have been produced in Kufic, this new script was widely used for most other literary publications.

The use of paper and the new Arabic hand in turn made writing accessible to those without private means. It could be argued that Baghdad under the Abbasid caliphate was the first society in the history of the world in which a man or a woman could make a living as an author. Of course, people had written books before, thousands of them, but they had always been wealthy in their own right, employed or subsidized by rich patrons, or attached to institutions, like Christian monasteries, which gave them the space and security to write. In the ninth century Baghdad could boast a Grub Street culture where a would-be author could write a work, have it copied and sell it in the hundred or more shops in the Book Suq (*Sūq al-warrāqīn*), and make enough money to stay alive. It was not easy to live off one's writing, any more than it is in Britain today, but it was at least possible. And if your own books were not selling well, you could always fall back on copying other people's work to tide you over in the lean periods.

The technologies were in place, the demand was there, so what did the writers, poets and artists of the Abbasid caliphate produce? In the second half of the tenth century a Baghdadi writer called Ibn al-Nadīm (d. 995) compiled a book called *Fihrist*, which can best be translated as 'The Catalogue'. We do not know whether this is a library or a bookseller's catalogue, but in it the author lists some 3,500 authors with the names of the books they wrote and some information about their contents. Many of these books must have been very short, little more than pamphlets, but equally many were more substantial works. The variety of subjects they covered was truly astonishing. He divides his list into ten chapters:

1 Languages and scripts: the scriptures of the Muslims and other people of the book (37 pages)
2 Grammar and lexicography (51 pages)
3 History, belles-lettres, biography and genealogy (73 pages)
4 Poetry (22 pages)
5 Scholastic theology (47 pages)
6 Law and Tradition (38 pages)
7 Philosophy and the 'ancient sciences' (62 pages)
8 Stories, legends, romances, magic and conjuring (32 pages)
9 Doctrines of the non-monotheistic religions (32 pages)
10 Alchemy (9 pages)

We might expect to find Islamic religious sciences and Arabic poetry in such a list, but what is more surprising is the amount of material relating to other religions, to non-Arabic scripts and to science and philosophy. It seems that all human knowledge, as it existed at the time, is there somewhere and there is no hint that any subject was banned, censored or felt to be forbidden.

The Abbasid Poets

Poetry was the queen of the arts of the time. Since the great pre-Islamic poets of the Jābiliyya, with their images of the lone warrior and his camel, riding, fighting and loving in the harsh environment of the Arabian desert, poetry had conveyed the aspirations of men who lived more prosaic lives. It had also intrigued grammarians and literary critics who sought in it the origins of the Arabic language and more obscure points of grammar and lexicography. But of course most readers and listeners in the Abbasid caliphate did not live in the wild desert and their knowledge of, and enthusiasm for, camels was probably almost as limited as ours, so the poets of the Abbasid age moved on from the ancient and revered paradigms to reflect the largely urban and courtly world in which they participated.

Panegyric poetry was still the best way to make money: it is also the most difficult form of verse for us to appreciate. The extravagant and complex metaphors seem simply contrived and insincere, clearly designed to encourage rewards from the caliph or other patron. People at the time, however, had a different opinion. Just as we today can admire the flattering portraits of the powerful and wealthy painted by Velázquez or Goya because we can say that they are superb examples of the painter's art, so contemporaries valued praise poetry in the same way, for the startling new image or the subtle variations of common tropes.

Hunting poetry can also leave many of us cold, and poetry in praise of wine we can no longer taste is not much better, but the poetry of love can still resonate through the centuries, even in translation. Perhaps the best known of Abbasid love poets was Abū Nuwās, the 'father of locks (of hair)'. He flourished in the reign of Hārūn al-Rashīd, and especially in the circle of the young prince Amīn, where his innovative and unconventional poetic talents could develop. He writes of wine and love, openly glorifying both. The tavern, and the groups of young men drinking there, are celebrated with uninhibited enthusiasm. It may come as something of a surprise to find that drinking poetry was so popular in the Muslim society of the time, but it was one of the measures of the confidence and diversity of this society that it could accept such challenging images if they were presented elegantly and wittily. Abū Nuwās presents a world of common taverns, but the enjoyment of wine was also a central part of Abbasid court culture. Some caliphs, such as Mahdī, did not drink out of religious scruples, but many others did as part of princely display and performance.

Abū Nuwās wrote love poetry about women, but more often about young men and boys. Nor are the poems abstract and chaste fantasies. He celebrates gay sex with unconcealed enthusiasm which can sometimes catch modern readers by surprise: poems by middle-aged men praising the sexual attractiveness of schoolboys would, after all, be regarded as dangerously transgressive even, or perhaps particularly, in the early twenty-first century, but the celebration of same-sex love was a widely accepted literary form in both Arabic and later Persian poetry in the Islamic Middle East.

It is easy to seize on Abū Nuwās because his poetry was clever, eloquent, original and very popular, but it would be wrong to assume that he was typical of all the poets and writers of his time. Some, like his contemporary and sometime rival Abū'l-Atāhiya, became deeply pious and devoted themselves to religious themes, while others, like Abū Tammām in the ninth century, found new and interesting ways of praising their patrons, in his case the warrior caliph Mu'tasim, and celebrating their victories over the Byzantines. Perhaps the most striking feature of this poetry to the modern reader is its sheer variety: all male human life is there, and there was no attempt, either official or unofficial, to censor it. Pious people certainly disapproved of some of the sentiments expressed, but, in general, books were not burned, nor were poets imprisoned and punished.

The majority of poets in this era were male, but women played an important role in the performance of the culture. The singing girl (*jāriya*) is a characteristic presence in descriptions of gatherings, whether domestic or public, in which poetry was discussed. Most poems were sung and the singers were mostly young women. It is easy to forget this because there was at the time no form of musical notation; so while we have the lyrics of hundreds of songs, the tunes are completely lost to us. The singing girls learned and passed on the musical tradition. They appear in countless stories. They are clever and sassy and, needless to say, beautiful. They are also learned not only in music but sometimes in the Traditions of the Prophet and the religious sciences. They were usually slaves, trained up by masters in the Holy City of Medina and sold on in Baghdad, but before we consider the implications of their servile status we should remember the anecdote of one of Zubayda's (Hārūn's wife) conversations with one of the girls in her entourage. 'Are you a slave or free?' the queen asks, to which the girl replies, 'I don't know,' and Zubayda responds, 'No, nor do I.' In their knowledge and personalities the singing girls were major figures in the artistic environment. They were an integral part of the court culture of the caliphate, and when the caliphate collapsed in the middle of the tenth century, the singing girls disappeared from the cultural landscape at the same time.

The richness and variety of this literary and musical culture is evoked in one of those great compilations which the new technologies of writing had made possible, the great Book of Songs (*Kitāb al-aghāni*). Abū'l-Faraj al-Isfahānī (d. 967) began his great work by selecting the hundred best songs he could find and used this list as a framework to attach numerous other poems and, just as important, prose anecdotes about the lives and deeds of many of the poets and singers. The result is fascinating. The stories about the artists are unusual in their detailing of non-elite lives. An abiding theme of the collection is the way in which people from low and even outcast social backgrounds can rise to fame and fortune through their artistic talents, and this means that tales of the struggling poor form a central part of the work. Isfahānī was writing after the collapse of the Abbasid caliphate in the tenth century and his collection is, in some aspects, a memorial to a culture which was vanishing, but the riches it preserves gives us a wonderful panorama of this world.

The Abbasid Scientists

If poetry and song were the only literary products of this caliphal culture, it would be interesting but limited. In fact, cultural activity spread in many different directions. One of the most famous achievements of the period is the translation of ancient Greek works into Arabic and the intellectual ideas that emerged as a result. The Greek-speaking and -writing Byzantines, the Rūm of the Arabic sources, were of course arch-enemies of the early Muslims and warfare against them was maintained as a regular and pious exercise. This did not prove an obstacle, however, to the acquisition and appropriation of Greek learning. Muslims wanted Greek learning because they believed it to be useful and they translated and read those parts of the Greek canon which are almost completely ignored by modern western readers. They wanted Euclid's geometry, Ptolemy's astronomy, Galen's medicine and Dioscorides' knowledge of the usefulness of herbs and plants. Above all, they wanted to acquire and use the philosophy of Aristotle, both as a way of viewing the world, and as a tool box of logical techniques for constructing arguments.

On the other hand, they had no interest in ancient Greek poetry: after all they had plenty of ancient poetry of their own, so the *Iliad* and the *Odyssey* and all later poetry were completely ignored. Greek drama was an unopened book to them and they had no interest either in historical works. The *Histories* of Herodotus, which would have told them so much about the ancient Persians who built the ruins they saw at

Persepolis and the ancient Egyptians who built the pyramids, were unknown to them.

Caliphs and others had commissioned translations from the Greek from the Umayyad period onwards and, as we have seen, Mansūr was credited with initiating this practice, but it was the personal enthusiasm of Caliph Ma'mūn that really gave impetus to the translation movement. He was perhaps the most genuinely intellectual of the caliphs we encounter in this book and the fashion he set encouraged his courtiers to patronize translators and other intellectuals, paying them for their work and employing them in their great households as tutors for their children.

There are mentions in our sources from this period of an institution called the House of Wisdom (*Bayt al-hikma*). Enthusiastic modern historians have taken this to be a sort of proto-university, a college where distinguished scholars could work and debate in peace and a measure of prosperity. In reality, the House of Wisdom was simply a library where books were stored. To find scholars at work you had to go to the great houses where patrons would maintain resident intellectuals. In this sense Abbasid Baghdad was a bit like London and Paris during the Enlightenment: it was in the salons and the studies of government officials, including, of course, caliphs and private individuals, that learning flourished.

Many of the works which were translated into Arabic had previously been translated from Greek into Syriac, another Semitic language. Syriac was the literary version of Aramaic, the Semitic lingua franca of the Middle East before the Muslim conquests, and the translations had mostly been made in Christian monasteries, which were centres of Syrian intellectual activity. In this way they had already been through a filter. The monks were mainly interested in the same sort of practical texts as the Muslim scholars were. They did not, on the whole, translate theological or devotional writings, as one might imagine, because they held the Byzantines to be heretics whose works were useless and corrupting.

The people who knew Greek and Syriac were mostly Christians and almost all the translations were carried out by members of the religious minorities. Let us take the example of Hunayn b. Ishāq (d. 873). Hunayn was a Christian from the city of Hira, near Kufa, in central Iraq. It had been a centre of Iraqi Christianity before the coming of Islam and the traditions of learning were clearly still alive. Hunayn was a skilled stylist in Greek, Syriac and Arabic and made a good living as a translator. A later biographer gives us a glimpse of his agreeable lifestyle:

> He went to the bath every day after his ride and had
> water poured on him. He would then come out wrapped
> in a dressing gown and, after taking a cup of wine with a
> biscuit, lie down until he had stopped perspiring.
> Sometimes he would fall asleep. Then he would get up,
> burn perfumes to fumigate his body and have dinner
> brought in. This consisted of a large fattened pullet stewed
> in gravy with a half kilo loaf of bread. After drinking some
> of the gravy and eating the chicken and the bread he would
> fall asleep. On waking up he drank four *ratls* [perhaps two
> litres] of old wine. If he felt like fresh fruit, he would have

some Syrian apples and quinces. This was his habit until the end of his life.[5]

Despite his relaxed approach, he was a prodigious worker. His output was enormous and his standards high.

The translation of Greek texts was much more than a passive reception of works from another culture. These writings stimulated a wave of new research and discussion in the Muslim world. Greek philosophy inspired Ya'qūb b. Ishāq al-Kindī, known as 'Philosopher of the Arabs'. Unlike many of the scholars who worked in Abbasid court circles, Kindī was an Arab from an ancient and aristocratic Bedouin lineage, but he spent his life in Baghdad and was a familiar figure at the courts of the caliphs Ma'mūn, Mu'tasim and Wāthiq. He also had a very extensive private library, which was a source of pleasure and pride until it was confiscated at the instigation of his intellectual rivals, the Banū Mūsā, though it was eventually returned to him. He was not himself a translator, but he was the first to use Aristotle's work to create an Islamic philosophical discourse in Arabic. He was also the first to grapple with the problem of reconciling faith with logical investigation.

This approach to Muslim doctrine aroused the suspicion and hostility of more conservative elements in society and there were continuous disputes between the philosophers and the Traditionists, who held that one should accept the teachings of the Qur'ān and *sunna* without further question. The issues were very similar to the discussions in twelfth-century France between the radical and flamboyant philosopher Peter Abelard and his opponent, the austere and dogmatic St Bernard, Abbot of Clairvaux. In both cases this was not a dispute about the truth of religion, between believers and atheists, but about ways of understanding and investigating religious ideas. For philosophers both in Baghdad in the ninth century and Paris in the twelfth, the ideals were *fides quaerens intellectum*, faith seeking understanding, and in both cases they came up against those who believed that investigating the divine mysteries could lead to heresy and unbelief. As long as caliphs like Ma'mūn and Wāthiq reigned, Kindī and those who thought like him were protected by the patronage of the court. But when in 847 Mutawwakil came to the throne, he reverted to strict orthodoxy, seeking the favour of the Traditionists, and the influence of philosophers was eclipsed.

Despite this hostility, the Arab philosophical tradition survived for centuries. In Andalus, at the time of the Almohad caliphs, the great Ibn Rushd (d. 1198) initiated the last original discussions in the canon. Arabic philosophy would ultimately survive the loss of caliphal patronage, but, without the initial protection and support of the court of the caliphs in the ninth century, it is unlikely that it would have developed and matured in the way it did. This openness to, and delight in, new ideas was fundamental.

The caliph Ma'mūn certainly showed a real interest in natural and experimental science. This can be seen in the story of his project to measure the circumference of the earth. There was no question that the earth was round: every educated person in ninth-century Baghdad knew that. But no one knew how big it was, and the caliph was determined to find out. He knew that the ancient Greeks had calculated it at 24,000 miles and he wanted to determine whether this was accurate. He asked the Banū Musa, who were his main scientific advisers, to investigate. As Ibn Khallikan recorded:

They enquired where a level plain could be found and were told that the desert of Sinjar [in north-west Iraq] was completely flat as was the country around Kufa. They took with them a number of people whose opinion Ma'mūn trusted and whose knowledge of this area could be relied on. They set out for Sinjar and came to the desert. They halted at a spot where they took the altitude of the Pole Star with certain instruments. They drove a peg into the ground and attached a long cord to it. They walked due north, avoiding as much as possible going off to left or right. When the cord ran out, they stuck another peg into the ground and fastened a cord to it and carried on walking to the north as they had done before until they reached a spot where the elevation of the Pole Star had risen one degree. Then they measured the distance they had travelled on the ground by means of the cord. The distance was $66\frac{2}{3}$ miles. Then they knew that every degree of the heaven was $66\frac{2}{3}$ miles on earth. Then they returned to the place where they had stuck in the first peg and continued to the south, just as they had previously done to the north, sticking in pegs and fastening cords. When they had finished all the cord they had used when going north, they took the elevation of the Pole Star and found it was one degree lower than the first observation. This proved that their calculations were correct and that they had achieved what they had set out to do.

Anyone who knows about astronomy will see that this is true. It is well known that the number of degrees in the heavens is 360 and that the heavens are divided into twelve constellations and that each constellation is thirty degrees. This makes 360 degrees in all. They then multiplied the number of degrees in the heavens by 66⅔, that is the length of each degree, and the total was twenty-four thousand miles. This is certain and there is no doubt about it.

Then the Banū Mūsā returned to Ma'mūn and told him what they had done, and that this agreed with what he had seen in the ancient books. He wished to confirm this in another location so he sent them to the Kufa area where they repeated the experiment they had conducted in Sinjar. They found the two calculations agreed and Ma'mūn acknowledged the truth of what the ancients had written on the subject.[6]

The account reveals the respect that intellectuals in the caliph's circle had for the ancients, whose works they could now read in the new translations. But their respect was not uncritical, and they needed to test what they had read rather than being overawed by the ancients' authority. We can also see their commitment to practical scientific method, the statement of a hypothesis and the use of experimental evidence to prove it and, perhaps most impressive, the care taken to make sure that the experiment could be replicated, in the same area and then in an entirely different one. All this demonstrates a truly scientific approach that has few parallels in the post-classical, pre-modern age.

The Religious Sciences and History Writing

The prolific literary culture of the Abbasid caliphate expressed itself in many different ways. For a lot of people in ninth-century Baghdad, both intellectuals and commoners, the most important of these were probably the collections of Traditions of the Prophet, which were being gathered and discussed in numerous assemblies in the city. People came from all over the Muslim world to the great city to listen to the masters expound and to garner new and unusual material. At the same time leaders of the emerging law schools, such as Ahmad b. Hanbal, lectured and wrote. At one level this activity was a result of the caliphal system of government. Without the financial impetus and the development of this huge city, the circles and gatherings would never have appeared. At another level, however, the Abbasid court in the ninth century was not where these Islamic sciences developed, and indeed the court and the scholars were in many ways at odds. Poetry and science could thrive in the Abbasid palaces and the homes of their rich and powerful courtiers, but the collection of Traditions did not. These religious studies were taught in mosques and private houses, not at court.

Abbasid court culture also encouraged the development of historical writing, though here again much of it took place in studies and libraries far removed from the palace. The greatest master of the age was Abū Ja'far al-Tabarī (d. 923). Tabarī was a Persian by origin from the area of Tabaristan (hence the name) on the southern shores of the Caspian Sea. He came to study in Baghdad when still a young man and lived there for most of the rest of his adult life. He seems to have led an austere bachelor life – there is no mention of any close family – and he lived off the rents of the family estates in his native Tabaristan, which were brought to him every year by pilgrims passing through the capital on their way to the Holy Cities. Despite his Persian origins, he wrote exclusively in Arabic. His *History of the Prophets and Kings* is a huge collection of material relating to the pre-Islamic and Islamic past, virtually a one-man library. In the English translation it appears in thirty-eight volumes, each of them more than 250 pages long. Nor was this all: Tabari also wrote a Commentary on the Qur'ān which was almost as long.

Tabarī's economic independence meant that he was not a court historian and there seems to be no record that he ever met any of the caliphs of his time or attended their courts. He did not actively criticize their regime, but he records with vivid honesty such discreditable episodes as Caliph Mansūr's execution of Abū Muslim or the avoidable disasters of the civil wars which followed the death of Hārūn al-Rashīd in 809. He also incorporates the biography of the Shi'ite Muhammad the Pure Soul, who led an uprising against Abbasid rule in 762, which is deeply sympathetic to the rebel. There is no evidence, either, that he denigrated the Umayyad caliphs whom the Abbasids had overthrown. In short, there is no evidence that he wrote to please the court or that he was subject to any sort of censorship. He had his prejudices – a dislike of popular rebellions and uprisings and extreme religious views – but they were essentially those of the pious Baghdad bourgeoisie of his era.

In the later parts of his chronicle, he does incorporate what might be called official history. This reflects the policies of Abbasid caliphs anxious to publicize their roles as military champions of Islam. The warrior caliph Mu'tasim appears to have commissioned long and detailed accounts of his campaigns against the Byzantines, notably the sack of Amorion in 833 and the campaigns of his generals against non-Muslim rebels in northern Iran. Later on Caliph Mu'tadid asked for his campaigns against the Zanj rebels in southern Iraq to be recorded with the same care. We also know that in the later ninth century letters from generals and provincial governors describing the defeats of rebels were read out in the mosque at Friday prayers and some of these were included by Tabarī in his great work. In general, though, Tabarī's multifaceted history reflects the pluralist society in which it was written, a society in which the caliphal government made no effort to control or dictate what intellectuals wrote.

The history writing of this period was deeply humanist, that is to say that it portrayed events as being caused primarily by human agency, and it attached enormous importance to human character, describing the main actors with all their faults and strengths. Direct divine intervention in the course of human affairs was rarely invoked. Of course, it was acknowledged that God protected some virtuous people and equally that he punished some wicked ones, but it was human beings who made the decisions about whether to act well or badly. The measure of good or bad behaviour among rulers was rarely that of strict piety, only the Umayyad caliph Umar II was credited with being motivated by religious goals and his reign was too short to come to any conclusions. The qualities expected of a good ruler were a concern to defend Islam and Muslims, wisdom and foresight, behaving in moderation in all things and dealing justly with all men. Caliphs and other rulers failed because of their stupidity, vanity and arrogance. It was a scale of values that Shakespeare, among others, would have recognized.

The Inclusiveness of Caliphal Culture

One important aspect of this cultural activity was its inclusiveness. The Abbasid caliphate was a deeply Muslim polity; it was ruled by Muslims and the caliph was, as we have seen, God's representative on earth. At the same time, it was broadly tolerant of religious difference and there is very little evidence for the ill-treatment of non-Muslim populations. The city of Baghdad itself had been founded as the capital for a Muslim dynasty and its official name, Madinat al-Salam, the City of Peace, suggested an Islamic identity. Yet within this new city a Christian community had developed. They built churches and monasteries and no one seems to have stood in their way. The hierarchies of the various Christian churches in the caliphate were recognized by the caliphs. One patriarch of the Church of the East, Timothy, was a regular visitor to the court of Caliph Mahdī. Christian administrators continued to work in the higher echelons of the bureaucracy, though vastly outnumbered by Muslims, and, as we have seen, Christians played an important part in translating Greek into Arabic.

By and large, churches and synagogues were respected and there are few reports of deliberate attacks on these places of worship. The cathedral in Damascus was demolished by the

Umayyad caliph Walīd, but that was because he wanted to build a (still surviving) mosque on the site and the Christians were amply compensated in cash and by the restoration of some churches which they had lost at the time of the original Muslim conquest of the city seventy years before. The great cathedral at Edessa (now Urfa in southern Turkey) was damaged when some of the marble columns were taken for building mosques. In Baghdad we hear of churches being attacked by mobs, but this was part of a general civil disturbance rather than a product of caliphal policy.

Just as there was no attempt to take over or destroy churches in general, so Zoroastrian fire temples continued to exist in areas like Fars, in southern Iran, where large numbers of them were still functioning in the tenth century. Indeed they were valued by at least some Muslims because the old soot from the eternal flames in the fire temples made the blackest and most permanent ink. Most were abandoned from the eleventh century onwards because increasing conversion to Islam meant that they no longer attracted worshippers, but there was no official move to close them.

The disused temples and other monuments of classical antiquity were often admired and, while they might also be used as quarries for building materials, there was no attempt to destroy them for ideological reasons. On this subject, Tabarī records an interesting discussion which is said to have occurred between Caliph Mansūr and his Persian adviser Khālid b. Barmak, who was one of the men in charge of the building operations in Baghdad. Mansūr suggested demolishing the huge brick palace of the Sasanian Persian kings in the old capital of Ctesiphon nearby and using the rubble in his new city. Khālid replied, 'I do not think that is a good idea, O Commander of the Faithful,' and when the caliph asked him why, he said, 'It is one of the proofs of Islam by which the observer is convinced that people like its lords were not swept away by the power of this world but only by the power of God.' The caliph said he was wrong and that he only said that because of his Persian connections.

Mansūr ordered that the palace be demolished and a section of it was, but it was soon apparent that the demolition and transport of the materials was more expensive than making them new on site. When he consulted Khālid again about what should be done, the reply was that he should complete the demolition or people would say he had given up. Once again, the caliph rejected his advice and the great Ctesiphon arch still stands to this day.

It would be misleading to say that this was an equal society where people of different faiths lived together as fellow citizens. Christians, Jews and other non-Muslim religious minorities were second-class citizens in a number of ways, not being allowed, at least in theory, to bear arms or ride horses, both public indications of status. At the same time, they participated in the economic and intellectual life of the society and their cultural contributions were accepted and admired as an important part of the vibrant mix which characterized the life of the Abbasid caliphate.

Abbasid Culture Remembered

The memory of the glories of Abbasid court culture lingered on in less expansive days. The personalities of the period, their characters, deeds and sayings remained part of the intellectual hinterland of Arabs writers and thinkers for centuries. An interesting example of this is Ibn al-Sāʿī's *Consorts of the Caliphs*. Ibn al-Sāʿī (d. 1276) lived in Baghdad and he was actually in the city at the time when it was sacked by the Mongols and the Abbasid caliph was put to death, in 1258. He himself survived this trauma and lived to a ripe old age. The book was probably written before that date. It consists of thirty-eight brief lives, some of them only a few lines long, of the female partners of the caliphs, celebrating their wit, their wealth and their piety. The author takes the story down to his own days, trying to show that the great women of the contemporary (thirteenth-century) Abbasid court were worthy inheritors of a great tradition, but the women of his own time lived virtuous and sober lives and talked only in prose. It was the women of the early Abbasid period who had panache and wit and the ability to make poetry come alive.

There are many memorable figures in the collection, but, to give a flavour, let us hear some of the story of Mahbūba, beloved of Caliph Mutawwakil. She was one of a group of 400 slave girls given to the caliph by one of his courtiers, but 'in his eyes she surpassed them all'. She was famous for her ready wit and clever ripostes. One of the courtiers tells the following story:

I was once in the presence of Mutawwakil when he was drinking. He handed Mahbūba an apple perfumed with a scented musk blend. She kissed it and took her leave. Then one of her own slaves appeared with a piece of paper which she handed to Mutawwakil. He read it, laughed, and tossed the paper to me to read. This is what it said:

> 'You-fragrance of an apple I had to myself
> You ignite in me the fire of ecstasy
> I weep and complain of my malady
> And of my grief's intensity.
> If an apple could weep, then the one I hold
> Would shed such tears of pity
> If you do not know what my soul has suffered,
> Look, the proof is in my body.
> If you gaze upon it you will see
> One unable to suffer patiently.'

The poem was set to music and became a popular song.

The same courtier remembered another occasion.

The caliph said, 'I paid Qabīha[7] the Poetess a visit and found she had written my name on her cheek using scented musk blend. I swear, Alī [the court poet who was sitting with him], I have never seen anything more beautiful than that streak of black against her white cheek. Go ahead and compose a poem about that!'

Mahbūba was sitting behind the curtain, listening to us talk and in the time it took for an inkstand and a scroll of paper to be brought and for Alī to formulate his thoughts, she had already improvised the following verses:

> 'She wrote "Ja'far"[8] in musk on her cheek
> How lovely that streak where the musk left its mark!
> On her face she wrote just one line,

But she etched many more on my heart.
Who can help a master in thrall to his slave,
Subservient in his heart, but plain to see,
Or one whose secret desire is Ja'far
May he drink his fill from your lips.'

Alī was dumbfounded by being upstaged like this.

In another story from the same courtier we hear:

Mutawwakil had a falling-out with Mahbūba and found it very hard to be apart from her. In the end the pair made up. Meanwhile I went to see him. He told me he'd had a dream that they had been reconciled, so he called a servant and said to him, 'Go and find out how she is and what she is doing.'

The servant returned and told him that she was just singing.

'Can that woman really be singing when I am so angry with her?' he said to me. 'Come on, let's find out what she is crooning about.'

We headed to her room and this is what she was singing:

'I wander the palace, but I see no one,
No one will answer my plaint it would seem.
I feel as though I've committed a sin,
One I can repent of but never redeem.
Will someone plead my case to a king
Who ended a quarrel when he came in a dream?
Yet when the dawn broke and the sun shone,
He forsook me again and left me alone.'

Mutawwakil was visibly moved. Realizing he was there, she came out of her room, and I made myself scarce. She told him she'd had a dream in which he'd come to her and they'd made up. That is why she had composed the poem, put it to music and sung it. Mutawwakil was so touched that he decided to stay and drink with her. She made sure I was well rewarded.

But the days of musk and wine were brought to a brutal end with the caliph's assassination in 861. For all her beauty, intelligence and wealth, Mahbūba was still a slave. When Mutawwakil was killed his slaves were divided up and Mahbūba went to a Turkish soldier, Wasīf, one of the conspirators who had plotted the caliph's death.

The courtier's account continues:

One day, as he was having his morning drink of wine, Wasīf ordered that Mutawwakil's slaves should be brought before him. They arrived in all their splendour, adorned, perfumed and dressed in brightly coloured clothes, bedecked with jewels, except for Mahbūba who came dressed in pure mourning white and not wearing any make-up.

The slaves sang, drank and made merry, as did Wasīf. Carried away by it all, he commanded Mahbūba to sing. She picked up her lute and sobbed as she sang:

'What sweetness does life hold for me
When I cannot see Ja'far?
A king I saw with my own eyes
Murdered, rolled in the dust.
The sick and the sorrowful

They can all heal;
But not Mahbūba –
If she saw death for sale
She would give everything she has to buy it
And join him in the grave.
For the bereaved
Death is sweeter than life.'

The song struck home. Enraged, Wasīf was on the point of having her killed when Bughā [another Turkish soldier], who happened to be present, said, 'Give her to me!'

Bughā took her, gave her her freedom and allowed her to live wherever she pleased. She left Samarra for Baghdad where she lived in obscurity and died of grief.

May God have mercy on her and reward her for her devotion to the memory of her beloved master.

The story is interesting in so many ways. The brilliant court culture where a quick wit and good poetic style were passports to success; the role of the women, virtually princesses and slaves as the same moment but major actors in court life; and the touching epitaph written by the author 400 years after the events but still remembering them as fresh and poignant.

The court culture of the Abbasids in their heyday had an unrivalled variety and éclat. It was an environment in which many different talents, from many different backgrounds, could flourish. Apart from the world of theology and the disputes about the createdness of the Qur'ān, disputes which were, as we have seen, as much political as intellectual, there was no official line which had to be obeyed, no censorship of views on a whole world of matters. It was the sheer vigour and variety of this culture which makes the Abbasid caliphate such an inspiring and powerful model.

For all its splendour, however, Abbasid culture has little resonance with modern audiences, both in the Muslim community and, more especially, beyond. In a world dominated by visual images the Abbasids have virtually nothing to offer. Abbasid Baghdad has left no traces and the detailed descriptions only mean that we can reconstruct it in our imaginations. The outlines of the great palaces at Samarra can be drawn in the dust and gravel of central Iraq, but the mud-brick of which they were built has dissolved into the soil from which it was made, while the plaster, mosaics and frescoes which covered and beautified the walls only survive in the smallest fragments. The gorgeous silks and intricate carpets which the sources constantly refer to have vanished without trace. Huge numbers of books were produced and read, but there were no illustrated manuscripts to preserve a visual image of the caliphal court. The Umayyad caliphs left their stone-built palaces in the Syrian desert which we can still admire. The courts of later medieval Iran are shown in the book-paintings so evocative of court life and the Ottomans have bequeathed not just illustrations of court life but the grand palaces in which they, their courts and their harems lived and moved. This great gap should not, however, blind us to the fact that the court of the caliphs was, in its time, the most important and the richest cultural centre on the planet.

CHAPTER 5

The Later
Abbasid
Caliphate

The Caliphs under Buyid Control

The coming of Buyid rule in Baghdad from 945 lead to the almost complete collapse of the administration of the Abbasid caliphate and ushered in two generations of obscurity and impotence in which the ancient office seemed to many an irrelevant relic. A succession of caliphs lived in the remains of the Great Palace of the Caliphate (Dār al-khilāfa) on the banks of the Tigris, but much of it lay in ruins and their authority was confined within its walls. The caliph no longer had a vizier to manage his affairs since there were so few of them to manage, nor *dīwāns* for his administrators, for there were none, or barracks for his soldiers, for they had gone to serve other masters. He had a secretary and a modest retinue of domestic servants, an exalted title and an ancient genealogy, and that was all. Nor was his person secure: Muttaqī was deposed and blinded in 944 and Mustakfī killed in 949 when they aroused the anger of their military 'protectors'.

The Buyids were complete outsiders in the world of the caliphate. They came from no famous tribe and until the beginning of the tenth century the family lived in obscurity as fishermen on the shores of the Caspian Sea. By a mixture of daring and ability, they took advantage of the debacle of the caliphate and by 945 made themselves masters of western Iran, Iraq and of Baghdad itself, and with it the person of the Abbasid caliph. The Buyids ruled in Shiraz, Rayy and Baghdad, but Baghdad was always the most prestigious, if no longer the most prosperous, of their capitals. They were also Shi'ites, though it is not entirely clear which sect of the Shi'a they belonged to. This meant that they had none of the respect for the Abbasids which other politicians and generals at the time had. It might have seemed logical for them to remove the Abbasids altogether and establish a caliph from the house of Alī. They chose not to do so, partly at least because they risked choosing a man whose authority and popular appeal would supplant their own, and who could dispense with them. Instead, it suited them to maintain an Abbasid presence. It attracted some support for their regime among the non-Shi'a population and it also gave them a constitutional legitimacy. They ruled as supporters of the *dawla* (the state or dynasty, meaning the Abbasids), and they took titles which meant 'pillar of the dynasty', 'support of the dynasty' (Rukn al-Dawla, Adud al-Dawla), and so forth. Everyone knew that this was at best a polite fiction, since the Buyids made all the decisions even in Baghdad, but it served its purpose. When the Fatimids conquered Egypt in 969, they made no effort to forge a Shi'ite alliance with them, instead remaining as protectors of the Abbasids.

Despite his powerlessness, the caliph could still be useful on some occasions to the Buyid rulers. In 980, when an ambassador from the rival Fatimid caliph in Cairo came to visit Adud al-Dawla, then ruler in Baghdad, the latter sought to impress him by the presence of his caliph, Tā'ī. The ambassador was led between serried ranks of troops to the presence of the caliph, hidden by a veil. When this veil was removed, the caliph could be seen, seated on a high throne surrounded by a hundred guards in brilliant robes with drawn swords. He wore the mantle of the Prophet and held his sceptre in his hands. Before him the Qur'ān of Uthmān was displayed. When the ambassador asked who this was, Adud al-Dawla replied, 'This is the caliph of God on earth,' a clear rebuke to the pretensions of the Fatimids. Adud al-Dawla made a huge show of respect, kissing the caliph's foot before being formally appointed to offices he already held: 'I entrust you with the charge of my subjects whom God has committed to me in the east and in the west, with the exception of my personal and private property. Do you therefore assume charge of them?' To which the Buyid replied in apparent humility, 'God aid me in obedience to our Lord the Commander of the Faithful.' The performance ended with the bestowal of robes of honour by the caliph.[1] The ostentatious deference of Adud al-Dawla to the caliph was, as everyone knew, a charade, but the Abbasid caliphs soon began to assume a new and significant role as leaders of the Sunni community in Baghdad and the wider Muslim world.

Important developments took place in Baghdad at this time, which have striking and unhappy parallels in our own day. In the year 900 the Sunni and Shi'i communities were not sharply differentiated. There were certainly enthusiastic, even fanatical, supporters of the Family of the Prophet who were prepared to risk their lives for the cause, but many Muslims were simply that, part of the broad consensus of the *umma*. The uncertainties caused by the collapse of government in the tenth century led men to seek the protection of other like-minded people. What had been differences in religious opinion now became differences in political life. Baghdad became divided into sectarian communities, each intent on defending its own district. The Shi'ites worshipped in their own mosques and developed their own, exclusive, festivals, especially the celebration of the Ghadīr Khumm, the pond between Mecca and Medina where, the Shi'a believe, Muhammad designated Alī as his heir. Their opponents, whom we can describe as proto-Sunnis, developed a rival festival of the Cave, the cave where Muhammad and Abū Bakr had hidden together to escape the persecutions of the Meccans. Graffiti artists wrote slogans on walls, cursing some of the early caliphs. Most people in Baghdad would accept the cursing of the Syrian Umayyad Mu'āwiya, but when the cursing was extended to Uthmān and, even worse, Abū Bakr and Umar (for depriving Alī of his rightful inheritance), anger rapidly developed into violence.

The Buyid regime became involved in these differences between the people, often supporting the Shi'a as a way of mobilizing popular forces against their enemies, who in turn began to look to the Abbasids for leadership. Until his death in 983 the greatest of the Buyid emirs, Adud al-Dawla, ruled the city with an iron hand, suppressing violence from whichever quarter it came: on one occasion he had the leaders of the Alid Shi'ites and the Abbasid party drowned together in the Tigris as a sign of his even-handed, no-nonsense justice.

When he died, his successors fought against each other to control his inheritance. As the power of the Buyid claimants was undermined by wars among themselves and increasing financial problems, the balance between the Buyids and the Abbasid caliphs began slowly to change. Increasingly Buyids needed the support in the city which the Abbasids were sometimes able to deliver and the caliph had much more scope for public action.

Reinventing the Abbasid Caliph

In late 991 the Abbasid caliph Tā'ī held an audience for the new ruler of Baghdad, Bahā al-Dawla. The caliph wore a ceremonial sword and sat on his throne. The Buyid approached and, as protocol demanded, bowed his head to the ground in front of the caliph before being invited to take a seat beside him: the Buyids, for all their power, were still in theory servants of the dynasty. What happened next was definitely not in the caliph's script. The Buyid troops approached the caliph, but instead of bowing down seized him by the strap of his sword, dragged him from his throne and took him prisoner to the Dār al-mamlaka, the Buyid centre of power in the city. Here Bahā al-Dawla declared the caliph deposed and announced that the new caliph was to be Tā'ī's cousin Qādir, who was then a refugee in the marches of southern Iraq.

It was a public and obvious humiliation for the Abbasids (even if the deposed caliph was more fortunate than those of his predecessors who were blinded or murdered). However, even though no one probably realized it at the time, the incident marked a new beginning for the caliphate.

We have some fairly detailed descriptions of how Qādir was accepted as caliph. There were two oaths of allegiance:

the first, a private oath (*bay'at al-khāssa*) taken among the Abbasid family and the members of the caliphal household, and the second a public oath (*bay'at al-āmma*) taken before a more general audience. The next stage was a ceremony at which the new caliph and his Buyid sponsor swore mutual oaths of loyalty to each other. In addition, a family agreement was made by which Bahā al-Dawla's daughter would marry the new caliph, though in the event she died before the wedding ceremony could take place. Such dynastic alliances were become increasingly important at this time as a way in which dynasties of outsiders, like the Buyids and later the Seljuqs, could attach themselves to the genealogy of the Quraysh and the Abbasids.

The mention of the caliph's name in the *khutba* (the Friday sermon) and on the *sikka* (coinage) were further acknowledgements of his status in the public eye. In the days when Umayyad and Abbasid caliphs were all-powerful, these symbols were more or less taken for granted, but by the end of the tenth century they were often contested and thereby more important. However, the Buyid army in Baghdad, demonstrating yet again the truculence with which soldiers at the time responded to their rulers, refused to allow the *khutba* to be made in Qādir's name until each of them had received eighty dirhams.

Although both sermon and coinage were significant indicators of the caliph's acceptance beyond the region of Baghdad and its immediate surroundings, there would be no such affirmations of loyalty, of course, in the areas of Syria and Egypt rule by the Shi'ite Fatimids, who had their own sermons and coinage proclaiming their caliphal title. The situation in Iran was even more complex and some, notably other members of the Buyid family, resented Bahā al-Dawla's high-handed treatment of the previous caliph. But by the year 1000 Qādir's name was almost universally acknowledged. In 1001 his position was further secured when his son was publicly accepted as heir apparent.

The naming of the caliph on coins is an invaluable piece of evidence for the historian. While chroniclers can make mistakes about complex events which happened long before their time, the evidence of the inscriptions on dated coins is more trustworthy and, by following them, we can trace the extent of the caliph's recognition and note who were the local rulers who acknowledged him.

So what real authority did this imply? From Qādir to the death of the last Abbasid caliph, Musta'sim, at the hands of the Mongols in 1258, caliphs exercised some limited power at two different levels. At one level they were, in a vague, undefined but still crucial way, heads of the Sunni Muslim community. Most thinkers believed that a caliph was necessary for the maintenance of the *sharī'a* and true Islam. In some respects the caliph was a bit like the Hidden Imam of the Twelver Shi'is, powerless but essential for the performance of true religion, except that the caliph was a live human being. At another level, the later Abbasids were rulers of a principality in central Iraq with its capital at Baghdad which became increasingly important within the regional politics of greater Mesopotamia, reaching its apogee in the long reign of Caliph Nāsir (1180–1225).

One of the ways in which Qādir could exercise real power was through the appointment of *qādīs*, or judges. While the appointment of local governors or military commanders was beyond his control, *qāḍīs* owed their position to the *sharī'a*, of which the caliph could claim to be the guardian. *Qāḍīs* were often important figures in their own right because they came from influential families in their localities. In the mid-eleventh century, indeed, we find them acting as virtually independent rulers of towns. In 999 Qādir made a number of appointments in the Baghdad area, Wasit and in distant Jilan, in northern Iran. In fact, he did not limit himself to appointments but also sent letters of instruction and guidance. This was soft power to be sure, but power nonetheless.

Within Baghdad, Qādir asserted his leadership of the Sunni community in the city. Sometimes this took the form of direct intervention in the conflicts which plagued the city. In 1007, for example, a dispute had broken out when Sunnis were accused of burning a recension of the Qur'ān which the Shi'ites held in great respect. The Shi'ites gathered in protest, publicly cursing those involved, even going so far as to proclaim allegiance to the Fatimid caliph in Cairo, but the Qādir acted to support the Sunnis, sending members of his household to help. In the end, matters quietened down and the Shi'ite leaders went to the caliph to apologize.

A much more important element of Qādir's policy was the staking of the claim to decide doctrine, and specifically Sunni doctrine, in distinction to any other forms of Muslim belief. The early Abbasid caliphs had not been, in the modern sense, Sunnis. Their claim to the caliphate was, after all, based on their membership of the extended Family of the Prophet and there was, at that time, no clearly defined body of belief which might be described as Sunni. Faced with the Shi'ite sympathies of his protectors the Buyids, and, much more challenging, the Fatimids claim to be the rightful caliphs of the whole Islamic world, Qādir decided to establish his leadership of the Sunni community in unambiguous terms. In 1017 he called on 'innovators', notably Mu'tazilite jurists (who believed in using philosophical logic to examine the mysteries of faith) to repent and stop their teaching. In 1029 he went much further in holding a series of public ceremonies in the Dār al-khilāfa, attended by the civil elite of Baghdad, in which a letter explaining correct beliefs and attacking Mu'tazilites and Shi'ites was read out. At the end of his life he had written a document in which he formulated Sunni beliefs in a clear and approachable way.[2]

The Qādiri Epistle (*Risālat al-Qādiriya*) is a comparatively short document and has none of the bombastic and convoluted language of, say, Walīd II's letter about the appointment of his heir discussed earlier. In fact, it was obviously written for public circulation and information.

Having started, as we might expect, with an affirmation of God's unity and eternity and a statement that He is the creator and lord of everything, Qādir denounces anthropomorphists, those who ascribe human attributes, especially speech, to God: 'He speaks but not with organs like those of human beings.' He also denounces in no uncertain terms anyone who believes in the createdness of the Qur'ān: 'He who asserts that it is in any way "created" is an unbeliever whose blood it is permissible to shed, should he refuse to repent of his error when called upon to do so.' After a general exhortation to faith, which can have no end because no one knows what God has recorded about him, he moves on to the most substantial issue which separated Sunnis from Shi'is:

One must love all the Companions of the Prophet. They are the best of human beings after the Prophet. The best and noblest of them after the Prophet is Abū Bakr al-Siddiq, next to him Umar [I] b. al-Khattāb, next to Umar, Uthmān b. Affān and next to Uthmān, Alī b. Abi Tālib. May God bless them and associate with them in paradise and have compassion on the souls of the Companions of the Prophet.

He then introduces two figures who are much more controversial. The first is Muhammad's wife Aisha, who had fought against Alī at the Battle of the Camel and whose alleged hostility to Alī made her a hate figure among the Shi'a: 'He who slanders Aisha has no part or lot in Islam.' Finally there is the first Umayyad caliph, Mu'āwiya, of whom 'we should only say good things and refuse to enter into any controversy about him'. This acceptance of Mu'āwiya was something none of the Shi'a, whatever sect they belonged to, could accept.

This uncompromising list is followed by a general plea for tolerance among Muslims: 'We should declare no one an unbeliever for omitting to fulfil any of the legal ordinances except the prescribed prayer', and a quote from the Prophet: 'Neglect of prayer is unbelief, whoever neglects it is an unbeliever and remains so until he repents and prays', to which he adds that the neglect of other injunctions does not make one an unbeliever. This seems to be a direct refutation of the Kharijites, and no doubt others, who held that sinners (that is, those who did not agree with them) were not Muslims but heathens, whom true Muslims should put to death unless they repented: 'Such are the doctrine is of the *sunna* and of the community.' Qādir then concludes with an invocation to God for forgiveness and what should perhaps be an indication of the role of the caliph: 'Let Him make us defenders of pious exercises and let Him forgive us and all the faithful.'

This is an interesting and impressive document, remarkable as much for what it does not say as what it does. There is no mention, for example, of the use of the Traditions of the Prophet as a source of law, no mention of fasting or the *hajj* or the prohibition of wine-drinking, all of which one might expect. Prayer is the only obligation absolutely incumbent on every Muslim. The reference to the caliph is understated and modest.

Just as important as the contents of the Epistle is the nature of its publication. It was read out in public assemblies, copies were sent to the provinces and Qādir's son and successor Qā'im reissued it under his own authority. No one could be in any doubt that the caliph claimed the right and obligation to decide on and communicate the basis of Sunni religious practice. This was something new and different in the development of his office.

This took place against the backdrop of a rapidly changing political situation. The death of Bahā al-Dawla in 1012 ushered in a period of chaos in the Buyid state as different members of the family tried to assert their leadership and win over the loyalty of the army. As short-lived and impoverished claimants succeeded each other, the balance between the caliph and his 'protectors' changed. Now it was not the case that caliphs were in the thrall of the Buyids, who could replace them and humiliate them at will, but the Buyid claimants increasingly needed Qādir's support and Qādir found himself in the position of being the intermediary between the Buyids and their armies as they tried to find a stable basis for their government, without any real success. The caliph did not, at this stage, have an army to call his own, but he was increasingly influential in Baghdad politics.

The Abbasids and the Court of the Ghaznevid Sultans

In eastern Iran, more important changes were afoot. At the end of the tenth century, the Samanid emirate which had controlled eastern Iran and Transoxania (modern Turkmenistan and Uzbekistan) from its capital Bukhara for the best part of a hundred years began to disintegrate. The western part of their lands, in eastern Iran and the north of modern Afghanistan, were taken over by one of their ambitious slave soldiers, Sebuktagin, and his son Mahmūd. They founded a dynasty known from the name of its capital Ghazni, in eastern Afghanistan between Kabul and Qandahar, as the Ghaznevids. This new dynasty, now powerful monarchs but only one generation from slavery and paganism, needed a legitimizing discourse, a position among the patchwork of Islamic dynasts who surrounded them and something to impress the religious dignitaries of the great eastern Iranian cities, such as Nishapur and Balkh, of which they were now the lords.

It was Mahmūd who decided that an alliance with the Abbasid caliph would serve his interests best. There was a lot to be said for this policy. The Abbasids could endorse his titles as no one else could, but they were a long way away and needing support; their overlordship would not be burdensome. Furthermore, there was a religious justification. The Ghaznevid defined himself not just as a Muslim but as a Sunni Muslim. This meant that he was totally opposed to the Shi'ite Buyids but even more to the Rāfidis, the Isma'ilis and other Shi'i popular groups in Iran.

Mahmūd's military power made him a formidable ally and enabled Qādir to appeal to him for support over the heads, as it were, of the Buyids. The alliance also introduced a major theme which would be important for the subsequent history of the caliphate: the connection between the Turks and the Sunni caliphate. It was with Mahmūd that this link first became established and to an extent the Seljuqs and Ottomans simply followed a pattern he had set. It is not easy to explain why Turkish dynasts were so drawn to these views and it may be that it was simply because the first Muslims the Turks came into contact with were Sunnis and they adopted their faith on conversion. Whatever the reason, Mahmūd made this connection with the reinvented Sunni Abbasid caliphate which was to be followed by the Turkish Seljuqs in the eleventh and twelfth centuries and the equally Turkish Mamluks in late medieval Egypt. The identification of the Turks with Sunni Islam has persisted to the present day: the modern Turkish republic and the Turkic-speaking areas of Central Asia – Turkmenistan, Uzbekistan, Khazakhstan and Kirghizstan – are firmly Sunni. Only in Iranian Azerbaijan do we find a substantial Turkish-speaking Shi'i population.

Qādir's original heir apparent had died, of natural causes, long before his father. In 1030 the caliph, now a man in his eighties, appointed a new heir with the title of Qā'im. A description of the ceremony tells of the caliph, now almost too deaf to understand what was going on, receiving the prostration of some of his old enemies before the curtain which hid him in the first part of the audience was drawn apart to reveal the old man on his throne. No Buyid approval was needed for this, the then Buyid ruler in Baghdad was informed by letter and had no choice but to acquiesce; the caliph could make up his own mind.

Qādir eventually died in 1031 at the age of eighty-six after a reign of almost forty years. This in itself was remarkable and his son Qā'im was to continue this tradition of longevity: he died in 1075 after a reign of forty-four years. Such biological events had a more than random importance. None of the 'great' Abbasid caliphs of the earlier period had lived beyond their early sixties and many had died in their forties or earlier. Qādir and Qā'im both outlived almost all their political contemporaries and rivals: Buyid kings and Seljuq sultans followed each other in rapid succession. Only the caliphs lived on, increasingly venerable and increasingly respected. What accounts for this longevity is quite unclear. It is possible that a moderate lifestyle and abstinence from alcohol may have played their part, but we have no evidence for this. Certainly their largely static lifestyle – neither of them seems to have travelled far from Baghdad – does not suggest that fresh air and exercise were important factors. Be that as it may, the long lives and reigns of these two caliphs were central to the revival of caliphal power and prestige in this period.

Qā'im continued most of the policies of his father,

including the alliance with the Ghaznevids. The importance of this relationship to both sides can be seen in the
account of the reception at the Ghaznevid court in Balkh of
the ambassador sent to announce the accession of Qā'im
and to receive the *bay'a* from the new Ghaznevid sultan
Mas'ūd, who had succeeded his father the previous year. The
reception, lasting from December 1031 to January 1032, is
described in the Persian history of Bayhaqi, a courtier of the
Ghaznevids and eyewitness, in which the importance of ceremonial in establishing legitimacy is described in fascinating
detail.

At this time the Ghaznevids, ruled by Sultan Mas'ūd
(1030–41), son of the great Mahmūd, were the most powerful
dynasty in eastern and central Iran and, from their base
in Ghazni, controlled much of northern India. Furthermore,
the dynasty had acquired huge prestige in the wider
Muslim world because of their role in this *jihād* (the 'Holy
War' of pillage and conquest) in the northern part of the subcontinent. With their powerful and well-organized army,
which included many elephants, their core of experienced
administrators and their resource base in the rich cities of
Khurasan, the Ghaznevids seemed to have little need of the
approval of the almost powerless caliph in distant, semi-
ruined Baghdad.

This appearance of invincibility did, however, hide some
significant weaknesses and anxieties. For all their military
power and their starring role in the *jihād* in northern India,
the Ghaznevids were still newcomers on the political scene.
In 1031 the newly enthroned Mas'ūd was the third generation
to hold power, but there must have been many in Iran who

remembered that his grandfather had been a slave from an obscure Turkish tribe in an out-of-the-way part of what is now Kirghizstan. Moreover, he was a first-generation convert to Islam. The family could claim no kinship with the Family of the Prophet or the heroes of the early Islamic state and they had no great pretensions to piety; indeed the public, formal consumption of wine in vast quantities at court was one of the defining features of their royal style. In these circumstances, it was very important to them to be granted the caliphal seal of approval. To be able to claim that they were servants of the Abbasid caliphs, who had appointed them to rule vast and populous areas of the eastern Islamic world, was of immense benefit. It gave them a recognizable position in the hierarchy of Muslim rulers, even if everyone knew that they had acquired their position by brute force and that the caliph had had little choice but to accept their position.

Mahmūd had forged close links with Caliph Qādir. They had mutual interests. The caliph, as we have seen, was intent on developing the religious and ideological aspects of his office and needed to find powerful supporters to accept this. Mahmūd of Ghazna, now firmly established as a ruler, had seen his opportunity. He proclaimed himself a loyal servant and protector of the caliph against the 'heretic' Buyids and pledged his loyalty to what was now clearly a Sunni caliphate. It was no coincidence that he also had his eye on many of the rich lands of western Iran presently slipping from the hands of the increasingly feeble Buyid princes. Who knows, he might well have had aspirations to establish his control in Baghdad itself and rule as a powerful Sunni protector of the caliph. Any such aspirations he may have had were ended by his death in 1030, but Mas'ūd, always his father's son, was determined to pursue the alliance with the Abbasids.

There were other, more specific areas in which caliphal support could be of benefit to the new Ghaznevid ruler. Mas'ūd's own accession had not been uncontested. He had been in central Iran with much of the army when his father had died in distant Ghazna. His half-brother Muhammad had taken control in the capital and was making a bid to be the next sovereign. There was no undisputed hereditary succession, no primogeniture to decide which of the two should succeed or, indeed, whether the Ghaznevid realm should be divided between them. For the moment, Muhammad had been defeated and was confined to prison in a castle near Ghazna, but he still had influential supporters and may well have been planning a comeback. Caliphal investiture of Mas'ūd might well have persuaded many waverers that he was the legitimate ruler.

But there was another problem too. When the Samanid state had disintegrated, the Ghaznevids had seized control of the western and southern areas, but Transoxania, including the old Samanid capital at Bukhara, had been taken by a Turkish nomadic group generally referred to as the Qara Khanids or Black Khans. They had converted to Islam and had claims to be powerful Muslim rulers. They were also powerful rivals and intent on expanding their influence to the west of the great river Oxus in the cities of Khurasan and especially the rich inland delta of the Oxus known as Khwarazm, which had its own lords, nominally vassals of the Ghaznevids but always careful to maintain their autonomy. If the Ghaznevids were to retain control of these areas, it was vital that they secured the caliphal investiture which would convince both citizens of the towns and local lords that they were the legitimate sovereigns. The new caliph, however, might take some persuading to put all his resources into the Ghaznevids.

Bayhaqi begins his account[3] with the report that the caliph Qādir had died and that his son Qā'im had been chosen to succeed him. The oath of allegiance had been taken by both the Abbasids and the Alids and all the people of Baghdad. Envoys had been sent out to the various provinces of the caliphate to request their oaths of allegiance and one Muhammad Sulaymānī had come to Khurasan for this purpose. The sultan and his counsellors met to decide what to do. There had not been a new caliph in the whole time of the Ghaznevid dynasty and there was no obvious precedent or rule to follow. They were really inventing a tradition which could be developed to boost the prestige of caliph and sultan alike and they realized this was a great opportunity to request the caliph's political support and to display the sultan's power to his subjects. Mas'ūd was staying at Balkh at the time. The Ghaznevid court was itinerant, like many contemporary monarchies in western Europe, and the ruler and his whole court moved between the cities and hunting grounds of his realm. Balkh, sometimes referred to as the 'mother of cities', had very ancient origins going back to Achaemenid times if not before. It consisted of an ancient citadel surrounded by a *shahristan*, an inner city roughly circular in shape. In the *shahristan* were the great mosque and the bazaars, while outside the walls there were gardens and the palaces of the elite. Mas'ūd chose to stay in a garden palace where there was space to house his troops and set up temporary offices for the government departments.

On Friday 3 December 1031 news came that the envoy was very close and the sultan ordered a reception committee of the *sharīfs* (nobles) of the Alids and other prominent citizens to go out and escort him in. It was important to send some men who spoke Arabic because there is no indication that the envoy spoke Persian, while many at the Ghaznevid court, including the sultan himself, had little or no Arabic. On 10 December, escorted by the notables of the town and a guard of honour of 1,000 troops, the envoy entered the city and was taken to his lodgings in a palace in the Alley of the Basket Weavers where 'much delicately prepared food was immediately brought in'.

The envoy was allowed three days to recover from the rigours of the journey and was lavishly entertained. The sultan then ordered that he be brought into his presence. Before he arrived, Mas'ūd had another private meeting with his main advisers to discuss how this encounter was going to be organized and how the letter pledging allegiance had been drafted. Thursday 19 December was the first day of the new Muslim year (423). Already by dawn 4,000 troops were on parade, all in full military regalia, including belts, swords, quivers and bow cases, and each soldier was dressed in a bro-caded coat from Tustar, a city in southern Iran well known for the production of fine textiles. They stood in two lines so that the envoy would pass between them and be left in no doubt as to the power of a state which could muster so many soldiers and equip them with such gorgeous uniforms. The procession which took him to the palace was accompanied by trumpets and various types of drums, including those which were carried on the backs of elephants – 'one would have said it was the Day of Resurrection' – and Muhammad Sulaymānī was much impressed, having never seen anything like this in the modest court of the caliph in Baghdad.

When Sulaymānī, dressed in Abbasid black, reached the palace, he found the sultan sitting on his throne surrounded by courtiers, the grand vizier standing by his side. He was invited to sit and the sultan asked him how the caliph was. This was the cue for him to announce the bad news of Qādir's death and the good news of Qā'im's accession. The grand vizier then requested that he present the letter he had brought and so he stood up and walked to the throne, taking the letter out of its black silk pouch. He then called on one of the courtiers to read out the latter in Arabic and then to translate it into Persian so that everyone (including the sultan himself) could understand. When this had been done, the envoy was escorted back to his lodgings with great ceremony.

The next day was to be the start of mourning for the dead caliph. The sultan wore a white headcloth and a white robe, white being the colour of mourning, and all his courtiers did the same. The bazaars were closed and people of all ranks came in groups to offer their condolences. After three days the mourning ended and drums were beaten to announce the reopening of the bazaars.

The next stage of the ceremonies was to acknowledge the new caliph. This was to take place at the great mosque in the centre of the city. The sultan summoned Alī b. Mikāl, a member of a well-known Persian family who held the office of chief of the notables of the city and who had been put in charge of the arrangements. Alī was ordered to decorate the street which led from the gate where the palace was situated to the great mosque. Ornamental arches were also to be erected on platforms. Alī summoned the leading citizens and for the whole week, Monday to Thursday, they transformed the street so that 'no one could remember seeing Balkh like it'. They carried on working all Thursday night and by dawn on Friday everything was ready.

That morning the sultan held court and gave instructions that the people should come in an orderly fashion to witness the procession, should be careful not to damage the arches and other decorations and should not make any noise or indulge in any jollity or merrymaking until after he and the envoy had passed. The onlookers could then do as they pleased, for he intended to return to his palace by another route outside the walls. Black-robed attendants were appointed to make sure the populace behaved themselves and played their part in this dignified pageant.

At noon the sultan mounted his horse. The 4,000 troops who had served as the guard when the envoy had first come to the city led the procession with their commander in the rear. They were followed by the sultan's personal guard, carrying his standard, the major dignitaries of the court and then the sultan himself. He in turn was followed by the grand vizier and Alī b. Mikāl escorting the envoy and the civilian elite of the city, the judges and learned *ulama*. It was all very sedate and disciplined, with not a sound to be heard apart from the drums and the attendants ordering people to stand back.

Once they reached the mosque they found the *minbar* covered from top to bottom with brocade woven with golden thread. The sultan and his courtiers sat at the foot of the pulpit while the *khatīb*, the official preacher, gave the sermon and formally invoked the name of the new caliph. After that the sultan's treasurers came up and laid purses full of coins by the *minbar*, first in his name and then in the names of his sons and his courtiers, until a vast sum of money had been collected. All this was to be taken to Baghdad and given to Caliph Qā'im. After that the court dispersed: the sultan and his immediate entourage made their way back to the palace while Alī b. Mikāl escorted the envoy through the bazaars past the stalls in the market, now thronging with people, back to his lodgings where an elaborate reception had been prepared. Meanwhile the people of the city celebrated enthusiastically.

The next day was reserved for business. The grand vizier and other advisers were to draw up the formal agreement (*ahd*) which Sulaymānī was to take back to Baghdad for the caliph to sign. After the vizier had consulted with his colleagues, Sulaymānī was summoned. It looks as if there was some fairly hard bargaining. The sultan would accept the agreement which had been brought from Baghdad, subject to certain conditions. Mas'ūd was to be invested with lands which were significantly more extensive than the ones he presently controlled. Among these were 'all of Sind and Hind [India]' and, more controversially, the whole of the western Iranian plateau as far as the pass of Hulwan. This would bring his forces to the edge of the Iraqi plain, only a short distance from Baghdad itself. The caliph was also to promise that he was not to enter into any direct correspondence with the Qara Khanids of Transoxania, nor to give them honorific titles or robes of honour, but was to use the Ghaznevids as intermediaries. This, the advisers claimed, had been the position under the great Mahmūd of Ghazna and they wanted it to be restored. In addition, the caliph was to give permission for Ghaznevid armies to attack Kirman in southern Iran and Oman on the other side of the Gulf. The Qarāmita heretics in Bahrayn were also to be annihilated. The sultan's officials were frank about their motivations: 'a vast army has been assembled and we need more territory. The army must be put to work.' An army which did not bring in more resources was an intolerable burden on the state.

There was more to come. If not for the respect Masʿūd had had for the caliph, he would have been forced to launch an attack on Baghdad itself. In fact, had it not been for his father's death and the need to return east, 'at the present time we would have been in Syria and Egypt'. The sultan explained that, although he was on good terms with the Buyid rulers of central and western Iran, they must be more vigilant in respecting the caliphate and restoring it to its former dignified state. Above all, they must protect the pilgrim route. The sultan's subjects had been instructed to prepare for the *hajj* and had been promised that they would be accompanied by one of his commanders. If they did not protect the pilgrims the Ghaznevids would 'act strongly'. For they were 'answerable to God Most High since there has been imposed on [them] not only great power and prestige but also countless troops all fully equipped and ready for action'. The mixture of pious justification and military menace was clear. Sulaymānī agreed that all this sounded fair and reasonable and the sultan's officials went to tell him, as he had not been present, everything that had been agreed.

With the business completed, it was time for the envoy to depart. The leading courtiers were assembled and the document pledging allegiance to the caliph, which had been drafted in Arabic, was translated into a Persian 'as fine and delicate as a Byzantine brocade'. The Arabic version and the Persian translation were presented to Sulaymānī, who read them both out and agreed that the Persian was an accurate translation of the text and that he would commend it to the Commander of the Faithful. Then the sultan read the Persian version with great eloquence: 'Amongst the monarchs of this house,' the author tells us, 'I have never known anyone who could read and write Persian the way he did.' When he had finished, the royal inkstand was brought and he signed his name at the foot of both the Arabic and Persian texts. Then the grand vizier and the officials present wrote their signatures as witnesses. The Turkish commander of the army, Begtughdī, did not know how to write, so a courtier signed for him.

Then the question arose of the presents Sulaymānī was to take back with him to Baghdad. The grand vizier replied, perhaps rather surprisingly, that generous amounts of indigo for the caliph and the courtiers was the traditional gift, though where he got this idea from is not clear. In addition, of course, the envoy was to take all the gifts which had been presented at the mosque. The grand vizier also looked back to precedents. He said that he had read in historical accounts that when Caliph Mu'tamid had sent an envoy to Amr b.

Layth the Saffarid on his accession a century and a half before, in 879, the envoy was sent back with a gift of 100,000 dirhams. When the envoy returned from the caliph, bringing with him the banner (*liwā*) which symbolized the conferment of office on Amr and a document from the caliph to that effect, he and his mission were given 700,000. This example was to be followed; Sulaymānī would be given 100,000 dirhams at this stage, but when he returned with the caliph's signature, then he would be given whatever the sultan saw fit. The sultan agreed that this was sound sense.

Then a list was made of further gifts: generosity was one of the hallmarks of a powerful ruler. There were to be 100 pieces of high-value clothing, ten of them woven with gold thread, fifty containers of musk, 100 pastilles of camphor, 200 bales of linen of the highest quality, fifty excellent Indian swords, a golden goblet filled with pearls, twenty fine rubies from Badakhshan (in north-east Afghanistan, then part of the sultan's domains), ten sapphires, ten Khurasani horses with satin brocade caparisons and head covers, and five valuable Turkish slaves. It was an eclectic list to say the least.

Then Sulaymānī was given personal presents, including riding animals and equipment and 100,000 dirhams for his personal use. On 9 January 1032 he finally set out, having spent some three weeks in Balkh. Typically for Masʿūd's court, a spy was attached to his retinue to report back on everything which went on.

At the end of his long account, Bayhaqi appends copies of the Arabic letters which were exchanged at this point. To say they are grandiloquent would be an understatement; they are a masterclass in classical Arabic epistolary rhetoric. At the same time the substance and detail are quite limited. The caliph's begins with a long, pious introduction about God's favour to Muhammad and the caliphs and the inevitability of fate. Blessings are called upon his father and predecessor Qādir. Eventually he explains how he became caliph because of the designation by his father. He then held a general court at which the prominent members of the court, the supporters of the dynasty and religious figures, judges, religious lawyers and court witnesses all stretched out their hands to swear allegiance. Finally he praises Mas'ūd for his qualities and his obedience and asks him to swear allegiance publicly through his envoy Muhammad Sulaymānī before calling down elaborate blessings on all concerned.

The sultan's reply is equally rhetorical, full of fine phrases and short of information. He swears genuine and unshakeable allegiance to the caliph, his lord (*sayyid*), though exactly what this might entail is not specified. Certainly, there is no concrete mention of military or financial support. He takes the oath by the Qur'ān, as one might expect, but also by the Jewish Torah, the Christian Gospels and the Psalms of David, and he finishes by a very extended indemnity clause in which he states that if he breaks this oath all his possessions, including slaves, should be given to the poor and any wives he has or will marry should be irrevocably divorced. Finally he will make the *hajj* to Mecca thirty times, on foot, not riding.

The sultan received the caliphal investiture in the time-honoured fashion for all his subjects to see. But however much the caliph's deed and banner meant to the Ghaznevids they could not save Mas'ūd from his fate. In the middle of the celebrations, news arrived of Turkmen raids from the desert on the eastern frontiers of the Ghaznevid state and many of the soldiers who had attended the celebrations were ordered to march out and confront them. It was a sign of things to come. Within a decade, the Ghaznevid army had been defeated and driven out of Khurasan by the Turkmen under their Seljuk rulers, the sultan was dead and the power of his successors was reduced to a small area of northern and eastern Afghanistan. The caliph, for all his high-sounding rhetoric, was neither willing nor able to help him and his investiture counted for nothing when the Ghaznevids were faced with the uncouth military power of the Turkish nomads.

Abbasid Caliphs and Seljuq Sultans

The caliphates of Qādir and Qā'im mark a moment when the Abbasid caliphs tried to assert a spiritual leadership in the Islamic world. The issuing of Qādir's Epistle, with its attempt to codify Sunni beliefs, the appointment of *qādīs* and the elaborate approval given to leaders such as Mas'ūd of Ghazna were all signs that the caliphate mattered, but they were not signs of military power.

In the almost two centuries between the death of Qā'im in 1075 and the Mongol conquest of Baghdad in 1258, successive Abbasid caliphs worked and struggled to maintain their position in a political world of almost mind-boggling complexity. In 1058–9 Qā'im had survived an attempted takeover of Baghdad itself by a military adventurer acting on behalf of the Fatimid caliph of Egypt and, for the only time in history, the pulpits of Baghdad had proclaimed a Shi'ite caliph. The coming of the Turkish Seljuq rulers, with their commitment to Sunni Islam and clear hostility to the Fatimids, put an end to that danger, but the Seljuqs could be demanding protectors. Fortunately for the Abbasids, they did not seek to make Baghdad their capital, preferring to rule from Iranian cities like Isfahan, Nishapur and Merv, but they did want to control the city and constrain the caliph.

In 1092 both the great Seljuq sultan Malik Shāh and his all-powerful vizier Nizām al-Mulk died and the Seljuq family embarked on a pattern of civil wars which was to last almost the whole of the twelfth century and destroy their once powerful state. Increasingly, as had happened with the Buyids, the Seljuq warlords became dependent on the Abbasids, not the other way round. The caliphs could give their mandate to one prince and remove it from another. They also controlled Baghdad and through the twelfth century built up what was effectively an independent state in southern Iraq, stretching from Takrit to the head of the Gulf. In Baghdad itself authority was divided, often uneasily, between the Dār al-khilāfa, the ancient palace of the caliphs, and the Dār al-mamlaka, the palace where the Seljuq military governor resided. Gradually the Abbasids began to recover some of the attributes of temporal sovereignty which their ancestors had enjoyed. The caliphs again had viziers to run an expanded administration and in 1125 Caliph Mustarshid (1111–36) led an army in the field against an aggressive prince of Hilla, who had attached himself to the Shi'ite cause. Caliph Muqtafī (1136–50) used his increased revenues to build up a new army recruited not from Turks but from Greeks and

Armenians who had converted to Islam. The caliphs often set themselves up as protectors of Baghdad and its inhabitants against the warring bands of Turkish troops. They claimed the moral high ground in the city as well, championing Sunni against Shi'ite and closing down wine shops, often run by agents of the Seljuq princes.

There were also advances on the international stage. In 1086 the new Almoravid ruler of Muslim Spain and Morocco, Yūsuf b. Tashfīn, who had just inflicted a major defeat on King Alfonso VI of Castile, was advised by the religious lawyers that 'It is proper that your authority should come from the caliph to make obedience to you incumbent on all and sundry.' So he sent an envoy to Caliph Mustazhir, Commander of the Faithful, with a large gift and a letter in which he mentioned the Frankish territories which God had conquered (at his hands) and his efforts to bring victory to Islam, and he also requested investiture with rule over his lands. A diploma granting him what he wished for was issued from the caliphal chancery and he was given the (newly invented) title of Commander of the Muslims. Robes of honour were also sent to him and he was greatly delighted with this.[4] In 1229 the ruler of Delhi, Iltutmish, requested investiture from Caliph Mustansir (1226–42). He was granted the title of Great Sultan and confirmed in all his possessions. The document was solemnly read out in a vast assembly and from then on Iltutmish put the caliph's names on his coins. His successors followed his example.[5] It is worth noting that neither Spain and Morocco nor northern India had ever been ruled by the Abbasids at the height of their political power.

In 1097 the first Crusaders, known to the Muslims as Franks, marched from France and other areas of western Europe and appeared in the Middle East. In 1099 they conquered the city of Jerusalem, holy to Muslims as well as Christians and Jews, and made it the capital of a new Latin Christian kingdom. Other Crusader principalities were created in the following decades in Tripoli, Antioch in the north of Syria, and even distant Edessa (Urfa in southern Turkey), until the whole of the eastern coast of the Mediterranean was ruled by these infidel intruders. For almost 200 years there was a Frankish military presence on the coastal areas of Syria and Palestine, an infidel presence in the heart of the Dār al-Islam. It would seem that this was an obvious opportunity for the Abbasid caliphs to seize the initiative and to lead, or at least coordinate, the Muslim response. Muslims at the time certainly thought so and groups of refugees from the occupied cities made their way to Baghdad in the hope of attracting caliphal support. In the event, no caliph participated actively in the campaigns or ventured far from Baghdad. None of them seems to have been prepared to take the leadership of Muslims or to undertake the traditional caliphal role of defending Islam against non-Muslim enemies. In hindsight it can perhaps be seen as a lost opportunity to revive the ancient role and prestige of the office. Instead the caliphs gave their blessings, but not much more, to those military leaders who attempted to combat the invaders. The great Saladin, ruler of Muslim Syria and Egypt from 1174 until his death in 1193, proclaimed that he was leading the Muslims in *jihād*, as the servant of Caliph Nāsir (1180–1225), but relations between the two men were generally cool and cautious, both sides being careful not to antagonize the other while not cooperating in any meaningful way. In a letter Saladin sent to Frederick Barbarossa, emperor of Germany, when he knew that Frederick was joining the Third Crusade, he threatened that 'If we instruct the Caliph of Baghdad, God save him, to come to us, he will rise up out of the high throne of his empire and he will come to aid our excellence'[6] – but he was 'calling spirits from the vasty deep': at no time did the caliph stir himself.

It was also during the Crusades that western Europeans began to hear about caliphs and the word begins to appear in Latin and Old French. Authors tried to compare the authority of the caliph with that of the pope over the Latin Church. The Arabic chronicler Ibn Wāsil, who had spent some time at the Hohenstaufen court in southern Italy in the early thirteenth century, commented: 'According to them [the Franks], the Pope in Rome is the *khalīfa* of the Messiah and the one acting in his place. He has the right to ban and to permit . . . He crowns the kings and nominates them. Nothing is done on their Holy Law [*sharī'a*] except with his consent. He has to be a priest.'[7] There were some similarities. Both ruled over a small state, the popes in Rome and the caliphs in Baghdad, but aspired to a spiritual leadership over a much wider area. Both could provide legitimacy by granting investiture to newly established rulers, as Mustazhir did to the Almoravid Ibn Tashfīn and Gregory VII did for Rudolf of Swabia in 1080. But there were many more differences. The popes, from Gregory VII to Innocent IV (1073–1216), built up a commanding authority over the western Church which enabled them to summon councils, decide doctrine and have a major influence on the choice of bishops throughout western Europe. The caliph, by contrast, had no authority over doctrine and little if any influence in the choice of *qāḍīs* or other religious leaders outside Baghdad and the immediately surrounding area.

In one way the twelfth century did see an expansion of the caliph's theoretical authority. In 1171 Saladin conquered Egypt, putting an end to the Fatimid caliphate, and one of his first actions was to arrange that the sovereignty of the Abbasid caliph be proclaimed from the pulpits of Cairo. The long years of struggle for power and influence in the Muslim world between the Sunni Abbasids of Baghdad and the Shi'i Fatimids of Cairo were brought to a close: there was now only one caliphate, the Abbasid, with universal pretensions – even if these meant little in practical terms.

None of the caliphs of the twelfth century had the opportunity or perhaps the personality to develop the sort of reputation that great rulers of the early Abbasid period, such as Mansūr, Hārūn al-Rashīd or Ma'mūn, had enjoyed, but some of them at least had a reputation for good government in their own area around Baghdad. Of Mustazhir (d. 1118) it was said:

> He was (God be pleased with him) gentle and noble in character. He loved to shower benefits on people and do good. He was eager to perform pious acts and good deeds. His efforts were appreciated and he never refused a favour that was asked of him.
>
> He showed great trust in those he appointed to office, not hearkening to any slanderer nor paying attention to what such a one might say. Capriciousness was unknown to

him nor did his resolution wilt under the urging of those with special interests.

His days were days of happiness for his subjects, like festive days, so good they were. When he heard of that, he rejoiced and was very happy. When any sultan or deputy of his set out to harm anyone, he did all he could to condemn and prevent it.

He had a good hand and his minuting of documents was excellent. No one came near him in that, which showed his rich culture and wide learning.[8]

He was also, and unusually for a ruler of his time, something of a poet:

The heat of passion melted what had frozen in my heart
When I stretched forth my hand for the formal farewell.
How shall I fare along the path of patient endurance,
Seeing my paths over the chasm of love to be cords?
A new moon whom I loved has broken his promise
After my fate had fulfilled what it promised.
If I break the compact of love in my heart
After this, may I never behold him more.

It is interesting to reflect on the love interests of caliphs and other elite figures as revealed in their poetry. It would apparently have been out of the question for any caliph to write poetry to a free woman. Early Abbasid courtiers and rulers could express their love for unfree singing girls, who might be slaves but who were, at least in the land of poetry, coquettishly free to reject their master's advances. In the more austere and military world of the twelfth century the singing girls are distant memory. Only the handsome young man is a proper and decent subject for a caliph's passion.

We have a revealing account of how the Abbasid caliph appeared to an outside visitor in 1184 in Ibn Jubayr's *Travels*.[9] Ibn Jubayr was an Andalusi (from Muslim Spain) and a pious but keen observer. He made the *hajj* from his distant homeland and after he had completed his pilgrimage made a sort of grand tour through Iraq, Syria and the Crusader states before boarding an Italian ship in Acre to take him home. As a secretary working for the government of the Almohad caliphate, one might have thought that he would dismiss the Abbasid caliphate. In fact, he is interested and respectful, although he reserves his real admiration for Saladin, then preparing for his epic struggle with the Crusaders.

He describes the city of Baghdad, partly in ruins but still boasting numerous baths and congregational mosques, including the one built by Mansūr, ancient but remaining in use, and the innumerable boats in which people crossed the river since the bridge of boats had been washed away by floods. He also mentions the 'famous Baghdad hospital':

> It is on the Tigris and every Monday and Thursday physicians visit it to examine the state of the sick and prescribe for them what they might need. At their disposal are persons who undertake the preparation of the foods and the medicines. The hospital is a large palace, with chambers and closets and all the appurtenance of a royal dwelling. Water comes into it from the Tigris.

He honours both of the tombs of the descendants of Alī, 'may God hold him in his favour', and also of the great Sunni legal scholars Abū Ḥanīfa and Aḥmad b. Ḥanbal. He even records, without passing judgement, seeing the tomb of the famous early tenth-century mystic Ḥallāj, executed for heresy on the orders of Caliph Muqtadir, before turning to the caliph himself:

All the Abbasids live in sumptuous confinement in those palaces, neither going forth nor being seen, having settled stipends. A large part of these palaces are used by the Caliph himself and he has taken the high balconies, the splendid halls and the delightful gardens. Today he has no vizier, only an official called the deputy of the vizierate who attends the council which deals with the property of the Caliph and who holds the books and controls the affairs. He has an Intendant over all the Abbasid palaces and an *amīn* over the harem, remaining from the time of the Caliph's father and grandfather, and all those included in the Caliph's own harem. He appears little before the public, being busy with his affairs concerning the palaces, their guardianship, the responsibility for their locks and their inspection night and day . . .

We saw him one day going forth, preceded and followed by the officers of the army, Turks, Daylamites and others, and surrounded by about fifty drawn swords in the hands of the men about him . . . He has palaces and balconies on the Tigris. The Caliph would sometimes be seen in boats on the Tigris, and sometimes he would go into the desert to hunt. He goes forth in modest circumstance to conceal his state from the people, but despite this concealment his fame only increases. Nevertheless, he likes to appear before the people and show affection to them. They consider themselves fortunate in his character for in his time they have obtained ease, justice and good-living and, great and small, they bless him. We saw this Caliph Ahmad al-Nāsir, whose lineage goes back to Muqtadir and beyond him to his ancestors the (Abbasid) caliphs, may God hold them in His favour, in the western part of his balcony there. He had come down from it and went up the river in a boat to his palace further up the east bank. He is a youth in years with a beard which is short but full, is of handsome shape and good to look on, of fair skin, medium stature and comely aspect. He is about twenty-five years of age. He wore a white dress like a full-sleeved gown embroidered with gold, and on his head was a gilded *qalansuwa* encircled with black fur of the costly and precious kind used for royal clothes, such as that of the marten or even better. His purpose of wearing this Turkish dress was the concealment of his state, but the sun cannot be hidden even if veiled. This was the evening of 6 Safar 580 [20 May 1184] and we saw him again the following Sunday, looking down from his balcony on the west bank. It was nearby this that we lodged.

Ibn Jubayr then describes the caliph's mosque next door to the palace, which was vast and had excellent ablution facilities. There was also a mosque of the sultan (that is the Seljuq rulers) outside the city walls where their palace had been. The Seljuqs used to control the affairs of the caliph but no longer had such influence. In another mosque, in Rusafa, were the tombs of the Abbasid caliphs 'may God's mercy rest on their souls'. He finishes his account with a poetic reflection on the vanished glories of Baghdad:

> The state of this city is greater than can be described. But ah, what is she to what she was! Today we may apply to her the saying of the lover:
>
> 'You are not you, and the houses are not those I knew.'

Ibn Jubayr points out the prosperity the caliph's rule brought to the city and there is no mention of any Seljuq officials: they are a thing of the past. When he leaves Baghdad with returning pilgrims, they are accompanied by a troop of the caliph's soldiers to protect them from the Bedouin – the caliph thereby fulfilling, at least in part, the ancient caliphal duty of safeguarding the *hajj*. On the other hand, there is no mention of him attending Friday prayers in his mosque, even though it was next door to his palace, or of any public receptions. Ibn Jubayr hears about him, no doubt because he asked lots of questions, and sees him in the distance, but there is no question of approaching him or having an audience.

This silver age of the Abbasid caliphate reached its apogee in the long reign of Nāsir (1180–1225), the caliph Ibn Jubayr saw as a young man. Nāsir went on to build a strong state in central and southern Iraq and to make the Abbasid caliphate an important regional power. And that is all it was. The Fatimids no longer provided a Shi'ite challenge to the Abbasids and the Isma'ilis were confined to their mountainous strongholds in coastal Syria and northern Iran. The revived caliphate no longer had any pretensions to universal power or wider religious authority, the Abbasid caliphs were simply one, and not necessarily the most powerful, of the dynasts who sought to expand their power in the Fertile Crescent.

Disaster: The Mongol Conquest of 1258

The later years of Nāsir's reign saw the emergence of a new threat to the entire political order in the Middle East: the invasions of the Mongols. Mongol power had been growing in eastern Asia from the end of the twelfth century and by 1206 Genghis Khan ruled over a nomad empire which dominated the steppes to the north of the Great Wall of China. The Mongols posed no threat to the Islamic world until 1217 when, in response to a foolish provocation by a local eastern Iranian ruler, Genghis launched a devastating attack on Iran. Great centres of Islamic civilization like Samarqand, Merv and Nishapur were destroyed and their populations massacred or driven west as refugees. For a generation or so the conquests stalled and then, from 1256, Genghis's grandson Hulegu renewed the push to the west. His intention was to secure Mongol control over the whole of Iran and Iraq. Two groups posed a challenge to this domination. One was the Isma'ili Assassins of northern Iran, who had successfully resisted all the attempts of the Seljuq Turks to subdue them, and the other was the Abbasid caliphs of Baghdad.

Two centuries before, the arrival of the Seljuq Turks from the east had presented both a danger and an opportunity to the caliphs, for they were, at least nominally, converted to Islam and their rulers sought to be integrated into the Muslim political world. The caliphs could, and did, do business with them. It was a very different story with the Mongols. They were not Muslims and sought domination rather than integration. For them the Abbasid caliphs, with their claims to be leaders of the whole Muslim community, were a threat they could not allow to remain. So it was that, in 1257, Hulegu directed his forces to Baghdad.

At the end of January 1258, after a siege of more than a month, the city was stormed and Caliph Musta'sim taken prisoner and brought to Hulegu's camp. What followed became the stuff of legend, or rather a number of different legends. We have few contemporary Arabic and Persian accounts which variously blame the Shi'ite vizier of the caliph for treachery, or the caliph himself for vacillation and miserliness, but none go into great detail about these terrible events. The earliest surviving narrative comes from the Frenchman Jean de Joinville, who participated in Louis IX's first crusade and who was in a position to have heard rumours while he was in the Levant, from Marco Polo, who travelled through the Middle East at the end of the thirteenth century, so the death of the caliph was soon reported in the west.

All of these western narratives tell essentially the same moral tale. The caliph was brought before Hulegu and shown all the gold and silver plate which had been taken from his treasuries. Then Hulegu told him that he had to eat the possessions he had loved so much. When the caliph objected that they could not be eaten, Hulegu asked why he had not used them to send him gifts to dissuade him from launching an attack or to raise more soldiers to defend his city. Then the caliph was confined in prison, surrounded by his treasures, and starved to death.

This edifying story of greed and miserliness does not find its way into the Muslim tradition. One of the earliest full Arabic sources is Ibn al-Furāt, writing in Cairo at the end of the fourteenth century. It was more than a century after the events, but survivors of the Abbasid court had fled to Cairo and might well have preserved genuine memories of what had happened. According to this account Hulegu did indeed offer dishes of gold and jewels to the starving caliph to make his point, but the execution was carried out by having the caliph and his sons put in two great sacks and trampled to death. In the Mongol scale of values, killing a man without shedding his blood was an expression of respect. But the thirty-seventh and last Abbasid caliph of Baghdad may have missed the point of this compliment as Hulegu's horses pounded him to extinction.

The fall of Baghdad and the brutal death of its caliph were at one level simply another grim incident in an era which had witnessed more than its share of massacre and murder. As we have noted, there was no widespread and immediate sense of shock or general lamentation in the Muslim world. But later generations looking back on these events would realize that they marked the end of a long story. Never again would the caliphate be a politically independent entity; as we shall see, it would always be subordinate to Mamluk or Ottoman rulers and priorities. While the papacy has, precariously at some times, maintained its political independence to this day, the caliphate lost it in 1258 and it was never revived. With this political independence, gone too were any real aspirations to a leadership which went beyond self-interested dynastic concerns.

CHAPTER 6

Three Authors in Search of the Caliphate

The state of the caliphate in these centuries of near power-lessness provoked considerable unease and soul-searching among intellectuals and political thinkers. Apart from a few Kharijites, everyone accepted that the community needed a caliph to govern men and keep them from going astray. Of course, an important part of this duty involved maintaining law and order, by force if necessary, so that Muslims could live together in peace and harmony. There was also a religious aspect to this office. In a memorable phrase which seems to date back to early Islam, the caliphs were said to be 'the tent pegs of our faith'. They were needed to hold up the whole edifice of the *shari'a*. All *qāḍīs* and preachers, it was argued, owed their authority ultimately to the caliph. Without him no marriages would be valid, no contracts enforceable and man would be bereft of spiritual guidance.

But there was a serious problem with this idea. The Abbasid caliphs themselves lacked the power and authority to do the job effectively. What was to be done? How could the institution be reformed or repositioned to make it worthy and capable of undertaking the heavy responsibilities the community demanded of it? Many scholars contributed to this debate, but in this chapter I will concentrate on just three of the most influential participants, Māwardī (d. 1058), Juwaynī (d. 1085) and Ghazālī (d. 1111).

Māwardī

The first and probably the most influential of these scholars was Māwardī, whose treatise *The Ordinances of Government* is, among other things, an attempt to make sense of the very ambiguous position in which the caliph now found himself.[1] At one level the caliph was the deputy of God on His earth, or the successor of the Prophet of God, and all men should obey him. At another level, he was the powerless inheritor of an ancient office without a single soldier under his command, entirely at the mercy of local warlords. Māwardī was an authority on these matters. He was no armchair academic but was active in the diplomatic service of Caliph Qā'im. In 1031 he was entrusted with the delicate mission of getting the *bayʿa* from the powerful Buyid sovereign Abū Kalijar in Shiraz and it is probably a measure of his diplomatic abilities that he succeeded and was able to return saying that he had been well treated. Later we find him negotiating agreements between Buyid princes at the caliph's behest; his last mission, in 1043, was to broker an agreement with the last effective Buyid sovereign, Jalāl al-Dawla, and the newly arrived Seljuk chief Tughril Beg. He thus had a keen idea of the political realities of his time.

Māwardī's treatise is in many ways a summing up of Islamic government practice, and much of it is concerned with details of tax collection, the powers of judges and other such matters, but in the first three chapters he directly addresses the questions of the choice of the caliph and the powers he could enjoy.

He begins with a discussion of the necessity of having an imam/caliph (he uses both terms interchangeably) for the Muslim community. This can be justified on the grounds of reason – men need to be governed to prevent disorder – or on religious grounds – because it is enjoined by the Qur'ān and the authority of Tradition. Having established this point, he then turns to the issue of choosing the caliph. He lists a number of obvious qualities that the candidate must have – a sense of justice, knowledge, physical ability and so on – and finishes with the assertion that the caliph must be descended from Quraysh. He justifies this, as he does most of his assertions, by reference to the deeds and utterances of the Orthodox caliphs. For him it is enough that Abū Bakr, quoting the Prophet's words, insisted that Quraysh were the only people entitled to the highest office.

Māwardī writes that the caliph can be chosen by election or by appointment by a predecessor but, he asks, if the caliph is to be chosen by election, who are the electors to be? Some say that all Muslims should be involved, but Māwardī looks to the choice of the Orthodox caliphs to refute this notion. Abū Bakr was chosen by a small group, Umar stipulated that there should be six in the *shūra* which was to choose his successor, while Alī was chosen by just one elector, Abbās (the Prophet's uncle and ancestor of the Abbasids), who simply said, 'Give me your hands so that I may pledge you my allegiance and let the people say, "The uncle of the Messenger of God, may God bless him and grant him salvation, has nominated his cousin." No two persons would then disagree about you.'[2]

But suppose there are two equally good candidates, Māwardī considers. The choice then depends on the situation. If Muslims are being attacked, then bravery in battle should be given priority; if popular lethargy and heresy are the main problems, then intelligence should be deemed more important. Age could be used to differentiate two equal candidates, but seniority, by itself, was not a decisive qualification. Casting lots should not be used in deciding these issues. Once the electors have decided and the candidate has agreed, then the decision cannot be undone unless the chosen candidate resigns. If two candidates are elected in different cities, then the one who was elected first has priority.

Māwardī then turns to nomination. Here the issue is whether the designated heir needs the approval of the electors. In general the answer is no, but some argue that approval is needed should the nominee be the son or, improbably, the father of the previous caliph.

The next issue is the permissibility of appointing two heirs, one to succeed the other. This had been common practice under the Umayyads and early Abbasids, but had also been the cause of dispute and violence in those dynasties. However, Māwardī argues that the selection of two heirs is valid by analogy with the behaviour of the Prophet himself, who appointed no less than three commanders to succeed each other in the military expedition he sent to Mu'ta in Syria at the end of his life.

Once chosen, the caliph's identity and title should be made known. Here Māwardī addresses the vexed issue of whether the caliph is deputy of God or successor to the

Prophet of God. He, like almost all later jurists, comes down firmly on the side who see the caliph as successor of the Prophet, citing Abū Bakr's alleged refusal of the title caliph of God as clinching evidence.

The final issue he deals with is the permissibility of removing a caliph who is wicked or inadequate. He considers three eventualities. The first is that a caliph has become unjust or fallen into heresy. In this case, the caliph must resign or be removed from office. Māwardī is very brief on this most difficult issue and he seems to be skating over it. He devotes much more space to physical incapacity as a disqualification, blindness or loss of limbs for example, yet he affirms that a eunuch can become caliph, though there is no record of this occurring in the history of the caliphate. A final sort of inadequacy is the caliph who is taken captive, whether by Muslims or non-Muslims, and here the answer depends on the nature of his captivity and his prospects of release.

Having discussed the qualifications required and the method of choosing the caliph, in his second chapter Māwardī considers the appointment of viziers. He looks at two different types. The first is the vizierate of delegation (*tafwīd*), in which the caliph essentially entrusts all his functions to an official who acts for him in every respect. Here Māwardī is giving a legal framework to a situation in which the caliph's real power has been usurped by officials, as with the Buyid emirs of his own day. In the second case (*tanfīdh*), the caliph simply appoints a vizier to execute his orders, whose role is therefore that of a prime minister, as it was at the time when the early Abbasids enjoyed real power. In the next chapter he turns his attention to the appointment of provincial governors. Here again he distinguishes two sorts of appointments. For the first, the caliph can choose whom to appoint and the official thereby entrusted with the office can be dismissed and recalled. This was the practice in the Umayyad and early Abbasid periods. The second kind is what Māwardī calls appointment by usurpation or coercion. In this case the caliph is obliged to give his approval to a local governor who has already seized power for himself. In this way Māwardī provides a legal stratagem by which the theoretical sovereignty of the caliph over the politically fragmented Muslim world can be maintained. In both the discussions of the vizierate and the governors we can see him devising a constitutional order which will safeguard the status of the caliph in an era of change. It is a synthesis which has been extremely influential in many subsequent discussions of caliphate.

Juwaynī

Abd al-Malik al-Juwaynī came from a very different background from that of Māwardī. His family originated from the small eastern Iranian town of Juvayn and his father had gone to Nishapur in 1016 to take up a position at a madrasa there. The young Juwaynī was brought up in this academic atmosphere and at the age of just nineteen succeeded to his father's position. In 1053 he left for Baghdad, still the greatest intellectual centre in the Muslim world, where he probably met Māwardī and certainly read his *Ordinances*. He may also have met Caliph Qā'im, then in the process of negotiating his relationship with the newly arrived Seljuq sultans. He went on to spend four years studying and teaching in Medina and Mecca. In 1063 he returned to Khurasan at the invitation of Nizām al-Mulk, at that time consolidating his position as vizier to the Seljuq sultan Alp Arslān, who appointed him as a professor in the Nizamiyya madrasa he had founded in the city, and Juwaynī remained there until his death.

Juwaynī wrote his political treatise *Ghiyāth al-umam* (Succour of the Nations) between 1072 and 1085 when the politics of the eastern Islamic world were dominated by the Seljuq sultan Malik Shāh and his all-powerful vizier Nizām al-Mulk. The Seljuqs wielded much political influence, but they needed caliphal recognition and wanted to extend their dominance even further. Above all, they wanted to found a dynasty which would combine the caliphate and the sultanate, that is, the religious and secular aspects of Islamic government. To that end the Abbasid caliph Muqtadī married the daughter of Malik Shāh and produced a son called Ja'far, who Malik Shāh was determined would be Commander of the Faithful. In 1092 Malik Shāh ordered the reigning caliph to resign and leave the city, paving the way for Ja'far to succeed him. In the event Malik Shāh died young and Nizām al-Mulk was assassinated and the whole scheme collapsed as the Seljuq princes and their supporters fought each other for the succession.

Juwaynī had been dead for seven years by this time, but his treatise could serve as the intellectual justification for the Seljuqs' plans. His ideas about the role of the caliphate differed fundamentally from Māwardī's. For Māwardī, with his Baghdadi education and background, Abbasid descent was a key element of the caliphate. The aim must be to restore the dignity of the caliphate and establish a system whereby the various sultans and emirs would function as subordinates to the caliph, even though much of the day-to-day power rested with them. For Juwaynī, with his eastern Iranian background, Abbasid descent was at best irrelevant and at worst a distraction which prevented the effective ruling of the community. The caliph should be chosen from the strongest and most powerful men among Muslims, no matter what his genealogical origins. Both caliphate and sultanate should be united under the rule of this new mighty caliph: the fact that the blood of the Family of the Prophet did not run in his veins was of no importance.

Juwaynī examines many of the points raised by Māwardī but often draws different conclusions. He begins his discussion of the qualifications for the caliphate, which he generally refers to as the imamate, by dismissing Shiʿi claims that the choice was dependent on designation by God; the Prophetic Traditions advanced by them to support this idea are false because, if they were genuine, the Sunnis would accept them too. This leaves Juwaynī in favour of the idea of election. The electors should be free men with experience in law, government and administration. Like Māwardī, he accepts the possibility of choice by just one elector, but for him the key qualification for this elector is that he has power and authority, what he calls *shawkat*. Although he does not say so, this allows the possibility that a powerful Seljuq ruler may quite legally appoint a caliph.

Juwaynī then examines the qualities which the caliph must possess: first of all, a caliph should be sound in body and mind, attributes all authorities agree on. As for Qurashi descent, Juwaynī finds that the Tradition quoted in favour of this has a weak transmission and he concludes that such descent is by no means essential. Although a caliph should ideally be learned in law so that he can make decisions and give guidance, he can, if he is not, rely on the *ulama*, with whom he should work in partnership. Juwaynī stresses that leadership and authority are required attributes for the caliph to be able to maintain the unity of the *umma*, organize armies and defend the frontiers. Here Juwaynī is breaking new ground: such attributes are not the result of being caliph but qualifications for the office. As Wael Hallaq, the great modern scholar of Islamic law puts it:

> Military and political power in Juwaynī's view take
> precedence over any other consideration, for power
> constitutes the only means by which the sovereign can
> properly run the affairs of the Community. A powerless
> ruler must therefore be replaced by a powerful one: 'If the
> imam loses his power and the flock disavow him for no
> obvious reason . . . and if his supporters abandon him' . . .
> he must be deposed and 'the imamate should be entrusted
> to an imam whom people obey'.[3]

The roles of caliph and sultan would be combined in the person of this one strong leader. Juwaynī makes it clear that the powerless ruler he has in mind is the Abbasid caliph Qā'im.

There seems to be a veiled encouragement to the Seljuq vizier Nizām al-Mulk to take over the caliphate. This would have been a very radical departure from the tradition and practice of the community but would be justified by Juwaynī's arguments. He praises the role of the Seljuqs, their organization of government and their leadership of the *jihād*, and argues that a usurper who has the power and the qualifications to lead the *umma* should be accepted. He should also include the *ulama* into the government structure because, Juwaynī says, they are the heirs of the Prophet and the guardians of the *sharīʿa*.

The implications of Juwaynī's views on the caliphate were nothing short of revolutionary. Taken to their logical conclusion, they suggest that military power and true belief are the only meaningful qualifications for the office and that, rather than being a divinely appointed ruler, the caliph should simply be the most powerful military figure, owing his rulership to the consensus of the Muslim community. Authority over secular affairs but also over the true maintenance of religion and *sharīʿa* should belong to him as of right.

Juwaynī's ideas were a product of his time and his close association with the Seljuqs and Nizām al-Mulk. He died in 1085 before they could be put into practice, but the debacle following the deaths of Malik Shāh and his vizier changed the balance of power between the Abbasid caliphs and Seljuq would-be sultans dramatically, and while Seljuq princes fought each other for the sultanate the Abbasid caliphs slowly recovered a measure of control.

Ghazālī

The third of our authors was also the most popular and widely read. Ghazālī was a pupil of Juwaynī's and like him came from an eastern Iranian background. He too enjoyed the support of Nizām al-Mulk, and he was appointed to an important teaching post at the Nizamiyya madrasa in Baghdad in 1091, just a year before Nizām's death. In 1095 he went through what has been described as a spiritual crisis and abandoned his successful academic career to return to his native Khurasan to concentrate on his Sufi and spiritual writings and it was here that he died in 1111.

Ghazālī produced an extensive body of work, and discussions of the caliphate, not always entirely consistent, feature in many of his books, but I shall concentrate on one of them, the Book of Mustazhir (*Kitāb al-Mustazhirī*), written in early 1095 when he was still in post in Baghdad and dedicated, as the title implies, to the reigning Abbasid caliph, Mustazhir (1094–1118). He explains that he was commissioned by the caliph to write a book which would refute the claims of the Shi'ite Isma'ilis to the caliphate. This was an issue of pressing importance: Malik Shāh and Nizām al-Mulk were dead, the Seljuqs were bitterly divided and both the Isma'ili Fatimids of Egypt and the Isma'ili Assassins of northern Iran were poised to take advantage of the chaos.

In his volume Ghazālī sets out first and foremost to challenge Isma'ili ideas of the caliphate. For the Isma'ilis, the caliph was the deputy of God and the only person qualified to interpret God's revelation; questions of *sharī'a* were to be decided by him alone, and not by jurists. The Fatimid caliph in Egypt was the one and only caliph admissible, and all mankind should obey him.

Ghazālī proceeds to demolish these ideas, elaborating an alternative legitimacy for the Abbasid caliphs. He maintains that there has to be a caliph to make the *sharī'a* effective: he is God's caliph and the mainspring for all that is right. Without a caliph all public functions would be void and the whole fabric of *sharī'a* in danger of collapse. This argument is based on the consensus of the *umma*, the actions of the Companions of the Prophet, who chose a caliph immediately on his death to safeguard the unity and future of the community, and the fact that there can only be one caliph, not a *shūra*, because that is the only way of preventing chaos.

The next question is the choice of the caliph. Having dismissed the Shi'i idea of divine appointment Ghazālī looks at mechanisms of election. Here he dismisses the idea of any sort of public participation, even one restricted to people of virtue and religious probity, and opts instead for having a single elector. The essential quality of this one elector is that he has power and authority to make the rule of the caliph effective. Ghazālī adopts the concept of *shawkat* already used by Juwaynī to express that combination of force and awe which is essential to enforce obedience, for a caliph who cannot command obedience is no use to anyone. It is God who provides and sustains this *shawkat*, thus expressing His support for the choice.

The implications of this doctrine are far-reaching. It comes very close to arguing that 'might is right', since political power is confirmed by God. In more practical terms, for Ghazālī's own age, it means that nomination by one Seljuq sultan, if that Seljuq sultan has *shawkat*, is completely legal. The problem, of course, is what happens if there is no figure who possesses this quality. Ghazālī does not appear to deal with this, except to suggest that two or three men might combine to, as it were, produce sufficient *shawkat* to enforce the authority of the caliph they choose. Such a system may well have seemed viable and workable when Malik Shāh was sultan and his all-powerful vizier Nizām al-Mulk (the one Juwaynī seems to have wanted as caliph) had all the *shawkat* needed. When they both died in 1092, just three years before Ghazālī was writing, there was no one else who could take their place, though he may have believed and hoped that one such would emerge.

Ghazālī goes on to discuss the qualities needed to be caliph. Some of these are uncontroversial, such as soundness of mind and body, and maleness (no discussion here), but he also insists, like Māwardī but unlike Juwaynī, on descent from the Quraysh. Then he describes a set of qualities which are acquired rather than innate. The first, which he calls *najda*, is a show of strength:

> A plentiful supply of equipment, seeking help of armies, the tying of banners and standards, possessing the ability, through the help of parties and followers, to subdue rebels and wrongdoers, to fight against infidels and those who are inordinately proud, to still the manifestation of discords and to stop the flow of the accumulated swell of trying afflictions before their evil becomes apparent and the harm they cause becomes widespread. This is what is meant by *najda*.

As the translator Carole Hillenbrand notes,[4] the passage is full of verbal conceits and rhetorical flourishes, but the basic meaning is clear: a caliph who cannot perform these functions is, for Ghazālī, no true caliph. In a long excursus, he explains how in his day the Turks, who made up most of the armies, were, for all their conflicts and disobedience, the source of the *najda* of Mustazhir's caliphate.

The last three qualities a caliph needs are competence (*kifāya*), piety (*wara*) and knowledge (*ilm*). Piety is difficult to combine with the exercise of power and depends on strict adherence to justice. As far as knowledge is concerned, the caliph does not need to be an outstanding scholar for he can ask the advice and opinion of the *ulama*. This is in contrast to the Isma'ili concept of a caliph who makes legal decisions on the basis of divine inspiration alone and who cannot err.

Ghazālī's overwhelming concern is to create a strong caliphate which will assure stability and unity within the Sunni world and make it able to resist the attacks of the Isma'ili Shi'is, whom, like his patron Nizām al-Mulk, he hates with a visceral passion. To achieve this, he needs to create a framework for cooperation between the caliph and the Turkish military, even if the Turks are sometimes (and, in fact, increasingly) themselves a source of disorder in the state.

All three authors were wrestling with the problems of reconciling the theoretical claims of caliphate and imamate with the realities of political power in their own time. The collapse of the Abbasid caliphate had led to a profound questioning of the nature of the office. All three agreed that a caliph was necessary for the proper ordering of the Muslim community. Beyond that these three pious and intelligent Muslims came to very different conclusions. For Māwardī the important thing was to restore the power and prestige of the Abbasid caliphate, while Juwaynī thought that the Abbasids were an irrelevant anachronism and that if the caliphate was to function it should pass to the most militarily powerful and effective ruler of the time, provided, of course, that he was a pious Muslim. Ghazālī tried to find a compromise, combining military power with spiritual leadership. The main point that we can take from this discussion is that, as early as the eleventh and twelfth centuries, there were profound differences among leading Sunni Muslim intellectuals as to what the caliphate could and should be. There was no one definitive answer or model.

CHAPTER 7

The Caliphate of the Shi'ites

The caliphates we have been discussing so far, the Orthodox, the Umayyad and the Abbasid caliphates, all belong to, or have been adopted by, the Sunni mainstream of Islam, but there is another tradition of caliphate, equally vital and varied, which we might define as the Shi'ite.

Islamic leadership in the Shi'ite tradition is described in terms of caliphate but also of imamate. The term imam has, as has already been noted, a whole spectrum of meanings in the discussion of Islamic society. In the context of this discussion it is used virtually as a synonym for caliphate, the religio-political leadership of the Muslims. The Twelver Shi'ites produced imams but, apart from the first Alī, no caliphs; the intention certainly was that at one stage in the future, with the help of God and the support of the Shi'a, these imams would also be caliphs. In the event this did not happen and the imams disappeared into hiding instead.

The Shi'ites are often described as heretics and it is worth pausing for a moment to see what this idea signifies in Islam. Heresy in Christianity, Islam and Judaism means believing the wrong thing in religious matters. It is the opposite of orthodoxy or right belief. Nobody ever claims they are heretics because nobody ever boasts that they believe the wrong thing and everyone thinks that they alone are orthodox. For Shi'ites of all persuasions, it is the Sunnis who are heretics. In ancient Christianity heresy was about theological issues, above all the relationship between the three persons of the Trinity and the nature of the incarnation of Christ. These abstract, and essentially unknowable, questions aroused fierce passions and, in the three centuries before the coming of Islam, a huge polemical literature was produced and much blood shed in debating them. From the eleventh century onwards the western Church was divided by another sort of heresy and that was the debate about the authority of the papacy of Rome, a controversy which in the end split the western Church from top to bottom and led to the Reformation in the sixteenth century.

The same issues still divide the Church today. The fundamental question is the role of the pope in defining true belief. For the Catholics it was clear that God's grace provided the pope with the authority to decide on controversial aspects of belief, and in the nineteenth century it became official doctrine that the pope was infallible, that is, he could not make a wrong decision when it came to pronouncing on questions of Christian belief. Protestants, on the other hand, rejected what they saw as papal authority, or what they considered to be papal dictatorship, and believed that matters of doctrine should be debated by learned men but in the end decided by individuals and churches. Ultimately, the key relationship was the relationship of the individual believer with God.

Islam was spared much of the speculative wrangling about issues of Trinity and Incarnation because the unity of God was paramount and indisputable; indeed Muslims defined themselves as those who rejected *shirk* (polytheism). There were, however, still two areas in which speculative theology crossed into wrong belief or heresy.

The first of these was the nature of the Qur'ān. All Muslims agree that the Qur'ān is the word of God; whereas most, though by no means all, Christians believe the Bible contains divine utterance but also a great deal of material, such as histories, proverbs and so forth, which is obviously composed by human beings. If you do not accept the Qur'ān as the word of God, you cannot be a Muslim. The question which separates Sunnis and Shi'as was whether the Qur'ān had existed through all eternity with God, or whether it had been authored by God at a particular moment in human history and revealed to Muhammad.

The second speculative issue which divided Muslims was that of anthropomorphism, the belief that God was in shape and form like a human (male) being, but much bigger and better. That is to say that He had arms and legs, sat literally on a throne and uttered words with His mouth in the way that we do. Nobody actually claimed to be anthropomorphist, but it was an accusation which could be levelled at Muslims who thought differently from true believers, and one which was used by the Almohads in the Maghreb to discredit the views of their enemies the Almoravids.

These were controversies which, though important at the time, were limited in scope and duration. The issue which really divided, and continues to divide the *umma*, is that of authority in the Muslim community. In this respect it is reminiscent of the controversies among Christians about papal supremacy, which proved equally divisive.

The Arabic word *shī'a* essentially means 'a party' in the sense of 'a group of supporters'. From this derives the Arabic *shī'ī*, meaning an individual member of such a party, and this in turn gives us the English Shi'ite, the term I shall use. In early Islamic political discourse there were a number of *shī'as*, the *shī'a* of Uthmān, for example, or the *shī'a* of the Abbasids, but by the tenth century the term generally referred to the party of Alī, or the party of the Family of the Prophet.

The fundamental idea to which all Shi'ites subscribe is that the Family of the Prophet has a special status in the Muslim community. This in itself was neither controversial or divisive. Most Sunni Muslims, at least in pre-modern times, would accept that the members of the Family should be honoured and perhaps given pensions or other benefits. What distinguished the Shi'ites is that they believed that the Family of the Prophet, and only it, had a God-given right to lead the Muslim community as caliphs or imams and to make decisions on matters of *sharī'a*.

This belief, if accepted, gave rise to a number of further questions. Who exactly belonged to the Family of the Prophet? Clearly this included the direct blood descendants of Muhammad through his daughter Fātima, her husband Alī b. Abī Tālib and their two sons, Hasan and Husayn. But could it also include the descendants of Alī's brother Ja'far, or the Prophet's paternal uncle Abbās, from whom the Abbasids were descended? Then there was the question of later descendants. Were all the offspring of Hasan and Husayn eligible to lead the community? If so, as the centuries rolled on, this provided a huge number of potential candidates – too many, in fact, for a proper choice to be made. But if the number of eligible members of the Family was to be restricted, who should do this and how? And even in the case of an imam who produced a number of sons, should it necessarily be the eldest who should succeed, or should the most able and suitable be selected? And what would happen if the presumed heir apparent seemed, God forbid, to behave in a wayward and un-Islamic way? Did this mean that he should be deposed and replaced by someone apparently more suitable as a candidate, or did it mean that God's decisions were inscrutable to men and should be obeyed whatever the apparent situation?

Then there was the further question of what this God-given authority amounted to. Virtually all Shi'ites believe that it means that the imam should be able to interpret uncertain and controversial passages in the Qur'ān and that it is him, not the scholars of Tradition, who had the knowledge to do this. The *sharī'a* of the Shi'ites is to be decided by the imam, not by the *ulama* or by the consensus of the community. Some took the argument further than that, saying that the imam should be able to change and even abrogate the *sharī'a* because of his superior judgement.

All these questions were serious and difficult and the answers to them had important implications for the leadership of the *umma*, so it his hardly surprising that they gave rise to a vast literature. Some of this literature took the form of heresiographies, or accounts of all the different sects which emerged. These numbered up to seventy-three, each named after a real or imaginary founder, each advocating a particular answer to the various questions. Some of these were clearly large groups; others amounted to little more than one lone individual proclaiming his own eccentric ideas.

This proliferation of such groups can give an impression of fissiparous chaos, or perhaps even frivolity, but most of them represent answers to the major questions which the idea of the God-guided ruler gives rise to. To understand these complex developments, we have to think of them as a result of pious, honest and intelligent men trying to find meaningful answers to difficult but very fundamental questions of belief and authority in the Muslim environment.

There were other, more mundane factors which accounted for the emergence of so many different groups among the Shi'ites. At times, adherence to Shi'ism was the result of social tensions. As already explained, much of the enthusiasm for Ali and his descendants in Iraq in the early Islamic period seems to have been experienced by those who felt left out and resented their status as second-class citizens. There were also regional differences. Again, it has been pointed out that from a very early period devotion to the house of Ali went along with, and was part of, Iraqi resentment of Syrian dominance. In later centuries we find Shi'ites ruling in marginal areas of the Muslim world, the mountains of northern Iran, for example, or Yemen, where Shi'ism has emerged as a signifier of local sentiment, and the official Shi'ism of modern Iran is an inseparable part of Iranian national identity.

Among the many different strands into which Shi'ism divided, three main sects emerged. The first are the Imami or Twelver Shi'ites, who are the most numerous at the present day, comprising the Shi'ites of modern Iraq and Iran; the second are the Zaydis, now only really active in northern Yemen but a group with a long and interesting history; and the third are the Isma'ilis, the group who founded the Fatimid caliphate of Egypt (969–1171) and are now represented in a world-wide diaspora, many of whom accept the leadership of the Aga Khan.

Imami or Twelver Shi'ism

Imami or Twelver (*ithnā asharī*) Shi'ism is defined by the fact that it recognizes twelve imams, descended from Alī through his son Husayn. None of these imams, after Alī himself, were caliphs or attained any significant political power, though their followers certainly thought that they should. After the failure of Husayn's attempt to seize power from the Umayyads in 680 and his death at Karbala, his son Alī (d. 712), known to later generations of Twelvers as Zayn al-Ābidīn (Ornament of the Believers), seems to have led a life of retirement. Although the biographies of these early imams were elaborated later to give an impression of continuous activity, there is no evidence that this second Alī played any part in the politics of his day or that he was respected as an authority on religious questions. The same was broadly true of his son Muhammad al-Bāqir (d. *c.*735). There were Shi'ite revolts in Iraq, notably that of Zayd b. Alī in Kufa in 740, but the line of the Twelver imams played no part in them. There are reports that at the time of the Abbasid revolution the organizer of the Abbasid movement in Kufa, Abū Salama, tried to interest the then imam, Ja'far al-Sādiq (d. 765), in putting himself forward for the caliphate, but Ja'far, perhaps wisely, declined to get involved and Abū Salama paid for his initiative with his life.

Despite this, it seems to be Ja'far who was the first of the Twelver imams to be more than a name in the genealogy. His status was certainly developed and probably exaggerated by later Shi'ite writers, but he is said to have distinguished himself as a dispenser of legal rulings and to have attracted a following which respected these rulings not just because he was learned but, more significantly, because he was a direct descendant of Alī and of the Prophet himself. Ja'far appears to have made it clear that one could believe in the spiritual authority of the Family without committing oneself to open rebellion. This meant that accepting the Shi'ite imam as spiritual leader did not necessitate violent opposition to the Abbasid caliphate but could be a matter of private conviction. It may have been in his time that the distinctively Shi'ite doctrine of *taqiyya* was developed. *Taqiyya* held that it was completely legal, and not blameworthy, for a man to disguise his religious belief if he felt that to proclaim it openly would put his life at risk. That meant that, although one could accept the Shi'ite imam as rightful leader of the Muslims and as a man who should be caliph in an ideal world, this did not entail rising up against existing authorities or taking violent actions.

Many looked up to Ja'far as a divinely inspired imam and learned authority and this is probably how he saw himself. But some, known to the Arab tradition as *ghulāt*, which can roughly be translated as 'extremists', believed that Ja'far and other imams including, rather improbably, his contemporary the Abbasid caliph Mansūr, were saviours and messiahs.

Their opinions were infallible and their lives were blameless. The two strands, the scholarly and the messianic, were in some senses contradictory, but they later came together as parts of the composite image of the imam.

It was under Ja'far's son and generally accepted heir Mūsā al-Kāzim that Twelver Shi'ism began to be organized as a political movement. Mūsā had agents who worked for him and collected money from his followers in what would seem to be preparations of a bid for political power in his name. He is one of the two imams commemorated at the great Baghdadi Shi'ite shrine at Kazimayn, which shows that his memory lingered on. He in turn was succeeded by his son, known as Alī al-Ridā (Chosen One: hence the name Reza, the Persian form of Ridā, being a common name for Iranian men, including the last two shahs). Alī was the only one of the Twelver imams to come anywhere near political power when he was adopted as heir, briefly, by the Abbasid caliph Ma'mūn in a bid to reunite the different branches of the Family of the Prophet and to attract much needed political support in Iraq. Alī, however, died before the caliph, some said of poison administered when he became politically inconvenient. His tomb, and the shrine that developed around it, at Meshed, in north-eastern Iran, is the largest and most opulent of all Shi'ite pilgrimage sites.

He was succeeded by a boy and the imams who came after him were more or less kept under house arrest by the Abbasid authorities. When the last generally accepted imam died in 874, his young son, if he ever existed, disappeared. His followers said he was in hiding: *ghayba*, the Arabic word, is rather disconcertingly translated into English as 'occultation'.

To Twelver Shi'ites this occultation of the imam meant, and still means, that there is an imam in the world, indeed there has to be an imam or Islam would not be possible, but he is hidden. It is impossible to have any direct communication with him or for him to issue any decrees. Instead, decisions have to be made by learned men on the basis of decrees passed down from Alī and the known imams. This gives enormous authority in Twelver Shi'ism to scholars, the most important of whom are known, from the nineteenth century onwards, as ayatollahs or 'signs of God', for their position does not depend just on their learning, as it does for Sunni scholars, but also on their status as representatives of the 'hidden imam'. Correspondingly, the existence of the 'hidden imam' leaves no space for a contemporary caliph: there is, so to speak, no vacancy. This is why Twelver and other Shi'ites will never be able to accept the pretensions of modern claimants to the caliphate. The Twelver Buyids who ruled Iraq in the late tenth and early eleventh century never appointed a caliph from the Family of the Prophet and the powerful and magnificent Safavid rulers of Iran were able to take the ancient Iranian title of shah but could not proclaim themselves caliphs.

The Zaydis

The Zaydis stand in clear contrast to this quietist tradition. The essential idea behind Zaydi belief as it crystallized in the ninth and tenth centuries was that the caliph, who must, of course, be a descendant of Alī and Fātima, had to distinguish himself by taking up arms against the unjust rule of Muslims who rejected the rights of the Family of the Prophet. Any one of the numerous males of the Family was entitled to put himself forward and risk his life assuming this role. In practice, in later Zaydism, the leadership became hereditary in certain families, but that was not the guiding principle in the beginning.

In terms of political action, then, the early Zaydis were much more radical than the Twelvers. In other ways they were much closer to the Sunni mainstream. The Twelvers were Rāfidis, that is, they rejected the claims of the first three caliphs, Abū Bakr, Umar and Uthmān, believing that they had usurped the right to the caliphate which properly belonged to Alī. Some but not all Zaydis, on the other hand, were prepared to accept the legitimacy of the first two caliphs (even though they were, of course, inferior to Alī) and believed that it was only with Uthmān things began to go wrong. The Umayyads and Abbasids were, without doubt, completely illegitimate and should be violently challenged by true Zaydis. An imam who sat at home dispensing wisdom to a few peaceful followers was no imam at all and no use to anyone.

Apart from Alid descent and courage, the other quality a Zaydi imam needed to have was learning. Zaydis discussed whether this learning was different to the learning of ordinary men because of the Prophetic descent of the imam, or whether it was like other men's learning only better. The imam was thus in a position to decide questions of *sharīʿa* and a fully qualified Zaydi caliph would not need to have *ulama* to advise him.

Zaydism takes its name from one Zayd b. Alī, a younger

son of the fourth of the twelve imams. While his elder brother Muhammad al-Bāqir stayed at home, and was later accepted as a true imam by the Twelvers, Zayd led a revolt in Kufa against the Umayyads in 740. Like so many Alid revolts it was, at a practical level, a complete failure. The Kufans did not rise up en masse against Umayyad rule and Zayd was soon cut down and killed by troops sent by the governor. The revolt did produce some of the earliest political rhetoric in the Shi'ite tradition, however. Zayd had called for acceptance of himself as caliph because of his membership of the Family, but he also laid out a practical programme. As caliph he would restore to the Kufans their rights to salaries and pensions, rights which had been guaranteed by his ancestor Alī and effectively stolen by the Umayyads. His recorded speeches play on the idea of the Zaydis as righters of wrongs and champions of the dispossessed.

Zayd's death did not spell the end of his ideas. His son Īsā took up his father's cause and led a small, secret cell of believers in Kufa. Constantly harried by Umayyad and later Abbasid police, they nonetheless kept the flame of revolution alive and formed the core of support for the most spectacular of all the early Shi'ite revolts of the early Islamic period. Muhammad b. Abd Allah, known as 'the Pure Soul' (al-Nafs al-zākiyya), was not, like the twelve imams, a descendant of Husayn but of his elder brother Hasan. He was named after his ancestor the Prophet and lived in the Prophet's city of Medina. Immediately after the establishment of the Abbasid caliphate he began preparations for revolt. His project was to restore the Islamic community to what it had been in the time of the Prophet and the earliest Muslims. Medina, which was remote from the main centres of Muslim power and population and dependent on food imported from Egypt, was a most impractical place to begin such a project. But that was not the point: the fact that it was the Prophet's city, the city which he had defended against the enemies of Islam, was more important. It was a pious and romantic vision, pursued with courage and defended with eloquence.

We know a lot about his project because of a remarkable narrative put together by one Umar b. Shabba after the failure of the revolt, which is preserved not only in Shi'ite sources but also in the great *History* of the staunchly Sunni Tabarī. It is a heroic account, constantly referring back to the example of the Prophet himself and featuring a correspondence between the rebel, when he had declared himself in the Holy City, and his opponent, the Abbasid caliph Mansūr, in which each defended their right to lead the Muslim community. In the end force prevailed, as it was bound to. A small professional army, led by a cousin of the caliph, attacked the city. Muhammad defended it, as the Prophet himself had done, by digging a trench to impede the enemy, but to no avail and Muhammad was killed, fighting bravely.

In the aftermath of this and later defeats of Alid military revolts, many of the supporters of the rebellion chose to flee to avoid the inevitable punishment. Two of these fugitives had a lasting effect on the religious geography of the Muslim world, establishing a link between the Family and groups of Muslims in regions far from the centres of power and population.

One of these was the area of modern Morocco. This was a land which had been nominally conquered by the Muslims by 700, but Muslim population and government had been concentrated across the Straits of Gibraltar in Andalus and the indigenous Berber tribes had been little affected by the coming of Islam. It was into this world that Idrīs b. Abd Allah fled, hoping to escape the long arm of Abbasid authority. Idrīs was able to establish his prestige as a holy man and descendant of the Prophet, attracting a following among the Berber tribes but not able to save himself from Abbasid retribution. He died, it is said, from the effects of a poisoned tooth-pick sent by the caliph. The Idrisids, as his descendants were known, were never able to establish a lasting, stable state, but they set a pattern for rulership in the region which still has power today, a pattern in which descent from the Prophet through Idrīs (which the present king of Morocco claims) brings unique political prestige. At the same time, the Idrisid view was not strictly speaking a Shi'ite one as they did not claim to have semi-divine powers or wisdom. Nonetheless, the idea of a caliphate combining religious and political leadership remained and still remains an important part of Maghrebi political discourse.

Zaydi beliefs also spread to the mountainous provinces at the southern end of the Caspian Sea: as so often, the mountains provided a refuge for ideas which were, so to speak, driven out of the wide plains and large cities of the central Islamic world. For eight centuries this area was home to a variety of Shi'ite communities, both Zaydi and Isma'ili. The Zaydis lasted as an independent group until the sixteenth century when they were absorbed by the Imami Shi'ism of the Safavid state and disappeared from history.

Still longer lasting were the Zaydi imamates of the Yemen.

Founded in the late ninth century, the Zaydi imamate survived invasions – by the Ayyubids in the twelfth century and by the Ottomans, twice, in the sixteenth and at the end of the nineteenth centuries – and continued to hold power until 1962 when the last imam was overthrown by a coup. The strongholds of the Zaydis were in the northern mountains of Yemen, around the city of Sa'da, and their control of the ancient capital at Sana'a and the south was always tenuous. The Houthis of this northern area, who are presently contending for power in Yemen, are Zaydis and it is surely only a matter of time before someone decides to seize the initiative, as Zaydis have always done, and revives their caliphate.

The Zaydi imamates remained a distinctly Yemeni phenomenon. The imams were, in a way, outside the tribal structure. They served as mediators, advisers, scholars and leaders of the Yemenis against invaders but not as rulers with absolute control over law and order and other aspects of everyday life: this was left in the hands of the tribes and tribal chiefs. It was a model of authority which worked well enough in Yemen for many centuries but could not be exported to other parts of the world.

The Early Isma'ilis

The last of the main Shi'ite groups we must consider are the Isma'ilis. Their importance lies partly in the number of manifestations of Isma'ili belief (Qarāmita, Fatimids, Assassins) and their extensive geographical spread (from Tunisia to Tajikistan and later into India) and long survival (the Isma'ilis emerged in the late ninth century and remain a very active part of the Muslim community today).

From our point of view, the significant feature of the Isma'ilis was that they generated the most important Shi'ite caliphate and with them we can see, as nowhere else, the advantages and problems caused by having a caliph chosen by God from the Family of the Prophet. The Imamis would have liked to have established a caliphate over the whole Muslim world in the name of the Family, but their attempts came to nothing. The Zaydis did produce effective rulers, some of them bearing the title of caliph, like the Zaydi imams of Yemen in the early modern period, but their influence was always confined to marginal and impoverished areas of the Muslim world. With the Isma'ilis, it was different: the Fatimid caliphs came to rule Egypt and much of Syria, their authority was even accepted in Baghdad for a short period and Fatimid missionaries and agents operated as far east as Afghanistan. The fundamental question we must ask is: to what extent and in what ways was this Shi'ite caliphate distinct in definition and purpose from its Sunni equivalents? Was this a radically different model or essentially the same one in a different guise?

The origins of the Isma'ili movement lie in the Imami Shi'ite environment of early ninth-century Iraq. The Isma'ili story is that the sect originates from a dispute about the succession to the imam Ja'far al-Sādiq (d. 765) and the reasons why his eldest son did not succeed him. The roots of the dispute are unclear: either Isma'il died before his father or he was deemed unsuitable and removed from his position. In any case he did not become imam, but, it is said, he left a son,

Muhammad, who was the seventh and last of the imams (hence the Isma'ilis are sometimes referred to as Seveners in distinction to the Twelvers discussed earlier).

The succession dispute goes to the heart of Shi'ite views of the imamate. For some, Isma'il's failure, for whatever reason, to assume the succession meant that his claims were invalid. For others, however, he was God's appointee. If he seemed to be morally defective, that was because men do not understand God's purposes; if he died before his father, it was similarly God's will and his son should certainly succeed.

Be that as it may, no one seems to have heard of Isma'il or his presumed heir until a century or so later when people in the villages of southern Iraq began claiming that the descendants of Isma'il were in fact the true heirs of the Family of the Prophet. This was, of course, in the aftermath of the occultation of the twelfth imam and it may have been a response to it by Shi'ites who wanted a real and present leader to follow. Shortly before 900 a man called Ubayd Allah, then living in the small central Syrian city of Salamiya, began to proclaim that he himself was a descendant of Isma'il and that people should swear allegiance to him as the living imam. Not all Isma'ilis agreed and a group of them argued that they should wait for the return of the real imam, Muhammad b. Isma'il, who was in hiding. They were known as Qarāmita (or Carmathians in western accounts) and set up a revolutionary state in eastern Arabia, pillaging the pilgrim caravans and eventually stealing, as we have seen, the Black Stone of the Ka'ba itself. But they did not found a caliphate, nor did their leaders take the title.

Ubayd Allah, however, continued to claim the leadership, but Syria was not a suitable base to mount a rebellion. The Bedouin of the desert had ideas of their own and the settled governments in Baghdad and Egypt remained powerful enough to prevent him taking over any of the cities. He began to send out agents to investigate the possibilities of attracting support in fringe areas of the Muslim world. Yemen and Ifriqiya (modern Tunisia) were the places he selected.

His agent, Abū Abd Allah al-Shi'i, arrived in Tunisia in 893 and began to preach, not in the towns like Qayrawan and Tunis, which were the centres of Arab Muslim population, but in the Kabyle mountains of what is now western Algeria. Here, among the Berbers of the Kutāma tribe, who generally resented the rule of the Aghlabid dynasty of Qayrawan, he found a ready audience. The Kutāma Berbers were to be the military backbone of the Fatimid caliphate until well after the conquest of Egypt in 969, as the Khurasanis had been for the Abbasids. Soon after his initial success Abū Abd Allah was joined by Ubayd Allah and in 909 they conquered the ancient capital of Qayrawan and proclaimed the establishment of a caliphate.

The Fatimid Caliphate

It was the first time a Shi'ite caliphate, led by a member of the Family of the Prophet, had been able to establish itself in power anywhere in the Muslim world. It was a momentous event, but it also meant that many questions which had previously been left unanswered had to be confronted. Was this new caliphate to be a radically different institution from the

Muslim governments which had preceded it, or was it to be a traditional state with, so to speak, a different management? It was fine to talk about a God-guided, infallible imam when such a figure was no more than a dream, but how would it work with a real human being wielding real power? How could there not be a sense of disillusionment when mundane matters of maintaining order and collecting taxes from reluctant payers had to be confronted. In the Arabic terminology, it was a move from *da'wa* (missionary activity) to *dawla* (state), a move from the era of miracles and wonder to the hard realities of government.

Ubayd Allah immediately set about establishing his authority with determination. The missionary Abū Abd Allah, whose preaching had done so much to mobilize the Kutāma in the Fatimid cause, was executed, much as the Abbasid caliph Mansūr had executed Abū Muslim. There could only be one focus of authority.

The new caliph took the messianic title of Mahdī and claimed to be the true leader of the Family of the Prophet. He and his descendants were known to themselves and others as Fatimids, to emphasize their descent from Fātima and hence from the Prophet himself. As such they were his legitimate successors in a way the Abbasids could never claim to be. Mahdī was to be much more than a local leader, however: the Fatimids were to be true caliphs, rulers of the whole Islamic world. But not everyone was convinced. Unlike the Twelver imams, whose genealogy was generally accepted even by Sunnis and other hostile observers, the Fatimid lineage had some possible holes in it. How exactly was Ubayd Allah related to Muhammad b. Isma'il, who must have died a century before he appeared on the scene, and who were the intermediary stages? This weakness made the Fatimids vulnerable to challenges from their enemies. Their whole claim to power rested on descent from the Prophet. If this was false or even doubtful, then the whole enterprise was a fraud.

To assert their claim the Fatimids would need to use force. The Kutāma were formed into a regular army and paid salaries, Greek and Slav slave soldiers were recruited to serve alongside them and a navy was created. It all looked very much like a conventional Muslim state apparatus of a sort which would have been familiar to the Umayyad and Abbasid rulers.

Attempts to seize the moment by invading Egypt ended in failure and from 920 the caliphate began to develop as local rulers in Tunisia. A new capital was founded on the Mediterranean coast and called Mahdiya. The remains of it can still be visited, a fortified seaport looking on to the Mediterranean and east to Egypt. Compared with Baghdad or later Cairo, it was built on a modest scale, but both its name and the prayers which were performed in its new mosque proclaimed its role as the first capital of a new caliphate.

It was at this time too that the arrangements between the Fatimids and their non-Shi'i subjects were worked out. Most of the population of Tunisia, especially in the Holy City of Qayrawan, remained Sunnis and the Fatimids made no attempt to convert them to their Isma'ili faith. But the new capital was Isma'ili and anyone who aspired to senior posts in army or administration had to accept that the caliph was the God-guided Mahdī. In practice, this was a successful accommodation. The Fatimids made no attempt at forcible conversion and, as a result, there was little public opposition to their rule. As long as they maintained law and order, defended the people from outside attack, allowed merchants to make money and were not too aggressive in their tax collection, they were accepted without any outward opposition. The caliphs of the new dynasty were soon forced to make those messy decisions and compromises which go with political power and even their closest admirers must have wondered whether they were always, as they claimed, sinless and infallible, but good government was enough for most people.

In 969 the Fatimid general Jawhar, an ex-slave of Greek origins, conquered Egypt with his army and the Fatimid caliphate was transformed from a provincial oddity into a world power. The conquest was not a violent and destructive military invasion. The post-Abbasid Ikhshidid regime that had been overthrown had little popular support: a series of low Nile floods had resulted in widespread famine and Fatimid agents had prepared the ground well in advance, assuring all sections of society that a Fatimid takeover would be in their interests. As a result, the conquest, if not entirely peaceful, was not actively opposed by the vast majority. As Jawhar approached with his huge army of perhaps 100,000, mostly Berbers, agreements were made with the leading figures in the administration and with the chief *qāḍī* of Fustat (Old Cairo), and the military forces of the old regime were easily defeated. In July prayers were said in the venerable Mosque of Amr, the heart of the spiritual life of the country, in the name of the Fatimid caliph Mu'izz, not the Abbasid Qādir, and the rule of the Family of the Prophet over a major area of the Muslim world had triumphantly begun.

One of the first and most important actions taken by Jawhar was the foundation of the new palace city of Cairo (in Arabic *Qāhira* means 'the Victorious') in 970. The first Islamic capital of Egypt had been Fustat, now often referred to as Old Cairo, which lay just outside the walls of the old Roman fort which formed the original nucleus of settlement in the area. The new Fatimid city was separated from Fustat by open spaces and gardens and formed a distinct city, surrounded by its own walls and gates. It was designed very deliberately and its construction began according to careful astrological observations. At the centre were two vast palaces, one on each side of the main north–south street. The palaces have long disappeared, but the street is still known to this day as Bayn al-Qasrayn (Between the Two Palaces). A new mosque was built, designed for the performance of Isma'ili rites, and it still forms the core of the present Azhar mosque.

It was very much a government city, a magnificent residence for a caliph who was God's deputy on earth and the direct descendant of His prophet Muhammad. This was no humble abode: God's favour was demonstrated for all to see by His generosity to the ruler and the wealth and splendours which were showered upon him. There were similarities with Mansūr's round city of Baghdad, except that palaces, rather than a mosque, lay at the centre. Elsewhere non-Fatimid life continued much as before. Fustat remained the centre of commercial life and home of the Christian and Jewish communities. It was in the old mosque of Amr that the *qādī* of Fustat sat dispensing Sunni law to a Sunni population. One could say the Fatimid caliphate presided over one country and two systems.

This dual system was one of the reasons for the success of the Fatimids. If they had tried to settle their Berber soldiers in the old city, there would have been inevitable tensions, riots and disturbances. If they had tried to foist their doctrines on a recalcitrant population, they would have faced the sort of resistance which forced the Abbasids to abandon the doctrine of the createdness of the Qur'ān.

The Azhar mosque is famous today as the foremost centre of Sunni religious scholarship in the whole of the Islamic world, but that was not how it began. The Fatimid caliphate was in many ways an intellectual project. From the very beginning of the state in 909 the caliphs and their advisers had worked to provide an ideological basis for the regime. This was central to the caliphate in order to justify its rule in Egypt and other areas it controlled, but also because the early Fatimid caliphs were determined to expand their authority over the whole Muslim world. Egypt was only a start and a base. Further to the east, in Iraq and Iran, they built up a network of *dāʿis*, missionaries who would preach to disaffected Muslims wherever they were to be found. In some cases these missionaries were sent from Cairo, in other cases they were men with Isma'ili convictions who came to Cairo to see the caliph in all his magnificence before returning to their homelands to spread the word. This network required a clear message and system of belief to sustain the missionaries in their work. In Cairo itself Isma'ili doctrine and law were taught in official sessions known as *Majlis al-hikma* (Assemblies of Wisdom), held twice a week on Thursdays and Fridays. No Umayyad or Abbasid caliphs had tried to instruct their subjects in this systematic way.

The fullest statement of this ideology comes in a remarkable work written by Qāḍī Nuʻmān (d. 974) called *Daʻāʼim al-Islam* (The Pillars of Islam). Composed before the Fatimid conquest of Egypt, this is, in the words of Wadad al-Qāḍī, ʻa clear, well-organized dogmatic exposition of the tenets of Isma'ili positive Law'.[1] The first volume deals with the seven pillars of the *ibādāt* according to the Isma'ilis, that is, devotion to the imams, ritual purity, prayer, alms, fasting, pilgrimage and *jihād*, while the second volume discusses more practical legal matters like sales, oaths, foods, marriage, divorce, thefts, testimonies and so forth. Nuʻmān treats his subject-matter very systematically, dividing each chapter into sections, and recording the legal decisions pertaining to each section in the form of Qurʼanic citations and Traditions transmitted from the Prophet, Alī b. Abī Ṭālib and the first five imams after Alī, that is down to Isma'il's father Jaʻfar al-Sādiq.

In most cases the positive law differs little from what was the general practice of the Sunnis and Twelver Shiʼites. Devotion to the imams and ritual purity are added to the other five pillars of Islam. However, there is one very important and original difference which marks it off from similar Sunni compendia of law and that is the sources which it uses. The Qurʼān, of course, is the foundation and the Traditions of the Prophet, as recognized in Shiʼite doctrine follow. After that come traditions passed down from Alī and the imams who followed. Their words are authoritative. By contrast there is no use of traditions from the Companions of the Prophet and, of course, no citations of the great scholars of Sunni jurisprudence like Shafi'i (d. 820) or Ibn Hanbal (d. 855). It is the

Prophet and his Family who decide law, not the Muslim community and its legal scholars.

The second defining feature of the work is that it became an official handbook, sanctioned and supported by the caliph and his government. It became, in fact, caliphal law. Even the strongest and greatest of the Umayyad and Abbasid caliphs, Abd al-Malik or Mansūr, had not presumed to produce an official law-book. The caliph sanctioned the law and it was to the caliph that difficult decisions should be referred. If the Abbasids had lost the struggle with the *ulama* for control of *sharī'a*, the Fatimids had clearly won it.

The new caliphate was faced with problems of a more political nature. The object of Fatimid policy remained the takeover of the entire Muslim world, but that was obviously a long-term project. More immediate was the issue of the government of Syria and Palestine. Both had been ruled, more or less effectively, by the Tulunid and Ikhshidid dynasties which had preceded the Fatimids in Egypt, so it was natural that the new caliphs should seek to do the same. There were also other reasons to be concerned with Syria and Palestine.

The first was economic. Egypt, of course, was dependent for its food supply on the Nile flood. The height of this varied from year to year, but in most years it provided sufficient water and silt for agriculture to feed the population. In other years it did not and there was no other source of water for the farmers. As the Bible describes, in the time of the pharaohs this could lead to serious famine and there was basically nothing the government, whether pharaohs or caliphs, could do about it. The agriculture of Syria, on the other hand, was dependent on rain brought in by western winds from the

Mediterranean. Of course, this too was changeable, and there were good years and bad, but the system was completely different from the Egyptian one and only at the most unlucky times did harvests in Egypt and Syria fail simultaneously. Food security was an important reason for the Fatimids to seek to control Syria or at least parts of it.

The second reason was that control of Syria brought the Fatimids into direct contact with the Byzantines, the foe of Muslim governments from the time of the Prophet onwards. Campaigns against the Byzantines were the only wars in which the Abbasid caliphs had taken part and the only ones in which they had led their troops in person. The failure of the Abbasid caliphs to protect the Muslims of the frontier areas in the first half of the tenth century had been in part the cause of the loss of confidence in their leadership.

The problem was becoming urgent. In the mid-tenth century, partly because of the weakness of the Abbasid caliphs, the Byzantines were beginning to make significant inroads into Muslim territory, which culminated in their capture of the ancient city of Antioch (in modern-day Turkey) in 969, the very year in which the Fatimids established themselves as caliphs in Cairo. Muslims were driven from their homes and mosques were converted into stables. For the Fatimids, anxious to establish their caliphal status in the wider Muslim world, this was both a duty and an opportunity. If the Fatimid caliphs could be seen to defend Muslims against the infidels, the most fundamental obligation of any Muslim leader, when the Abbasids had so obviously failed, it would be an enormous boost to their prestige.

The Fatimids also seized the initiative from the faltering

hands of the Abbasids regarding the protection and leadership of the *hajj*: both Umayyad and Abbasid caliphs had made a point of doing this. As we have seen, along with leading the *jihād*, this was one area of public performance in which the caliphs themselves or members of their families could be seen to be the real leaders of the Muslim community. The Abbasid caliphs were manifestly failing in their duties in this respect too. No Abbasid caliph after Hārūn al-Rashīd had made the *hajj* in person. From the late ninth century the pilgrims on the long and often waterless route across the Arabian desert had been attacked by Bedouin, robbed or made prisoner, and their women sold as slaves. These assaults culminated in the taking of the Black Stone from the Ka'ba by the Qarāmita, who were often at odds with the Fatimids. It was the Fatimid caliph, still based in Tunisia, who negotiated the return of the stone to Mecca so that the pilgrimage could again be performed according to the proper rites.

Now that they ruled in Egypt, the Fatimids were able to protect the *hajj* by subsidizing the Bedouin so that they would not attack. The 'official' *hajj* now started not from Iraq but from Egypt and Syria. The route lay through the Hijaz and along the west coast of Arabia, or up the Nile to the great bend at Qus and across to the Red Sea ports where pilgrims would take ships to Jar or Jedda. Pilgrims from all over the Muslim world would witness the magnificence of the Fatimid caliph, travel under the protection of his banner and hear his name pronounced in the pulpits of the Holy Cities of Mecca and Medina.

The rule of the Fatimid caliphs saw a period of great prosperity in Egypt, which came to replace Iraq as the wealthiest

province of the Muslim world. The maritime trade of the
Indian Ocean came up the Red Sea to Egypt rather than travelling up the Persian Gulf to Basra and southern Iraq. Italian
merchants from Amalfi and other ports began to arrive at
Alexandria to purchase spices from the Indian Ocean area,
such as pepper, cinnamon and cloves, which were so highly
prized by the increasingly wealthy elites of western Europe.

The caliphs were the beneficiaries of fortunate circumstances, but they made their contribution to the prosperity
of the country too, above all by providing security and an
excellent coinage. Here again, they took over one of the symbols of the caliphate from the Abbasids. The minting of
gold coins was clearly linked to caliphal status. When Abd
al-Rahmān III proclaimed himself caliph in Córdoba in 929,
one of his first acts was to begin the minting of a gold coinage. At the same time the Abbasids lost the ability to mint a
gold coinage and their Buyids protectors could only issue
debased and distorted versions of the old silver dirhams.
Fatimid dinars, by contrast, are some of the finest and most
beautiful Islamic coins ever minted, advertising to the world
the splendour of this Shi'ite caliphate.

The Fatimids made Cairo the centre for great public displays of power on a scale which never seem to have occurred
before in the Muslim world. We know surprisingly little of
the public performance of monarchy in the Umayyad and
Abbasid caliphates. We hear of audiences (*majlis*) where
appointments were made, ambassadors received and poetry
recited. The Umayyad caliphs may have visited the great
mosque in Damascus which bears their name, but we never
hear about it. We know Mansūr preached in the mosque in

Baghdad, but it is not clear that any of his successors did. One of the immediate causes which led to the death of Mutawwakil in 861 was a change in the order of the procession to the mosque on Fridays, effectively demoting the heir apparent Muntasir, but this is the only indication we have that such a procession was part of the public life of the Abbasid caliphate.

The Fatimids, however, evolved a whole new language of public ritual. They made celebrations like the opening of the dykes at the time of the Nile flood into public events, presided over by the caliph himself or a member of his family. Here the caliph could be seen as guardian of the people and show his public concern for their welfare.

We can see something of the impact that the Fatimid caliphs had on their subjects and other Muslims from the travel account of Nāsiri Khusraw.[2] He was an Isma'ili from what is now Tajikistan, then as now a remote area of the Muslim world. A philosopher and intellectual, he travelled to Egypt in 1045 to visit the Fatimid court. He is one of the liveliest and most engaging of Muslim travel writers, and his writings are full of vivid first-hand accounts and personal reactions. He was hugely impressed by what he found in Cairo, both the city's wealth and the firm but benign nature of the caliphal government. He constantly contrasted the prosperity of Egypt with the poverty of his native Iran. Of course his is a *parti pris* – he is writing to convince his fellow countrymen (the book is in Persian not Arabic) of the excellence of Isma'ili rule – but the picture rings true or at least gives us one version of reality.

After a vivid and eloquent description of Cairo, including

the opulence of its markets and the number and splendour of its mosques, he turns to a discussion of the role of caliph, whom he often refers to as sultan.

> In the year 1047 the sultan ordered general rejoicing for the birth of a son. The city and markets were so arrayed that, were they to be described, some would not believe that drapers' and moneychangers' shops could be so decorated with gold, jewels, coins, gold-spun fabrics and linen so that there was no room to sit down.
>
> The people are so secure under the sultan's reign that no one fears his agents or informants, and they rely on him neither to inflict injustice nor to have designs on anyone's property. I saw such personal wealth there that, were I to describe it, the people of Persia would never believe it. I could discover no end or limit to their wealth, and I never saw such ease and security anywhere.
>
> I saw one man, a Christian and one of the most propertied men in all Egypt, who was said to own untold ships, wealth and property. In short, one year the Nile failed and the price of grain rose so high that the sultan's grand vizier summoned this Christian and said, 'It has not been a good year. The sultan is burdened with the care of his subjects. How much can you give, either for sale or as a loan?' The Christian replied, 'For the happiness of the sultan and the vizier, I have enough grain in readiness to guarantee Egypt's bread for six years' . . . What a lucky citizenry and just ruler to have such conditions in their days. What wealth must there be for the ruler not to inflict injustice and for the subjects to hide nothing!

Later Nāsiri Khusraw adds: 'The security and welfare of the people of Egypt have reached a point that drapers, money-changers and jewellers do not even lock their shops: they just lower a net across the front and no one tampers with anything.' Of course, we should take his account with a pinch of salt, but the point is clear: the caliph feels a responsibility for the welfare of his subjects and religion is no barrier to participation in society.

He also describes the Fatimid caliph as playing a very public role, at prayers in the mosque and leading the popular ceremonies which marked the opening of the irrigation canals at the time of the Nile flood. He saw the caliph in person:

> a well-built, clean-shaven youth with cropped hair, a descendant of Husayn son of Alī. He is mounted on a camel with a plain saddle and bridle with no gold or silver and wears a white shirt, as is the custom in Arab countries, and a wide belt. The value of this [belt] alone is said to be ten thousand dirhams. On his head he has a turban of the same material and in his hand he holds a large, very costly whip. Before him walk three hundred Daylamites wearing Byzantine goldspun cloth with belts and wide sleeves as is the fashion in Egypt. They all carry spears and arrows and wear leggings. At the sultan's side rides a parasol-bearer with a bejewelled gold turban and a suit of clothing worth ten thousand dinars. The parasol he holds is extremely ornate and studded with jewels and pearls . . . to his left and right are thurifers burning ambergris and aloe. The custom here is for the people to prostrate themselves and say a prayer as the sultan passes.

This was performance monarchy: the ruler, descendant of the Prophet and God's representative on earth, guarantor of the prosperity of the country, showing himself in public to all his people.

Unlike anything recorded of the Umayyad and Abbasid caliphs, the Fatimid ruler played the generous host to his subjects:

It is customary for the sultan to give a banquet twice a year, on the two great holidays [the *īd* which marks the end of the fasting of Ramadan and the *īd* which marks the day of sacrifice at the time of the *hajj*] and to hold court for both the elite and the common people, the elite in his presence and the commoners in other halls and places. I was very anxious to see one with my own eyes, so I told one of the sultan's clerks I had met and with whom I had struck up a friendship that I had seen the courts of such Persian sultans as Sultan Mahmūd of Ghazna and his son Mas'ūd, who were great potentates, enjoying much prosperity and luxury, and now I wanted to see the court of the Commander of the Faithful. He therefore spoke a word to the chamberlain.

The last day of Ramadan 440 [8 March 1049] the hall was decorated for the next day, which was the festival, when the sultan was to come after prayer and preside over the feast. Taken by my friend, as I entered through the door of the hall, I saw constructions, galleries and porticos which would take too long to describe adequately. There were twelve square 'palaces', built next to each other, each more dazzling than the last . . . hunting and sporting scenes

[were] depicted and also an inscription in marvellous calligraphy. All the carpets and pillows were of Byzantine brocade and *buqalamun* [a richly embroidered fabric], each woven exactly to the measurement of its place. There was an indescribable latticework of gold along the sides. It is said that fifty thousand maunds of sugar were bought for this day for the sultan's feast. For decoration on the banquet table I saw a confection like an orange tree, every branch and leaf executed in sugar, and thousands of images and statuettes in sugar.

The sultan's kitchen is outside the palace and there are fifty slaves always attached to it. There is a subterranean passageway between the building and the kitchen. Every day fourteen camel loads of ice have to be provided for use in the royal kitchen. Most of the emirs and the sultan's entourage receive allowances there and, if the people of the city make requests on behalf of the suffering, they are given something. Whatever potion or medication is needed in the city is given out from the harem and there is also no problem in the distribution of other ointments such as balsam.

In 973, four years after Jawhar had taken Cairo and established Fatimid rule, Caliph Mu'izz came to Egypt in person for the first time. He brought with him his entire court and the coffins of his ancestors: he was moving to Egypt for good. In May he held court at the foot of the Pharos in Alexandria, which had been restored under Muslim rule and was still largely intact. Here he met with the leaders of the civil elite of Fustat and of the Bedouin tribes. He was conciliatory, saying he had only come to pursue the *jihād* against the infidels and safeguard the road to Mecca for pilgrims. Both these were recognized as caliphal duties to which no Muslim could object.

The safeguarding of the *hajj* was the easier of these two obligations and in 975 the *hajj* caravan was able to reach Mecca overland and the name of the Fatimid caliph was read in the pulpits of the Holy Cities. The Fatimids did not take over political authority in Mecca, which remained in the hands of a family of Alid *sharīfs*, as it did until the beginning of the twentieth century, but the Fatimid ruler was proclaimed as caliph in front of pilgrims from all over the Muslim world. The caliphs subsidized the *hajj* and provided the *kiswa*, but, unlike the Abbasids, they never led the *hajj* in person.

The *jihād* against the Byzantines was much more difficult and required an enormous input of resources. One of the problems was, of course, the strength of the Byzantine forces. The empire was now at the height of its medieval power and the emperor Basil II and his successors in the first half of the eleventh century were able to lead their armies deep into Syria and dominate Aleppo and the surrounding country. It was not, however, the Byzantines who were the main opponents of the Fatimids in Syria but the Bedouin tribes, who were increasingly aggressive, pushing further into the settled lands, destroying agriculture and ravaging cities. It took all the military resources of the caliphate to keep these tribes at bay and even then the Fatimid armies were only intermittently successful. On the other hand, direct conflict with the Byzantines was rare and for long periods the

Fatimids and Byzantines maintained cordial diplomatic relations, much to the disgust of some of the Fatimids' Muslim subjects.

The Fatimid caliphs raised and paid armies and appointed generals to lead them, but they never commanded them in person. The caliph remained in Cairo, always figurehead and sometimes mastermind of these expeditions but never participating. Their armies had originally been made up of Kutāma Berbers, who were by and large loyal to the caliphate and religiously committed to the Isma'ili cause. They were not the easiest troops to manage and frequently caused conflict with the population of Syrian cities like Damascus. To counterbalance this, the Fatimids began to employ increasing numbers of Turkish troops, recruited from the eastern part of the Muslim world. The greatest Fatimid general of the first half of the eleventh century, Anūshtakīn Dizbari, for example, came from the small principality of Khuttal in modern Tajikistan. There he was captured by slave raiders and taken to be sold in Kashgar, the great Muslim trading city now in western China. From there he escaped to Bukhara and was sold on to masters in Baghdad before reaching Damascus, where he came to the notice of the Fatimid governor and entered the caliph's service.

Dizbari's story shows how military slavery gave opportunities for social mobility and how the caliphs were always on the lookout for talented young men, whatever their background. This boy of obscure origins from a remote part of the eastern Islamic world would rise to be the second most powerful man in the great Fatimid caliphate after the caliph himself. He had either been brought up a Muslim or converted in his youth, but he did not come from an Isma'ili background. Though he no doubt accepted the claims of the caliphs to rule as members of the Family of the Prophet, his primary allegiance, and those of many of his fellow Turks, was to the caliph as a strong ruler, not the caliph as a spiritual guide. Increasingly with the coming of the Turks, the Fatimid caliphate looked less like a revolutionary new beginning and more and more like a conventional Middle Eastern state.

The Fatimids pursued their religious policies. In Egypt they only made occasional attempts to enforce typically Shi'ite rituals, as when the newly arrived caliph Mu'izz forced the shopkeepers in Sunni Fustat to close on 10 Muharram to commemorate the death of Husayn. He also decreed that the call to prayer should be given in the particularly Shi'ite formula, which includes the words 'Come to the best of works!' but that was about the limit of the public proclamation of the new faith. Caliph Hākim (996–1021), in one of his periodic bursts of religious fervour, decreed the public cursing of the *salaf*, the first generation of Muslims, including the first three caliphs, Abū Bakr, Umar and Uthmān, and Aisha, all of whom had failed to recognize Ali's superiority. The cursing of the *salaf* was extremely provocative and in contemporary Baghdad inevitably led to bloodshed. To add force to the insult, he decreed that the curses should be written on the walls of public buildings in gold letters. Like most of the caliph's decrees this only lasted a short time and two years later he issued a general edict of tolerance specifically ordering that the offending curses should be painted out.

The Isma'ilis remained a small ruling elite and therefore needed allies among the Egyptian population. They made close links with the non-Muslim communities, the Coptic Christians and the Jews, who probably made up the majority of the population. Senior posts in the administration, particularly the all-important financial administration, were entrusted to Christians, whom the Fatimids seemed in general to prefer to Sunni Muslims. In turn the Christian bureaucrats served the caliphs loyally. A unique view of this multicultural society can be found in the material from the Cairo Geniza. The Geniza was the store room of a synagogue in Old Cairo in which the Jewish community used to deposit their papyrus and paper refuse. They believed that it was wrong to throw away any writing which might contain the name of God and, since most letters, accounts and so on usually did, they just kept everything, from elegant Fatimid royal decrees, issued by the chancery and reused when they became out of date for legal documents and letters, to scraps of paper which were little more than shopping lists or short notes sent to other members of the community. This Jewish community had many international contacts and some of the most interesting letters relate to long-distance trade, but the greatest part of the material deals with the everyday life of Jews under Fatimid rule. They reflect good times and bad, and occasionally difficult relations with the authorities, but the general impression given is one of a tolerant society in which a moderately benign government allowed different communities to manage their own affairs. There is certainly no indication of systematic persecution of the Jews or of any attempt to convert them to Islam.

It was outside Egypt that the Fatimids made real attempts to spread their religious views. The Fatimids had arrived with the intention and expectation of conquering the whole Muslim world and bringing it under the government of the Family of the Prophet. In the event, these aims were thwarted by the intractable problems of Syria and later by the coming of the Seljuqs, but the *da'wa*, the Isma'ili missionary organization, remained active in areas like Iraq and Iran and many of the leading Isma'ili writers of the period were drawn from the ranks of these missionaries.

The most famous, or infamous, of the Fatimid caliphs was Hākim. He came to the throne at the age of eleven on the death of his father Azīz, in 996. At the age of fifteen he first showed his taste for absolute power by ordering the execution of his tutor and mentor Barjuwān. Having found at this early age that he could, literally, get away with murder, he allowed his autocratic impulses to go unchecked. He terrorized the leading members of the Isma'ili hierarchy, ordering the execution of many, like the family of Qādī Nu'mān, who had served the dynasty well, and groups of the population began to ask him for guarantees for their safety, hoping, sometimes mistakenly, that it would spare them from his unpredictable violence.

The caliphate of Hākim is interesting because he took the idea of the God-guided caliph to its furthest conclusion. He made decrees and new laws entirely on his own initiative, neither taking advice nor supporting them with Traditions and precedents. No other caliph in the Sunni or Shi'ite traditions created law in this way. He seems, in fact, to have made law on a whim and some of his decrees were very strange indeed. Both contemporaries and modern historians have searched for some element of consistency and purpose in his actions. Paul Walker divides them into four categories: 'the prohibition of food and drink, the imposition of a strict moral code, the restriction and alteration of religious practice and various modifications in the way he presented himself to his public and what he expected in return'.

In the first category we find the strict prohibition of alcoholic drinks, even for Christians to use in the sacraments. This is in accordance with generally accepted Islamic norms, but he also banned the sale and consumption of certain sorts of green vegetables and fish without scales, measures which have no support in Islamic law, or common sense.

The most important in the second group were laws strictly limiting the public movements of women.

The third category concerned relations with the non-Muslim elements in the population of the caliphate. Here again unpredictability was the most noticeable feature of his policy. He ordered that Christians and Jews should wear distinctive clothing and ride inferior animals. He embarked on a campaign of destroying churches and synagogues, including, most famously, the Church of the Holy Sepulchre in Jerusalem. By the end of his reign he had rescinded these policies and even allowed those who had converted to Islam under duress to return to their old faiths without being considered apostates.

His public appearances became rarer and in his final years he abandoned much of the pomp and display which had characterized Fatimid rule and took to riding a donkey and wearing shabby clothes. His end was as mysterious as the rest of his life. One day in 1021 he set off into the Muqattam Hills to the east of Cairo on his donkey and was never seen again.

Inevitably the mystery of his disappearance gave rise to speculation that he was not really dead but was simply hidden like the Twelfth Imam; there were even those who claimed that he really was the embodiment of God on earth and would never die. (It was from these groups that the Druze faith emerged, first in Cairo and later in Lebanon and southern Syria, where it still flourishes today. But the Druze did not found a caliphate and thus their history lies beyond the scope of this book.)

The bizarre behaviour of Hākim caused something of a crisis in the Isma'ili community in Egypt and a *dā'ī* from Iraq who came to Cairo at this time, Kirmānī, had to set about convincing them that the vision was still alive and that the Fatimid caliphs would still be able to unite the Muslim world under their rule. In the mid-eleventh century it seemed for a moment as if this might really happen. Important leaders of Arab tribes in Syria and Iraq had the Fatimid caliph proclaimed in the *khutbas* in their territory instead of the feeble Abbasid and in 1058–9 an adventurer called Basasīrī even took Baghdad in the name of the Fatimids. But these gains were based not on conquest or real power but on shifting temporary alliances. They soon broke up with the arrival of Seljuq Turkish power, firmly committed to the Sunni cause, from the late 1050s onwards. For the last century of its existence, from around 1070 to 1171, the Fatimid caliphate was competing with the claims of the Seljuqs and their Abbasid protégés. Increasingly the peculiarly Shi'ite nature of the caliphate declined and the struggle was one of great-power politics rather than fundamental differences about the nature of the caliphate. When the Crusader armies reached the east in 1097, the first Fatimid response was to see them as potential allies against the Seljuqs.

In the end, when Saladin abolished the Fatimid caliphate in 1171 and had the names of the Abbasids proclaimed in the pulpit of Cairo, the Shi'ite caliphate disappeared. It had been a bold experiment aiming to bring the whole of the Muslim world under the leadership of a caliph from the Family of the Prophet. Ultimately it succumbed because of the contradictions inevitable when a human being tries to take on the role of the infallible representative of God on earth whose every action is divinely inspired. The messy, often brutal, exigencies of government meant that many people became disillusioned with the idea. The Fatimid power became a regional power. Firmly established in Egypt, it became essentially an Egyptian empire representing Egyptian interests and as such it had little to offer the Muslims of Iraq and Iran.

Even in Egypt, though, the Isma'ili Shi'ite community disappeared with the abolition of the caliphate, though Isma'ili communities survived with the Assassins in northern Syria and northern Iran. But they were not caliphs. With the end of the Fatimids, the dream of a caliphate led by a divinely inspired leader from the Family of the Prophet was effectively dead.

CHAPTER 8

The Umayyads of Córdoba

While the struggle for leadership of the Islamic community continued between the Abbasids and Fatimids, a third caliphate was being proclaimed and established in Andalus. This was the far west of the Islamic world: those areas of Spain and Portugal under Muslim rule. Most of the Iberian Peninsula had been conquered by Muslim forces in the years 711–16, which left only a few impoverished, isolated areas of Cantabria and the Pyrenees under Christian rule. Muslim raiding parties then pressed deep into France, up the Rhône valley in the east and in the west through Aquitaine almost as far as the Loire valley. In 732 a raiding party led by the governor of Andalus, Abd al-Rahmān al-Ghāfiqi, was defeated by Charles Martel and a Frankish army. The defeat, though probably not disastrous in military terms, marked the end of Arab-Muslim expansion into France and the beginning of a period of consolidation when there was no more easy booty to finance the Muslim elite and systems of taxation and settled government had to be developed.

Initially Andalus formed part of the Umayyad caliphate, and rule from Damascus was surprisingly effective. Governors were appointed and dismissed with great frequency, only enjoying a few years' tenure at most, but the province was far from peaceful. The conquerors were a mixture of Berbers and of men of Arab descent and language whose families had originally come from Arabia, mostly from the settled areas of Yemen in the south, but who had stayed in Egypt for a couple of generations before joining expeditions to the Maghreb. They were Arabic-speaking but not, by and large, nomad Bedouin, and were used to urban and agricultural environments. The Berbers, however, outnumbered the Arabs. The indigenous people of north-west Africa, Berbers spoke their own language and, in contrast to the Arabs, were largely rural pastoral people living outside the few small towns of the Maghreb. In Andalus they tended to gravitate to the upland, rural areas of the peninsula.

The Arabs had settled as well, but they were divided by fierce tribal loyalties. As in modern Yemen, living in small towns and villages did not mean that tribal links lost their importance, far from it. Tribal rivalries dominated the politics of Andalus, all the more so when the revenue from booty dried up. In 741 the demographics of the Muslim population there were changed fundamentally. In 740 the Berber tribes of North Africa had rebelled against the Umayyad-appointed governors in Qayrawan. The grievances were against the imposition of *kharāj* by the authorities and the taking of slaves, especially girls, for the households of the caliphs and their supporters in the Middle East. Both the great Abbasid caliph al Mansūr and Abd al-Rahmān b. Muʿāwiya, the first of the Umayyad rulers of Andalus, had Berber mothers.

To combat the rebellion, a large army was recruited in Syria and sent to the west. Many of the troops came from the Arab tribes there, the backbone of the Umayyad army, but a considerable number seem to have been *mawālī* of the Umayyad family, that is to say that they were not Arabs by descent but people who had converted to Islam and taken service with the Umayyads as soldiers or civil servants. They owed their loyalties not to their tribes, or even to the wider *umma*, but to their patrons, the Umayyad family. The campaign was not a success and many of the Syrian troops were cut off by the rebels in Ceuta, just across the Straits of Gibraltar. In Spain too there was unrest among the Berbers and the governor reluctantly allowed the Syrians in Ceuta to cross the Straits and help suppress the rebellion. Their task completed, many of the Syrians settled in the south of Andalus in different *junds*, military divisions named after the areas of Syria they had come from. Needless to say, there was conflict between the various elements of the Syrian army and between them and the long-established Arabs of the first conquest.

The Umayyad Emirate of Córdoba

Such was the position when the Umayyad caliphate in Syria was overwhelmed by the advances of the Abbasid forces from the east between 747 and 750. The Abbasids set about exterminating the Umayyad family with single-minded ruthlessness and many of them were massacred on the spot or hunted down and killed. Among the few who escaped was Abd al-Rahmān b. Muʿāwiya, a grandson of the last great Umayyad caliph, Hishām. After some desperate adventures, including swimming across the Euphrates to get away from his pursuers, Abd al-Rahmān made his way to North Africa, presumably to take refuge with this mother's kin. Here he could feel safe from the Abbasids.

The Abbasids made no serious attempt to conquer Andalus. It was too remote and they had other more pressing concerns. But that did not mean the province was peaceful and fierce infighting continued. Meanwhile, Abd al-Rahmān's attempt to establish his power in North Africa had been thwarted by tribal rivalries and he sent his *mawlā* and right-hand man Badr to Andalus to make contact with the Umayyad *mawālī* there. After some negotiation, Abd al-Rahmān crossed the Mediterranean to the little port of Almunecar in 755 and, supported by the *mawālī* of his family, said to have been 2,000 in number, and elements of the Syrian Arab population, who retained their loyalty to the Umayyads, he entered Córdoba in May 757 and was proclaimed emir. Umayyad rule was to continue for over two and half centuries, until the abolition of the caliphate in 1031.

The long struggles by which the Umayyad emirs established and maintained their control over the unruly Muslims of Andalus are beyond the scope of this book, but some points must be noted. Until 929 the Umayyads ruled as emirs and did not claim the title of caliph. Everyone knew that they were descended from the tribe of Quraysh and were therefore eligible for the title. Everyone knew too that they were descended from the great Umayyad caliphs of Damascus; they called themselves 'sons of the caliphs', and this attracted the loyalty of many Syrians, whose ancestral homeland had been subdued and impoverished by Abbasid governments.

The Umayyads were probably restrained from taking the title of caliph partly because it would have been an open challenge to the Abbasids, who at least until the end of the eighth century maintained powerful forces in Ifriqiya. In fact, the Abbasids never mounted an expedition against Andalus, their hostile actions never amounted to more than abusive letters, and by the ninth century they had ceased to be a real threat. The Umayyads of Andalus may also have been dissuaded by the generally accepted idea that there could be only one caliph in the Muslim world and, clearly, they were in no position to march on Baghdad and overthrow the Abbasids. So they kept to the modest title of emir, but this in itself posed problems. At least in theory an emir was a commander or governor appointed by the caliph. To be legitimate he would require a deed of appointment and a banner of office sent from the capital. As we have already seen, long after the political and military power of the Abbasids had waned, these formalities remained very important. Obviously the Abbasids were not going to recognize an Umayyad ruler, even over their remote part of the caliphate. So the title remained in a sort of constitutional vacuum.

Such considerations did not deter the Umayyads of Andalus from developing a strong and effective state, probably richer and certainly more long-lasting than any of the emirates which had formed following the break-up of the Abbasid caliphate in the east. This was not due just to their standing army but to their increasingly elaborate administration and their minting of coins. The peninsula was ruled by local governors, usually but not always chosen and dismissed by the emir in Córdoba. Umayyad power was also reflected in the architecture. The Great Mosque of Córdoba, begun by Abd al-Rahmān and expanded by his namesake Abd al-Rahmān II in the ninth century, was of a scale and richness which rivalled anything in contemporary Baghdad or Samarra. Its design and masonry were a clear testament to the Syrian heritage of the Umayyads. Beside the mosque there was a lavish Amiral palace, of which almost no traces remain, and an extra-mural retreat at Rusafa (named after the Umayyad caliph Hishām's Syrian palace).

Despite the ideological differences and bitter hatred between the Abbasids and the Umayyads, the court at Córdoba in the ninth century looked to and emulated the court at Baghdad when it came to royal style. By the mid-ninth century the emir lived a secluded lifestyle in his luxurious palace, surrounded by a household of slave girls and eunuchs. The connections with Baghdad were intensified by the catastrophe which overwhelmed the eastern capital in the civil war between Amīn and Ma'mūn from 811 to 814 and the ensuing anarchy. A number of intellectuals and poets abandoned the city and sought opportunities in Andalus. Among these was Alī b. Nāfi', known as Ziryāb. He was from Iraq and had been a pupil of Ishāq al-Mawsili, one of the most prominent poets and cultural leaders of the Abbasid court. After a spell in North Africa, he arrived in Andalus in 822 and rapidly established himself as an arbiter of style and taste in such matters as dress and the way in which meals should be served. Abd al-Rahmān II maintained a lively interest in both the arts and sciences and was the patron of poets and scholars, among them the eccentric scientist Abbās b. Firnās, who made himself wings and attempted to fly.

The Umayyads were the proud rulers of one of the most powerful states in the Muslim world. Their capital had a population which may have rivalled Fustat, and they presided over a court as lavish as that of Baghdad, but, until the reign of Abd al-Rahmān III, they never aspired to the caliphal title.

Abd al-Rahmān III, who succeeded as emir in 912, came to the throne after a long period when the power of the ruler in Andalus was challenged by local Muslim lords and when it seemed as if the rule of the Umayyads was about to come to an end. Slowly and methodically the new young emir set about establishing his authority over his unruly subjects in a series of annual military campaigns. By 929 he had regained control over almost all Andalus.

The Caliphates of Abd al-Rahmān III and Hakam II: The Glory Days of Córdoba

It was at this point that Abd al-Rahmān III proclaimed himself caliph and Commander of the Faithful in the Friday sermon given by the chief judge Ahmad b. Bāqī in the Great Mosque of Córdoba. Letters were sent to all the provinces telling them of his new status. He asked no one's permission to claim the title, he was not designated by anyone and there was no question of election. He was very much a self-made monarch. What prompted this new departure and what difference did it make?

To understand this change we have to see it in the context of politics and developments in the wider Muslim world. Perhaps most obviously there was the enfeeblement of the Abbasid caliphate under the rule of Muqtadir (908–32), which made the Abbasids' claims that they were the only caliphs and leaders of the *umma* seem increasingly unrealistic, even absurd. Despite the huge distance between Córdoba and Baghdad, people in Andalus were very well informed about what was going on in the east (though no eastern writer seems to have attached any importance to events in distant Andalus). Indeed, one of our main sources for the complex history of the reign of Muqtadir was written by an Andalusi, Arib b. Sa'd al-Qurtubi (the Córdoban). As far as we know, he never visited the Middle East, but he was astonishingly well informed about events there. He took it upon himself to write a continuation of the great Arabic chronicle of Tabarī, which took the history of the Abbasids down to 910 and which must have been available in the libraries of Córdoba. He records events in Baghdad and the debacle of the caliphate with almost diary-like precision. The troubles of the Abbasids were public knowledge and provided an opportunity for Abd al-Rahmān to assert his claims to the title of caliph.

But there was another change which made the proclamation of the caliphate both more possible and more pressing. In 909, just three years before Abd al-Rahmān became emir in Córdoba, the first Fatimid had proclaimed himself caliph in Qayrawan. This was a major development. Of course, Shi'ite pretenders and rebels had proclaimed themselves caliphs before, but they had always in the end been crushed and their pretensions brought to nothing. This time, however, it was obviously different. The Abbasids were in no position even to think of invading Ifriqiya and destroying this new caliphate. It was clearly here to stay. This meant that the reservations about having two caliphs at the same time were effectively out of date. And if there could be two, why could there not be three? It was evident that the Sunni Andalusis could never acknowledge the authority of, or pay allegiance to, a Shi'ite caliph.

And there were more practical matters. The Fatimids and the Umayyads soon became rivals for the allegiance of the tribes of the largely Berber populations of the western Maghreb (roughly speaking modern Morocco). Clearly if there was going to be this sort of competition, the Umayyads of Córdoba needed to improve their ideological armoury to compete on equal terms. The Berber tribal leaders could now choose between two caliphs, not just a caliph and a simple emir, when they debated to whom they should offer their allegiance.

There were aspects of this inauguration of a new caliphate which had never occurred before. The Umayyads were not claiming to be successors to the Abbasids or the Fatimids. The proclamation, as far as we can tell, did not involve cursing the Abbasids or impugning their right to rule. Unlike other caliphs, including the contemporary Abbasids and Fatimids, the Umayyads of Córdoba did not claim to be rulers or leaders of the whole Muslim *umma*. The boundaries of their caliphate were not formally defined, but it seems to be understood that they would include Andalus and such areas of the Maghreb that accepted their rulership.

The Umayyads based their claim to legitimacy firstly on their descent. As their name indicated, they were indisputably members of the Prophet's tribe of Quraysh and the genuineness of their lineage was generally accepted, by contrast to the Fatimids, whose claim to be descendants of Isma'il and hence of the Prophet Muhammad and his daughter Fātima was challenged at several points. Not only were they members of Quraysh, they were also descendants of the Umayyad caliphs. This obviously carried weight, but there is no evidence that they claimed to be reviving or restoring the old Umayyad caliphate in its whole, wide geographical extent.

Another important claim to the caliphate was the role of the Umayyads in leading the *jihād* in Andalus. They were the acknowledged leaders of the Muslims against the Christian kingdoms and countries to the north and Abd al-Rahmān III had kept up and publicized this role when he was still emir. In 920 he led the Muslims in person for the first time. He went north through Toledo, where he received the allegiance of the semi-independent local leader Lubb b. Tarbīsha, and then struck north-east to Medinaceli, taking San Esteban de Gormaz and the now deserted city of Clunia. He then pressed on to the upper Ebro valley at Tudela and marched into the heart of the Christian kingdom of Navarre, defeating its army and Leonese allies near Pamplona. In 924 he was on the move again, marching up the east coast of Andalus and receiving the allegiance of the Muslim lords of Lorca and Murcia. From there he went to the Ebro valley again and marched into Navarre, sacking the city of Pamplona and burning the cathedral.

These, and other expeditions, had a three-fold purpose. The first and most obvious was to secure the safety of Muslim populations that had been attacked by the increasingly aggressive and powerful Christian kings of Pamplona and León, though it was noticeable that very little new territory was conquered or settled. The second objective was to meet in person and secure the allegiance of local Muslim lords, like those of Toledo, Murcia and Zaragoza, who had in effect become semi-independent in the disturbed conditions prevailing in the late ninth and early tenth centuries. The fact that Abd al-Rahmān was leading a large army against the unbelievers in the north made his demands difficult to resist. Not only would the recalcitrant nobles be defying the demands of their legitimate emir, they would also, and this was much worse, be undermining the Muslim military effort. The final purpose was to show that the emir, and the emir alone, was able to lead all the Muslims of Andalus against the non-Muslims, clearly confirming his status as leader of all the Muslims of the peninsula. Furthermore, this was a time when the Byzantines were making increasingly aggressive moves against the Syrian frontiers of the Muslim world, capturing Malatya in 934. The contrast between the Abbasid caliph, who never ventured to lead his army in the *jihād* and whose armies were unable to protect his Muslim subjects, and the emir of Andalus, who was fulfilling that role publicly and successfully, was plain for all to see. Of course, the other caliphal duty, that of leading and protecting the *hajj*, was way beyond the powers of the ruler of Córdoba, but this does not appear to have been a serious handicap.

It was important too that they owed no allegiance to any other power, so no authority was in any position to object. Nor do they seem to have felt it necessary to ask for the approval of their subjects: there was, in fact, not even the pretence of an election. It was simply announced that the prayer was being said in the name of the caliph and letters were written to the provinces. In this rather ad hoc manner, a caliphate was founded which was to last for a century and earn the respect of the Muslim world and of posterity.

The next question to ask is whether Abd al-Rahmān's style of rulership altered as a result of his assumption of the new title. The first and perhaps most obvious point is that he changed his name. The Umayyad emirs of Córdoba, like the Umayyad caliphs of Damascus, had simply continued to use their own names when they became caliphs, but the Abbasids, apparently from the beginning of their rule, had adopted the practice of having formal titles (Mansūr, Mahdī, etc.) by which they were usually known in official parlance and by which they appear in the historical record. The Fatimid caliphs in Tunisia imitated this practice, and so did Abd al-Rahmān III and his successors. Abd al-Rahmān himself becoming Nāsir li'dīn Allah, Victorious for the Faith of God.

Another outward and visible change was the minting of gold coins. Whereas many of the dynasts who took power from the Abbasids in the east minted silver coins, of very variable quality, in their own names, none of them minted gold dinars. This was partly, no doubt, because they did not have access to sufficient quantities of gold to be able to do this, but also because this was generally felt to be a caliphal prerogative. The only exceptions to this rule were the Fatimids of Egypt, as we have seen, and their minting of very fine gold coins was a clear indication of their exalted status. The opening up of trans-Saharan trade routes to both the Umayyads of Córdoba, through their North African connections, and the Fatimids of Egypt had given them both access to gold, and new-found wealth.

The proclamation of the caliphate reflected wider changes in Andalusi society. We cannot be sure of the numbers, but the late ninth and tenth centuries likely saw a rapid increase in the rate of conversion to Islam in the Iberian Peninsula, as more and more local people wished to join the Muslim community. By the time Abd al-Rahmān proclaimed his caliphate it is probable that a majority of the population were Muslims. The coming of the caliphate was a sign that he was not an emir ruling over an elite minority of Muslims but rather a caliph ruling over all Muslims in a largely Muslim society. Still, there were many distinctions and divisions within that society. Not only were there ancient tribal and regional loyalties, but there had also been considerable friction between those Muslims who claimed Arab or Berber descent and the *muwalladūn*, the descendants of the pre-invasion Christian and Jewish populations who had converted to Islam. In the years of the first two caliphs (912–76), loyalties to tribe and region were replaced by loyalty to the caliph and the increasingly powerful state apparatus and the distinction between Arabs and Berbers and *muwalladun* became gradually irrelevant.

In his long reign of almost fifty years, Abd al-Rahmān's style of government changed and evolved significantly. As we have seen, much of the power and prestige which had enabled him to claim the caliphate in the first place had been the result of his leadership of the *jihād* against the Christians of the north. For the first ten years of his caliphate (929–39), he continued this campaign, leading the Muslim army in person and cajoling and persuading those lords in the frontier areas, like the Ebro valley, to join him in the Muslim enterprise. In 939, however, he suffered a serious reverse. That year he led an expedition against Ramiro II, the Christian king of León. As he had done in previous years he marched through the Ebro valley, recruiting the reluctant lords of Zaragoza and Huesca to join him. He then embarked on an unsuccessful and demoralizing siege of the castle at Simancas. After this setback he turned south through rugged country to lead his army back to Muslim territory. It was here, that at an unidentified place which the Arabs simply called the trench (*khandaq*), that he engaged a force of Christian irregulars. The Muslim army was soundly defeated, many were killed and others taken prisoner. The humiliated caliph led his shattered army south to the safety of Muslim territory at Guadalajara.

The fundamental cause of this defeat seems to have been that the lords of the Ebro valley, ever resentful of the caliph's attempts to control them, deserted at a crucial moment, leaving Abd al-Rahmān to his fate. This reverse resulted in a profound change in his government. In the immediate aftermath he seized and executed Fortūn b. Muhammad, lord of Huesca, one of the leaders who had betrayed him, but he made no effort to destroy the power of the other rebellious lords. He himself never led another campaign to the north, and neither, in the last twenty-two years of his reign, did he lead Muslims in *jihād*. Instead he retired to Córdoba where, three years before in 936, he had begun the construction of the great palace complex at Madinat al-Zahra outside the city. Here he developed a lavish caliphal style in a large palace-city whose ruins can still be seen today, with its gardens, its courts and pools and a sumptuously decorated throne hall with mosaics and marbles. He welcomed visitors and used these magnificent surroundings to display the caliphate in all its glory. The court, its luxuries and its culture, attracted lords from all over the peninsula and Berber chiefs from North Africa, especially at the time of the two great *īds* (festivals) of the Muslim calendar. Rather than taking the caliphate on tour, so to speak, he created a court to which notables were drawn and wanted to belong, and where they wanted their sons to be educated. It was a pattern which, many centuries later, Louis XIV was to adopt in the palace and court at Versailles: autocracy by attraction rather than by the naked use of force.

This wealthy and apparently stable state elicited much admiration at the time and nostalgia for the lost glories of Andalus has remained a minor but continuing motif in Arabic culture ever since. In recent years, in fact, there has been a renewed interest, especially in the west, in the concept of *convivencia*. *Convivencia*, 'living together' in Spanish, has come to be applied to the perceived situation in Andalus at the time of the caliphate when members of the three great monotheistic faiths, Muslims, Christians and Jews, lived together in harmony and, at least to some extent, shared a common culture. In the aftermath of the 9/11 attacks on New York and Washington, some commentators looked to Andalus as a historical example and, possibly, as a model showing that hostility between the faiths was not inevitable, a view most eloquently espoused in the writings of Rosa Maria Menocal of Yale University.[1] Not everyone saw it this way: for Usāma b. Lādin and the ideologues of Al-Qaeda, the story of Andalus was a terrible warning. Muslims had tolerated Christian and Jewish elements in the population and allowed them rights and positions. The result was plain to see: Muslims ended up driven out of their own country and the Iberian Peninsula was permanently lost to the Dār al-Islam.

The historical reality is a bit more mixed. It is true that there seems to have been very little active persecution of Christians in Andalus. They were allowed to continue to worship in churches and monasteries and Christian bishops played an important role in the administration of the Christian population. Caliph Nāsir used the Christian Recemundo as his ambassador to both Aachen and Constantinople, and in the next century the administration of the kingdom of Granada was largely entrusted to powerful Jewish officials.

Relations between the faiths were not static. In the ninth century there was some opposition to Muslim rule. The so-called 'martyrs of Córdoba' were a pious group of Christians who courted death by openly insulting the Prophet Muhammad and the Islamic faith. Despite the intervention of the bishop of Córdoba, who was firmly opposed to the movement, and the attempts of the Muslim authorities to persuade them to recant, a number of them were put to death. In the first decades of the tenth century a rebel leader in the mountains of southern Spain, Ibn Hafsūn, attempted to rally support by claiming to be a champion of the Christians. In the period of the caliphate, however, we find nothing of this.

There are no accounts of Christian or Jewish resistance or of any persecution at that point. The reality was probably that, with a growing proportion of the population converting to Islam, both Christians and Jews were less important and posed little threat. This position changed in the eleventh century when growing Christian military pressure from León, Castile and Navarre meant that Christians could be seen as a potential fifth column and, under the rule of the Almoravids in the early twelfth century, many of them left for the north. Although *convivencia* meant peaceful co-existence, it did not mean equality. Christians and Jews were second-class citizens and a peaceful co-existence was only possible as long as they accepted an inferior status. When this was no longer the case and the Muslims felt threatened, then *convivencia* was doomed.

It was not only Muslims who came to pay their respects to the caliph in Córdoba and left impressed. Nāsir initiated a 'foreign policy', as befitted a caliph. In about 950 there began an exchange of ambassadors with the most powerful ruler in western Europe, the German emperor Otto I (938–73). Otto wanted the cooperation of the caliph against Muslim pirates who had seized the southern French city of Fréjus and used it as a base to terrorize the surrounding country and prey on shipping. No Arab source records this mission, but we know about it from a Latin account of the life of the German ambassador Abbot John of Gorze, which gives an outsider's view of the magnificence of the caliphal court.[2] John was a very undiplomatic ambassador, determined not to be impressed or intimidated, and progress was slow. He was scathingly dismissive of the local Christian bishop when he described the compromises Christians had to make to survive in Muslim-ruled Córdoba. Eventually Abd al-Rahmān sent an ambassador, a Mozarab (Arabized Christian) known by his Latin name of Recemundo or his Arabic one of Rabīʿ b. Zayd, to Aachen. Finally, after a three-year wait in Córdoba, John was granted an audience.

The account of this meeting, written by a fellow monk, is the only first-hand report of a pre-modern caliph we have by an outsider to the Muslim world. Before he met the caliph (who is called *rex*, king, throughout), John was meant to make himself 'presentable to royalty by cutting his hair, washing his body and putting on clean clothes'. He refused, even when the caliph sent him ten pounds in coin to smarten himself up, thanking him for the gift but suggesting that it would be better spent on alms for the poor: 'I do not despise royal gifts,' he wrote in response, 'but it is not permitted to a monk to wear anything other than his usual habit', and eventually the caliph gave in, saying, 'Even if he comes dressed in a sack, I will most gladly receive him.'

When the day came for John to meet the caliph, he was treated to the full display of caliphal power:

Ranks of people crowded the whole way from the lodging to the centre of the city and from there to the palace [presumably they met at Madinat al-Zahra, hence the walk along the dusty road from the city]. Here stood infantrymen with spears erect; beside them others brandishing javelins and staging demonstrations of aiming them at each other, after them others mounted on mules with their light armour; then horsemen urging on their steeds with spurs and shouts to make them rear up. In this startling way, the Moors hoped to put fear into our people by their various marshal displays, so strange to our eyes. John and his companions were led to the palace along a very dusty road, which the very dryness of the season alone served to stir up (for it was the summer solstice). High officials came to meet them, and all the pavement of the outer area of the palace was carpeted with most costly rugs and coverings.

When John arrived at the *cubiculum* where the Caliph was seated alone, almost like a deity accessible to none or very few, he saw everything draped with rare coverings and floor-tiles stretching evenly to the walls. The Caliph himself reclined upon a most richly ornate couch. They do not use thrones or chairs as other peoples do but recline on divans [*lectis*] or couches when conversing or eating, their legs crossed one over the other.

Then the Caliph signed to John to be seated. A lengthy silence ensued on both sides. Then the Caliph began: 'I know that your heart has long been hostile to me, and that is why I refused you an audience till now. You yourself know that I could not do otherwise. I appreciate your steadfastness and your learning. I wish you to know that things which may have disturbed you in that letter were not said out of enmity towards you and not only do I now freely receive you, but I assure you that you shall have whatever you ask.' John who, as he later told us, had been ready to say something harsh to the Caliph, since he had long harboured such resentment, now became very calm and was perfectly at ease.

John explained to the caliph that he had now banished these hostile sentiments and the latter was

greatly pleased with these sentiments, and talked to John about other things. Then he asked him to hand over the presents from the Emperor. [Sadly we are not told what these were.] When this was done, John instantly asked permission to leave. The Caliph asked in surprise: 'How does this sudden change come about? Since both of us have waited so long for a sight of each other, and since we have only just met, is it right for us to part as strangers? Now that we are together, there is an opportunity for each of us to acquire a little knowledge of each other's mind and we could meet again at greater length, and on a third occasion forge a truly firm bond of understanding and friendship. Then, when I send you back to your master, you could go there with all due honour.' John agreed to this. They ordered the other emissaries to be brought in and the presents which they were carrying were handed over to the Caliph.

The Christians returned to their lodging, and when after a time, John was again called to see the Caliph, he conversed with him on a number of subjects of mutual interest: the power and wisdom of 'our Emperor', the strength and numbers of his army, his glory and wealth, events of war and many things of that kind. The Caliph for his part boasted that his army exceeded that of any other of the rulers of the world in strength. John made little answer to this in order not to annoy the Caliph, but eventually he added, 'I speak the truth when I say that I know of no monarch in the world who can equal our Emperor in lands or arms or horses.

Here this fascinating account breaks off and we have no idea what, if any, results were achieved. It may be that the report of this friendly man-to-man conversation between monk and caliph should be treated with some scepticism, but much of the rest of the description rings true, for instance the rugs and tiles in the palace and the way in which the caliph sits cross-legged on a couch (which would be called *sarīr* in Arabic). It shows a degree of mutual respect between the two most powerful rulers in western Europe, the emperor in Aachen and the caliph in Córdoba.

At the same time, the caliph also began diplomatic relations with the Byzantine Empire. Constantinople and Córdoba were the two biggest and most sophisticated cities in Europe at that point; both states had highly developed and literate administrations, regular systems of taxation and the the use of coined money was widespread. They were in a different world from the peoples of northern and western Europe, with their war-bands, primitive castles and Viking invasions. It was natural that they should be aware of each other and make contact. The vast distance between the two meant that military conflict, even naval conflict, was out of the question so there were no obstacles to alliances based on mutual esteem. As we have seen, the Abbasids had tried to use Byzantine embassies as a way of demonstrating their leadership of the Muslim community and the caliph in Córdoba was now attempting to do the same. In the summer of 949 an embassy from Constantinople was received in Córdoba and in October of the same year an embassy led by Recemundo was in Constantinople. Although both parties came to share a common enemy in the Fatimids, this diplomacy seems to have been more about display and prestige than about making a military alliance.

There was an important cultural aspect to this exchange. Under the reign of the caliph's son Hakam, Byzantine mosaicists came to work in Córdoba and the brilliant results of their labours can still be seen around the *mihrab* of the Great Mosque and in the domes in front of it. Of course, the mosaics in Córdoba were very different in their iconography and images from the mosaics being created in Constantinople to decorate the churches of the city. The images of Christ and his apostles and saints were replaced by scrolls of vegetation and golden calligraphy but all showed consummate, and expensive, craftsmanship. Mosaic work was a luxury product and only Byzantine craftsmen could deliver the best. Just as fine and exotic textiles, including Byzantine silks, were signs of royal status in the Muslim world, so were these mosaics very public affirmations of the caliph's place among the monarchs of the world. The difference is that, except for a few rare fragments, the textiles survive only in descriptions in literary sources whereas we can still see the mosaics today, very much as the subjects of the caliphs did in the tenth century, and we can draw the same conclusions about their position in the world.

The cultural exchanges were not confined to public displays. In 951, presumably at the request of the caliphal court, a Greek monk called Nicholas was sent there to work on and interpret a manuscript of Dioscorides' ancient book on herbal and medicinal plants, apparently because no one in Andalus had sufficient Greek to do it. Here again the caliph was following the example set by the Abbasid court in the eighth and ninth centuries when the collection and interpretation of ancient Greek scholarship was an important aspect of the performance of caliphate.

Abd al-Rahmān al-Nāsir was succeeded by his son Hakam, who had long been groomed for the inheritance and had been given the title of Mustansir. He was an able and intelligent ruler (961–76) and followed his father's example in most of his policies. It was in the fifteen years of his stable administration that the civilization of Córdoba reached its zenith. He collected a vast library of books and it was he who created the *mihrab* and the domes, already mentioned, in the mosque of Córdoba. He also held court at Madinat al-Zahra, the scene of many glittering gatherings.

We know a great deal about these events because they are recorded in meticulous detail by a writer called Īsā al-Rāzī. Īsā came from a family of Persian origin (his name shows that they were originally from Rayy, in northern Iran). Like many other inhabitants of the eastern Islamic world, his family was attracted to the rich and cultured court of Andalus where their expertise in Arabic literature and history would be valued and well rewarded. Īsā's record is more a court diary than a universal chronicle: he describes who the main courtiers were, who came to the palace, where they stood in the formal *majlis*. Hakam continued his father's policies and ruled over a glittering and cultured court; the lords of the frontiers of Andalus and the Berber tribal leaders of Morocco came to pledge allegiance and were rewarded with gifts and a public acknowledgement of their status.

Hakam's reign saw important changes in the politics of North Africa. In 969, after the Fatimid conquest of Egypt, we saw that the caliph and his court established themselves in their newly founded capital of Cairo – Madinat al-Zahra on the Nile, so to speak. From now on the Fatimids were inextricably linked to Egypt. No Fatimid ruler visited the original power base of the dynasty in Ifriqiya ever again. They entrusted the province to a Berber family known to history as the Zirids, but while they recognized the Fatimids as their overlords, as mere emirs they were not in any sense a threat to the Umayyad caliphs. Morocco was never an easy country to control, however, and Hakam and his government spent a lot of money and resources to very little effect trying to do so.

The Umayyad caliphs main rivals were the various branches of the Idrisids. The Idrisids were Alids, direct descendants of Alī and Fātima and hence of the Prophet himself. They traced their origin to Idrīs b. Abd Allah who had fled from Arabia in 785 when a Shi'ite rebellion, of which he had been one of the leaders, was crushed by the Abbasids. Idrīs went to the Maghreb to seek both refuge and support. The family never managed to establish a stable state in this pastoral and tribal environment, some of its members attempted to exploit their status to attract followers. They did not claim the title of caliph – their poverty and marginal position in the Islamic world would have made that untenable – but their Alid antecedents were not contested. Unlike other Berber chiefs, they could use this status to appeal to followers beyond their own tribal networks. In the end, the

Idrisid challenge could not undermine Umayyad rule in Andalus, but it did pose both an ideological and political threat which prevented the caliphs from establishing real control in the Maghreb.

The Amirids and the End of the Caliphate of Córdoba

Although the Umayyads of Córdoba were in many ways rivals of the Abbasids of Baghdad, as we have seen, they did emulate their politics and political structures, and this wasn't always beneficial to the long-term political health of their caliphate. Hakam seems to have been devoted to his young son Hishām, who was invested as heir apparent when only seven years old. He was just fourteen when his father died in 976. His accession to the caliphate was by no means a done deal. Many in Córdoba were very reluctant to accept this inexperienced youth as ruler and a group among the Siqlabi (Slav) officials who formed the elite of the Córdoban army[3] attempted to secure the appointment of the dead caliph's brother Mughīra, son of the first caliph, Nāsir. However, they were soon outmanoeuvred by an ambitious courtier called Muhammad b. Abī Āmir and the unfortunate Mughīra, though he seems to have been innocent of any political ambition, was strangled in his own house in front of his family. The events were uncannily reminiscent of the circumstances surrounding the accession of Muqtadir as Abbasid caliph in Baghdad seventy years before in 908. In both cases ambitious politicians, the vizier Ibn al-Furāt in the case of Muqtadir, Ibn Abī Āmir in the case of Hishām, sought the appointment of a young and inexperienced caliph whom they could control. In both cases too a rival, both adult and respected – Ibn al-Mu'tazz in Baghdad, Mughīra in Córdoba – was put forward by another group, but the supporters of the youthful candidates were quicker and more ruthless and both Ibn al-Mu'tazz and Mughīra lost their lives.

In a sense, both accessions represented the triumph of the hereditary principle over any idea of election or *shūra*. In Baghdad and Córdoba, powerful women played an important role. In the Abbasid court it was the queen mother who dominated her son right up to his death. In Córdoba it was the Basque princess Subh, mother of the young Hishām, who worked with Ibn Abī Āmir closely, too closely for propriety, some rumours said, to secure her son's succession, though once this had occurred she seems to have found herself increasingly sidelined. Finally, in both cases, the accession of the young boy had a catastrophic effect on the power and prestige of the caliphate, an effect from which the institution never recovered. Ironically, as we have seen, people in Córdoba must have been fully aware of what had happened in Baghdad and the disastrous consequences that had ensued, but they were powerless to prevent it happening to them.

The reasons for this debacle lay in the changing political system. The caliph had absolute power, at least in theory, and winning the caliph's favour or, even better, controlling the person of the caliph was the most effective route to power. The increasing isolation of the caliph within the walls of massive palaces was an important part of this. It meant that those courtiers with immediate access could prevent the caliph exercising his own judgement and prevent anyone with whom they disagreed having access to him.

In Cordóba it was announced that the new caliph Hishām wanted to devote himself to prayer and pious exercises. So that he would have the solitude to permit him to do this, he was installed, not in the great expansive palace of Madinat al-Zahra, but behind the high walls of the old Alcāzar in the centre of town by the Great Mosque. Nobody came and nobody went and even when he did visit the mosque, just across the narrow road, the caliph was so secluded that none of his subjects could glimpse him, still less communicate with him.

Meanwhile Ibn Abī Āmir set about making himself caliph in all but name. He recruited new elements into the army, notably Berber tribesmen from North Africa who were brought in not as individuals, like the Slavs from eastern Europe who formed the other main contingent in the army, but in tribal groups operating under their own leaders. His aim was to create an army of many different factions, none of which would be powerful enough to challenge him on their own. He also completed the demilitarization of most of the indigenous Muslim population of Andalus. The military might of the caliphate was now almost entirely composed of foreigners, Slavs, brought in from eastern Europe, and Berbers, brought in from Morocco, just as in the Abbasid east it was largely composed of Turks brought in from Central Asia. It was a system which boosted the power of the rulers in the short term but had very deleterious consequences in the long run. This was especially true in Andalus where, in the thirteenth century, Slavs and Berbers were no longer available and the local people had neither the resources nor the skills to defend their towns and villages against the advancing Christians.

To begin with, however, the new army was powerful and effective. Ibn Abī Āmir claimed he belonged to a family descended from the first generation of Muslim conquerors, but he could not claim Qurashi antecedents. As he himself realized, this meant that he could never aspire to the caliphate, but he did arrogate to himself a caliphal honorific title: Mansūr, the Victorious. Not only did this have caliphal pretensions, but it was also the title of one of the greatest of the Abbasids: the symbolism could not have been more explicit. He also made a point of demonstrating his traditional piety. Hakam al-Mustansir had been a great book collector and it is clear that some at least of the tomes in his library were not acceptable to the rigorists among the religious classes and their followers among the ordinary people of Córdoba. What these books were we cannot know, but we can imagine that at least some of them were translations of Greek philosophy and science, deeply suspect material. Ibn Abī Āmir made a point of clearing out the library and destroying any work which might seem to threaten a strictly orthodox view. Nor were there any more embassies or craftsmen coming from western Europe or Constantinople. The Dār al-Harb (the lands beyond the Dār al-Islam) was a field for *jihād* and unrelenting hostility not cultural interchanges. Ibn Abī Āmir claimed to model himself on the Buyid sovereigns of Iraq who had 'protected' the Abbasid caliphs in Baghdad just as he 'protected' the Umayyad Hishām.

To justify his own position and his new title, and assert the legitimacy of his new army, he began a series of campaigns against the Christians of the north. He launched raids almost every year and no one could doubt his commitment to the *jihād*. The campaigns were largely successful on their own terms, as many prisoners and a certain amount of booty were taken. Mansūr also made sure that his subjects were aware of his achievements and letters describing his victories were read out in the mosque in Córdoba at Friday prayers. His greatest public relations coup was when he sacked the shrine at Santiago de Compostela, then just emerging as a major pilgrimage centre, and had the bells of the cathedral carried back to Córdoba on the backs of Christian prisoners. But in a larger strategic sense, the campaigns were less effective. Little or no new territory was occupied and the Christian kingdoms of León and Navarre, and the emerging county of Castile, were still strong, as events after his death showed.

When Mansūr died, he was succeeded by his son and designated heir, who was also given a quasi-caliphal title, in this case Muzaffar, yet another word meaning 'Victorious'. For the six years of his reign (1002–8), Muzaffar continued in his father's tradition, leading frequent campaigns against the Christians and keeping the nominal caliph carefully hidden. When he died, power passed to his brother Abd al-Rahmān, known as Sanchuelo, or Little Sancho, after his Christian Basque grandfather, the king of Navarre. He abandoned the delicate balancing act which had kept his father and brother in power. One of his first acts was to oblige the captive caliph Hishām to appoint him as heir apparent, meaning that there would soon be a non-Umayyad, non-Qurashi caliph.

It was not a wise move. It aroused the deep hostility of

the religious classes and the people of Córdoba who supported Umayyad claims and, of course, the numerous members of the Umayyad family themselves, who feared that they
were going to be deprived of wealth and status. The reaction
was swift. The new ruler decided to establish his position in
the traditional way, by leading his army against the Christians.
He chose to disregard his advisers and launched an expedition in the winter. No sooner had he passed into enemy territory than conspirators struck in Córdoba. The leader of the
rebels was one Muḥammad b. Hishām, an Umayyad and a
great-grandson of the first caliph, Nāsir. He had a clear plan
to restore the Umayyad caliphate as a reality. The useless
Hishām was obliged to abdicate in his favour, and he took the
title of Mahdī, following the third Abbasid caliph, a title
which stressed that he was God-guided rather than militarily
victorious. He recruited other members of his family and
appealed to the loyalty of the people of Córdoba to join a
militia to protect the new regime. At first all went well – the
capital was secure and the new caliphate proclaimed – but
the regime immediately faced the hostility of established
military groups, notably the Berbers. The events which followed were complicated and very destructive. The Berbers
themselves adopted another member of the Umayyad family
as 'their' caliph. Córdoba endured a three-year siege by the
Berber troops and when it was forced to surrender the city
suffered a terrible sack.

The end days of the caliphate dragged on as a number of
different members of the Umayyad family and others
attempted to establish their power, but the divisions were
too deep and different military leaders concentrated on

securing their positions in their own areas rather than rebuilding the central government. To make matters worse, Christians began to intervene on a large scale in the affairs of Andalus, demanding payments and territory in exchange for their support. It was the shape of things to come.

In 1031 a group of Córdoban notables came together and abolished the caliphate, preferring one of their own, unrelated to the ruling family, as local governor. The abolition of the caliphate was an unusual move in a society which valued traditions and titles, particularly a title with such a history and resonance. What is even more surprising is that no one seriously attempted to revive it. The Umayyad family just disappeared from the political scene. One important reason was the destruction of Córdoba and its Campiña, the rural area which surrounded it. The fate of the city and that of the Umayyad caliphs were closely bound up. After the siege of 1010–13, many of Córdobas people were dead and many others had emigrated, while the luxurious villas and estates which had provided the settings for so much of the social and cultural life of the caliphate were ruined and abandoned. The surviving inhabitants seem simply to have concluded that the caliphate was more trouble than it was worth. And they were probably right.

CHAPTER 9

The Almohad Caliphs

The collapse of the Umayyad caliphate of Córdoba in the first decades of the eleventh century led to the period of the Taifa kings in Andalus. These kings, whose power was confined to one city or region, were never able to claim caliphal status, both because their power was too limited to make such an assertion plausible and because they lacked the important attribute of Qurashi descent. The most powerful of them, the Abbadid rulers of Seville, took quasi-caliphal titles, Mu'tadid (1042–69) and Mu'tamid (1069–91), and for a while maintained the fiction that they were ruling in the name of the vanished Umayyad Hishām, until the passing of the years made such a claim ridiculous.

Christian advances in the late eleventh century, especially the conquest of Toledo by Alfonso VI of León-Castile in 1085, meant that the position of the Taifa kings became impossible to sustain and, with some reluctance, most of them accepted the overlordship of the Berber Almoravids (Ar. *Murābitūn*) from Morocco. The Almoravids were a coalition of Sanhaja Berbers from the western Sahara who had been brought together by the religious reformer Abd Allah b. Yāsin. Ibn Yāsin had travelled in the Middle East and returned to his native people with a clear message that the Islam they practised was at best corrupt and at worst heretical. Ibn Yāsin's puritanical reform movement soon spread to most of Morocco and, between 1086 and 1090, established its rule over most of Andalus except for the northern kingdom of Zaragoza. Under the rule of Yūsuf b. Tashfīn the Almoravids were able to stem the Christian advance, defeating Alfonso VI at the Battle of Zallaqa in 1086. However, under the rule of Yūsuf's pious but ineffective son Alī (1106–43), the military position in Andalus deteriorated and the Almoravids were faced by a major new ideological and political challenge from another group of puritanical reformers, the Almohads (Ar. *Muwahhidūn*).

The Almoravids, despite the extent of their empire, including as it did at its height most of Andalus, and Morocco as far south as the Sahara, never claimed the title of caliph. Instead they acknowledged the overlordship of the Abbasid caliphs of Baghdad, bringing the Maghreb back into the wider *umma*. They themselves took the title of Emir al-Muslimīn. Strangely, this rather obvious title, meaning simply 'Prince of the Muslims', was very seldom used by Muslim monarchs, the caliphal title always being *Amīr al-Mu'minīn*. The implication was that while they appealed to all Muslims they nonetheless remained emirs under the overall authority of the caliphs in Baghdad.

Ibn Tūmart and the Rise of the Almohads

Almoravid rule was challenged in Morocco from 1120 on by the emergence of the Almohads. As with the Almoravids, the movement was begun by a religious reformer, Muhammad b.

Tūmart, who had travelled to the east and returned with a mission for religious change. Ibn Tūmart was a Berber, but unlike the Almoravids he hailed from one of the Masmuda tribes of the Atlas Mountains and his followers were people from mountain villages rather than nomads from the desert. In the east he claimed to have been taught by the great Ghazālī (d. 1111), whose book *Reviving the Religious Sciences* had argued strongly that simple obedience to the strict laws of Islam was not enough and that Muslims should follow the spirit of Islam if they wanted to be good Muslims. Combining Sufism with traditional legal scholarship, his writings were widely circulated and complete anathema to the rigorist legalistic authorities of Almoravid Andalus, who ordered his books to be burned.

Ibn Tūmart claimed that the great man had given him his blessing and asked him to avenge the burning of his works. Whether any of this is true is quite uncertain, but it did mean that he could claim to be the disciple of the greatest religious thinker of his age. Ibn Tūmart's life became the subject of an account, almost like the biography of the Prophet Muhammad himself, and truth was embellished by piety so that we cannot be sure of all the details. What is clear is that he returned in the years 1117 to 1119, pausing along the way to preach a simple and puritanical Islam criticizing the wearing of bright clothes, the mixing of the sexes at festivals, the playing of musical instruments and the selling of wine.

By 1120 he had returned to his native Morocco and is said to have preached to the Almoravid ruler Alī b. Yūsuf in his capital at Marrakesh. His appeal for a reformed Islam was rejected and he made his way to the mountains where he had been brought up, to continue his mission from the safety they provided.

Ibn Tūmart had failed to win over the Almoravid leadership and became determinedly hostile to them. Both movements were intent on establishing a reformed Islam, free of what they regarded as the laxities and abuses which had crept in. It is difficult to see what divided them. Ibn Tūmart demanded that Islamic law be based on the Qur'ān and *hadīth*, rather than the reason and argument which were used to support it, and this seems to have aroused the opposition of the legal scholars whose work was the ideological foundation of Almoravid doctrine. He insisted on the absolute unity of God and accused the Almoravids of anthropomorphism, of representing God as a human being. This insistence on the unity of God gave the Almohads the name by which they are generally known to history, *Almohade* being the Spanish version of the Arabic *Muwwahidūn*, meaning those who assert the unity of God. He also attacked the Sanhaja Berbers who formed the backbone of the military support of the regime: like many of the Touareg of today, the men wore veils to protect their faces from the blowing sand and fierce heat of the desert. This enabled Ibn Tūmart to accuse them of effeminacy.

These were differences which could be stressed and used to dismiss the Almoravids as heretics and morally corrupt, but what really distinguished the Almohads from the Almoravids was the style of leadership. After his rejection by the Almoravid court, Ibn Tūmart determined to break with them completely. He began proclaiming that he was the infallible Mahdī who would lead the Muslims to true Islam. He also developed a genealogy for himself which showed that he was descended from the Prophet Muhammad through the Idrisids who had come to settle in North Africa. You could not be a member of the Almohad movement unless you accepted Ibn Tūmart as the God-appointed leader whose word was law. There was no room for compromise.

In 1122 Ibn Tūmart established his base in the little town of Tinmal, to the south of Marrakesh, which was accessible only through a narrow mountain pass. This was to become his Medina, the place to which he made his Hijra and where he established his regime. The mosque that was built there still exists, recently restored, a physical witness to the early days of the movement. He also set up a remarkable hierarchy among his followers, which aimed to supplement or even replace the tribal loyalties which were so strong among these mountain people. The Mahdī himself was, naturally, the head of the organization. Below him were the Council of Ten, all early followers of Ibn Tūmart, either people who had joined him on his journey west, like Abd al-Mu'min, or local tribal leaders. Below them were a Council of Fifty, mostly Berber tribal leaders from the Atlas region. They were assisted by a corps of people known as *talba* (sing. *tālib*). This term is usually translated as 'students' and, in its Persian plural, gives us Taliban. The *talba* were one of the most distinctive features of the Almohad regime. They were, in a sense, political commissars, ideologues who expounded Almohad ideology but also fulfilled a number of what might be described as civil service roles. Adherence to Almohad ideology was enforced with bloodthirsty severity. In 1129–30 there was the first *tamyīz*, or purge, among the Berbers, which resulted in the deaths of many who were thought to be opposed to Ibn Tūmart's authority or simply showed insufficient enthusiasm.

Another distinctive feature of the Almohad regime was its Berber identity. Berber was a vernacular which was, and still is, widely spoken in North Africa, but it had never been a written language nor, as far as we can tell, the language of religion and preaching. Ibn Tūmart not only preached in Berber, but he also produced a Berber version of the Qur'ān. Arabic was still used as an official language and remained the language of high culture, but a knowledge of Berber was essential for anyone who wanted to progress in the Almohad hierarchy and there are examples of *qādīs* and other officials in Andalus losing their jobs because they could not understand the language. This was the first time in the Muslim world that a regime had promulgated a non-Arabic Islam. Persian was widely spoken and written by the twelfth century and the great Ghazālī himself wrote religious tracts in Persian as well as Arabic, but there was no attempt to use a Persian translation of the Qur'ān, still less to make the learning of Persian compulsory. This Berber identity produced a sense of solidarity among the various Berber tribes committed to the movement, but it also alienated many Muslims, especially in Andalus where Berber was not really spoken at all. When the military power of the movement began to fail in the early thirteenth century, the Almohads were easily distinguished by their disgruntled subjects and this certainly contributed to the decline of the dynasty.

From his base in Tinmal, Ibn Tūmart launched a series of

attacks on the Almoravid capital of Marrakesh, but in 1130 the movement suffered what might have been a deadly blow. Ibn Tūmart was fatally wounded in an unsuccessful attack on the city. With the Mahdī gone, leadership passed to one of his earliest followers, Abd al-Mu'min. Abd al-Mu'min established his control over the movement and, crucially, took the titles of caliph and *Amīr al-Mu'minīn*. Whether consciously or not, he was casting himself in the role of Abū Bakr to Ibn Tūmart's Muhammad. Ibn Tūmart seems to have had no sons and his brothers were systematically removed from any positions of responsibility and influence. It was the family of Abd al-Mu'min who were to provide the caliphs until the end of the Almohad regime.

Like Abū Bakr, Abd al-Mu'min was determined to continue the expansion of the Almohad movement. In a series of campaigns in the 1140s he systematically subdued the cities of Morocco, and on 24 March 1147 Marrakesh was finally captured. It soon became the most important capital of the new caliphate and the real centre of Almohad power.

After the conquest of Morocco, it was inevitable that the Almohads would become involved in the affairs of Andalus. The collapse of the Almoravid regime in Marrakesh had left the Muslims in the Iberian Peninsula exposed to the depredations of Christians. Without military support from North Africa, Andalus was hardly viable. The pursuit of the *jihād* was a core function of caliphate and Abd al-Mu'min would certainly have been aware not only of the duties this involved but also the opportunities it would provide for developing the prestige of his office among his own followers and in the wider Muslim world.

His military support was urgently needed in Andalus. In 1147, the same year in which the caliph conquered Marrakesh, the king of the newly established kingdom of Portugal, Afonso Henriques, conquered Lisbon with the help of warriors from northern Europe sailing to join the Second Crusade. At the same time the Castilians contrived to capture, and hold for the next decade, the port of Almería, right on the south coast of the peninsula and an important centre of communication with North Africa. Throughout Andalus, the advances of the Christians provoked uprisings against the remaining Almoravid governors and garrisons. That year, invited by local leaders, Abd al-Mu'min sent the first Almohad forces to the Algarve.

The advance into Andalus was slow. This was partly because of strategic factors which made the Almohad state very different from the Almoravid. The Almohads were always active on two fronts. The Almohad empire at its height included all of modern Tunisia, Algeria and Morocco as well as a large part of modern Spain and Portugal. It was never easy to control these far-flung territories: distances were long and much of the land was wild and sparsely populated. In the 1150s Abd al-Mu'min devoted much of his military energies and resources to driving out the Normans out of Sicily, who had conquered the important seaports of Tunisia. It was not until 1160 that they were finally dislodged from their last stronghold, in Mahdia, and the caliph could devote his attention more completely to the *jihād* in Andalus. He took care to write to the people of Seville and presumably others in Andalus with a grandiloquent account of his victory over these infidels. The Almohads always paid great attention to what we might describe as the public relations aspect of caliphate, but at the same time the letter could hardly disguise the fact that he was giving them no real support against the increasingly aggressive Christians who were raiding right up to the gates of the city. Even with the Normans gone, the east was far from easy to control. Abd al-Mu'min had to deal with the numerous and powerful Arab tribes who had migrated to the area. He tried to do this by force but also by incorporating many of the tribesmen into the Almohad armies. Here they were a disruptive presence, resented by many of the Almohads and by the Andalusi military in the army. Their presence also led to an increasing Arabization of the Maghreb: it is ironic that this most Berber of dynasties should have facilitated the spread of the Arabic language.

Abd al-Mu'min was also busy restructuring the caliphate. He decided to build a new military base and centre of operations on the Atlantic coast where he could assemble armies and supplies for the *jihād* in Andalus. This base was called the *ribāt*, an Arabic word which means, among other things, a fortification, where men could go to practise religious exercises, particularly fasting and praying during Ramadan, and confronting the infidel. He constructed a massive fortification on a rocky headland on the other side of the river Bu Regreg from the ancient city of Salé and began work on a huge mosque. The city became the core of what is now the modern capital of Morocco, Rabat.

He also took time to establish his own family firmly in control of the caliphate. It helped that he had no less than fourteen sons, and most of the main provincial centres were governed by them. Other members of the old Almohad families were also given prestigious and lucrative positions and this consolidated the hereditary nature of the regime.

There was no pretence here that all the Muslim subjects of the caliphate were in any sense equals. This was a caliphate with a strict hereditary structure. It also had no pretensions to be a universal caliphate. Abd al-Mu'min never declared any intention to conquer the rest of the Muslim world or challenge the Abbasid caliphs of Baghdad. In this he was perhaps helped by the fact that the Fatimid caliphate of Cairo had been abolished in 1171. There were now only two caliphates in the Muslim world, both with very separate spheres of influence. There was some limited communication between them. At one stage in the 1180s, Saladin, who of course claimed to be in loyal service to the Abbasids, tried to negotiate a naval alliance with the Almohads against the Crusaders. Although this never came to anything, it shows that people in the eastern Islamic world both knew of and, at least at one level, respected the Almohads.

Stability in Andalus was frequently disrupted, not just by the aggressive Christians but also by groups among the Muslim population of the country who were bitterly opposed to the Almohads. This was especially true of one Ibn Mardanīsh, who effectively ruled Valencia and Murcia and the whole of the Levante and was quite prepared to ally with the Christians in his struggle with the Almohads. The rhetoric of caliphate cut very little ice with such men when they could see that it was no more than a cover for Almohad dynastic control.

Abd al-Mu'min tried to counter this by incorporating local

Andalusi lords into his army and paying them salaries, but though they often fought well they were usually excluded from the hierarchy and the best paid jobs. He also attempted to reorganize the administration of Andalus. The Almohads were always conscious of the legacy of the Umayyad caliphs of Córdoba and they attempted to harness this memory to boost their own prestige. After a triumph over Muslim rebels in Granada in 1162, the caliph ordered that the capital and all the government offices should be transferred from Seville to Córdoba. Seville had been chosen as the centre of Almohad administration in the Iberian Peninsula because of its good communications with Morocco. The river Guadalquivir was navigable as far up as Seville but not up to Córdoba. Córdoba was also by this time an impoverished and underpopulated city whose few inhabitants tried to make a living by farming deserted plots within the old city walls. The decision to move to Córdoba showed that prestige triumphed over logic and practical considerations.

Another attempt to harness the Umayyad legacy was by taking possession of the Qur'ān of Uthmān. The so-called Qur'ān of Uthmān was, as we have seen, used as a legitimizing relic by the Abbasids, but it would seem that this was another copy preserved by the Umayyads of Córdoba. It had been of special significance to them because Uthmān was himself an Umayyad and it represented evidence of their connection with one of the great figures of early Islam. This Qur'ān was now brought to from Córdoba to Marrakesh to form part of the spiritual armoury of the Almohad caliphate, symbolizing the transfer of the caliphate from the Umayyads to the Almohads. Nothing seems to be known about the fate of this volume after the fall of the Almohads in the late thirteenth century.

Despite the caliph's administrative reforms and the appointment of his sons as governors of the cities, the situation in Andalus remained precarious. In 1163 he prepared a huge expedition, gathered at his new stronghold of Rabat. There were said to have been 100,000 horsemen and 100,000 foot soldiers and the camp stretched for some nineteen kilometres. The intention was to attack all the main Christian states, Portugal, León, Castile and Barcelona, simultaneously. It would certainly have been a major invasion and might have secured the future of Andalus under Almohad rule, but the problems of supplying and directing so large a force would have been formidable.

The Later Almohad Caliphs

In the event all the preparations came to nothing because the caliph himself died in 1163. Abd al-Mu'min was the real founder of the Almohad caliphate. He had taken the legacy of Ibn Tūmart the Mahdī and transformed his religious vision into a powerful state, by far the strongest power in the western Islamic world, and established himself and his family in firm control.

He had chosen his son Muhammad as his heir in 1154 and had him publicly acknowledged. In the Almohad tradition Muhammad had rendered himself unsuitable for the position by drinking wine and other lapses. In the last years of his life, another brother, Umar, had become the caliph's chief adviser and he was with Abd al-Mu'min when he died in Rabat.

Umar now kept his death a secret while he arranged the succession, not of Muhammad, but of his own full brother Abū Ya'qūb Yūsuf, who was then governor of Seville. Yūsuf and Umar shared the same mother. They effectively took power and pushed their other brothers aside. From then on only the descendants of Umar and Yūsuf counted in power and succession.

The new caliph was a rather unusual character among the military and political leaders of his time. He was around twenty-five years old and had some political experience as governor of Seville and military experience serving in his father's armies. He was, however, a very different man from his father. He was bookish and intellectual, but he was not a natural military leader and at crucial moments seemed to lose his nerve and fail to take advantage of opportunities. We can observe his caliphate in action because we have part of a very full chronicle compiled by an Andalusi bureaucrat working for the Almohad government in Seville, Ibn Sāhib al-Salāt. His chronicle is full of lively, first-hand observations and enables us to see Almohad society and the interaction of personalities with rare intimacy.

Like his Umayyad predecessor Hakam II, Yūsuf built up a most impressive library. As caliph, he had ample authority to do so and sensible men did not refuse his request for books. A private collector in Seville remembered how this was done:

> The Commander of the Faithful came to hear of my
> collection so he sent Kāfūr the Eunuch with a selected
> group of slaves to my house when I was in the government
> offices and knew nothing about it. He ordered him not to

frighten anyone in the house and not to take anything except books and threatened him, and those with him, with the direst punishments if the people of the house lost so much as a pin. I was told about this while I was in the office and I thought he intended to confiscate all my property so, almost out of my mind, I rode to my house. There was the eunuch Kāfūr standing at the door and the books were being brought out to him. When he saw that I was obviously terrified he said, 'Don't panic!' and added that the caliph sent me his greetings and had mentioned me favourably, and he carried on smiling until I relaxed. Then he said, 'Ask the members of your household if anyone has frightened them or if anything is missing,' and they replied, 'No one has frightened us and nothing is missing.' Kāfūr then said we were free to go. Then he himself went into the library store and ordered that all the books be removed. When I heard this, all my anxiety disappeared.[1]

The caliph's interest in books was certainly genuine and other members of the Almohad elite seem to have shared his enthusiasm, but he was taken away from his studies by the need to assert Almohad control over those parts of eastern Spain ruled by Ibn Mardanish and to unite the Muslims against the persistent Christian aggression. Unlike his firm action in appropriating his subjects' books, he was less resolute in leading the Muslim armies. It was not until 1171, eight years after his accession, that he finally crossed the Straits and landed in Seville. He decided to launch a major campaign to retake the small frontier town of Huete, south-east of Toledo, which had recently been captured by the Christians.

It was a modest objective, but a large army of Almohad and Arabs was assembled and in the summer of 1172 the siege of the little town began.

What happened next is related by one of the Spanish Muslim commanders engaged in the campaign, Ibn Azzūn:

> When I was fighting with the Christians in the tower, which was the heart of their resistance in the city of Huete, and victory and triumph over them were within our grasp, I saw none of the valiant Almohad soldiers or commanders who were supporting me. I ran in person to the caliph who was in session with his brother and the *talba* of the court discussing questions of religious dogma. I said to him, 'My lord caliph! Send me reinforcements for I am on the point of victory!' I only wanted him to show himself on horseback so that the people and all the people would see him and they would enter the city there and then. But he did not answer me and carried on with what he was doing. I realized that the intention of the *jihād* had been corrupted and that the expedition had failed. I returned, despairing of victory and very preoccupied and thoughtful.[2]

As Ibn Azzūn predicted, the campaign was a failure. The huge army broke up and retreated with nothing achieved. The caliph himself returned to Marrakesh, leaving his ineffective deputies to try to organize the defence of Andalus. He busied himself with the politics of Morocco and the eastern half of his caliphate in Tunisia. It was not until 1183 that he came back to Andalus. The next year he attempted a campaign to recon-quer Lisbon, which had been conquered by the Portuguese in 1147. His second attempt at leading the *jihād* was even less successful than the first. In an abortive attempt to take the city of Santarem on the river Tagus, a sortie by the defenders caught the caliph and his followers by surprise. He himself, conspicuous in the red tent which marked his post, was wounded and died shortly afterwards.

His successor, who took the ancient and majestic title of Mansūr, was much less of an intellectual and much more of a warrior. His regime was less interested in intellectual activity and he devoted himself to defending Andalus against the Christians and led the last substantial Muslim victory over Christian forces when he defeated King Alfonso VII of Castile at Alarcos in 1195.

The early decades of the thirteenth century brought home the vulnerabilities of Andalus and the inability of the Almohad caliphate to deal with them. When Mansūr died in in January 1199 he was succeeded by his son, then only seventeen years old, who took the title (ironically given what was to come) of Nāsir, the Victorious. The first decade of his reign was spent in North Africa, stabilizing the situation in Tunisia by entrusting the country to a prominent Almohad family, the Hafsids, who later established themselves as independent rulers, taking the title of caliph. In 1211 the young caliph assembled an army at Rabat and crossed the Straits to Seville. In 1212 he was faced by a Christian expedition which included King Alfonso VIII of Castile, King Pedro II of Aragón and numerous other Christian notables, including French barons. This display of Christian unity was supported by Pope Innocent III, always eager to encourage crusading.

The Christians made their way through the rugged mountains of the Sierra Morena and encountered the Almohad army, led by the caliph in person, at Las Navas de Tolosa on 16 July 1212. It is unclear why the Muslim army performed so badly; at the time there were stories of disputes within the ranks and resentment at Nāsir's erratic and sometimes cruel leadership. By nightfall the battle was over, the Almohad army broke in full flight and the caliph rushed to the safety of the fortified city of Jaén. From there he returned to Marrakesh where he died shortly afterwards. Some said he was murdered by his dissatisfied officers. Meanwhile the magnificent banner of the caliphs was taken north by the victorious Castilians and placed in the monastery of Las Huelgas outside Burgos where it can still be seen today, a genuine relic of the Almohad caliphate.

The Battle of Las Navas de Tolosa spelt the end of the Almohad caliphate as a successful protector of the Muslims of Andalus. The defeat of the army and the death of the caliph led to rivalry and strife among the Almohad elite in Marrakesh, which allowed the Christians to consolidate and advance. The ancient capital of Córdoba, seat of the Umayyad caliphs, fell to Fernando III of Castile in 1236, and Seville twelve year later in 1248. At that point the majority of the territory and population of Andalus were lost to Christian rule and the caliphate disappeared from European territory. The Almohads now retreated to Morocco, but the various pretenders to the caliphal title fought each other and the Berber tribes increasingly rejected their authority. In 1269 the last caliph of the dynasty, Wāhid, was ignominiously murdered by a slave in Marrakesh. Neither the Nasrid kings of Granada, who ruled what remained of Andalus from their stronghold in the southern mountains until 1492, nor the

Merinids, who came to control most of Morocco, aspired to the caliphal title. The attempt to unify the Muslims of the west in an independent caliphate had failed and there was never to be another in later centuries.

The Culture of the Almohad Caliphate

Before leaving the Almohad caliphate, we should remember the important cultural legacy which survived long after it had disappeared. The dynasty were great patrons of architecture. In the beginning, as we saw, they built a new mosque in their mountain stronghold at Tinmal. As rulers of Marrakesh they constructed a new mosque in the old town. The ruins of the mosque at Rabat show the scale of Almohad architectural ambitions, but perhaps the finest surviving example of their work can be seen in Seville, the capital of their Andalusi domains. Apart from some work in the courtyard, the mosque has been replaced by the late Gothic cathedral, but the minaret, now a bell-tower called the Giralda, still remains in all its glory as the symbol of the city.

We have already seen that the caliph Abū Ya'qūb Yūsuf was an eager collector of books. He was also a committed supporter of writers and thinkers and can perhaps be numbered with the Abbasid Ma'mūn and the Umayyad of Córdoba Hakam II among caliphs who were genuine intellectuals. There was an established tradition of philosophical thought and discussion in Andalusi cultural life, but there were also strong currents, notably among the conservative legal scholars, that were fiercely opposed to questioning or even discussing anything which might touch on issues of faith. It was caliphal patronage which enabled the flame of enquiry to burn brightly in the last quarter of the twelfth century.

Yūsuf's main intellectual adviser was the writer and philosopher Abū Bakr b. Tufayl. Ibn Tufayl was born in Guadix, north-east of Granada, and first attracted attention as a physician. In 1154 he secured an appointment as secretary to the governor of Tangier, who was a member of the ruling dynasty. From there he graduated to becoming Yūsuf's doctor and adviser until his death in Marrakesh. Ibn Tufayl is best remembered for his philosophical story *Hayy b. Yaqzān*, about a young man growing up alone on a desert island and finding wisdom for himself, a book that has been widely translated and commented on and was one of the earliest classical Arabic texts to be translated into English, by Edward Pococke at Oxford in 1671.

Ibn Rushd, known in the western tradition as Averroes, was born in 1126. He came from an old family of religious scholars and jurists from Córdoba and was introduced as a young man to the caliph by Ibn Tufayl. When he first met Abū Ya'qub he was given a sort of interview in which the caliph asked such questions as whether the sky has existed throughout all eternity of whether it had a beginning. Encouraged by Ibn Tufayl, Ibn Rushd went on to display his immense philosophical and religious learning. The caliph was impressed and encouraged the young scholar to comment on and explain the texts of Aristotle, which he himself had difficulty in understanding. He also appointed him *qāḍī* of Seville and later Córdoba, offices which, Ibn Rushd complained, kept him away from his books. The death of Abū Ya'qub and the accession of Mansūr in 1184 led to a change of atmosphere at court. The new caliph's main concern was the *jihād* against the Christians and later in his reign he responded to demands in conservative circles that Ibn Rushd's kind of philosophical speculation should be forbidden. Ibn Rushd was summoned to a sort of inquisition before the chief jurists of Córdoba and his work was condemned and his books ordered to be burned, though he himself was unharmed and simply exiled to the little town of Lucena. In the end he retired to Marrakesh where he was free to return to his writing and where he died in 1198.

Ibn Rushd is an important figure in his own right because of the advances he made in the understanding of and commenting on Aristotle; but his influence was mainly felt in western Europe, while as a thinker he was largely neglected in Andalus where the caliphal patronage of intellectual life died in the chaotic circumstances of the thirteenth century. Even before his death, his works were being translated into Latin, usually at the city of Toledo, by now of course under Christian rule, where scholars from northern Europe came down to take advantage of the new Arabic learning. The writings of Ibn Rushd also had a major impact on the teaching of philosophy and logic in the newly developing universities of Paris, Oxford and Salamanca. Such characteristically 'Averroist' ideas as the eternal existence of the world and the possibility of attaining true happiness in this world, by philosophical contemplation of course, led to Averroism being linked to atheism and as such condemned by the Church for much the same reasons as it was attacked by rigorist Muslims. On the other hand, in Dante's *Divine Comedy* he, like other non-Christian sages, escapes the Inferno and spends his eternity in Limbo.

The detailed philosophical arguments need not concern us here. The flow of ideas from classical Greek to Arabic in Abbasid Baghdad in the ninth century, and their flourishing in Almohad Andalus in the twelfth, brought them to the attention of western scholars long before translations directly from the Greek were available in the fifteenth century. In terms of philosophy, medicine and science, Averroism had a profound influence on the intellectual history of Christendom. This kind of intellectual enquiry, if not always initiated by the caliphs themselves, was at least given crucial support by men like the Abbasids Mansūr and Ma'mūn and the Almohad Abū Ya'qūb Yūsuf.

We should remember the great caliphs of the Almohad dynasty for all sorts of reasons, and the encouragement of enlightened learning and the defence of philosophers and others against their enemies are not the least of these.

CHAPTER 10

The Caliphate under the Mamluks and Ottomans

The collapse of the Almohad caliphate in the thirteenth century spelt the end of attempts to build a caliphate which would embrace the whole of the Muslim west. True, there were dynasties like the Hafsids of Tunisia (1229–1534), who appropriated the title, but their power was too local to enable them to present themselves as real caliphs beyond the borders of their own statelets. In the east, however, the idea of the caliphate was too entrenched and its history too venerable for it to disappear completely. Baghdad may have fallen and the Abbasid caliph may have died a horrible death, but attempts were still made to revive or at least continue the office in one form or another.

Abbasid Caliphs, Courtiers of the Mamluks

The tragic death of the last Abbasid caliph of Baghdad at the hand of the Mongols and the devastation of his capital city in 1258 marked the abrupt end of the caliphate which had begun more than 600 years previously with the oath of allegiance to Abū Bakr in 632, and which had continued, with ups and downs, ever since. Never again would a caliph lead the

Muslims in prayer, defend them against the unbelievers or safeguard their *hajj*. Never again would the palace of the caliph be a centre of power, wealth and culture.

But the idea of caliphate never completely died. Four years after the catastrophe, a distant cousin of the last caliph of Baghdad made his way, aided by the Bedouin tribes of the Syrian desert, to Cairo where he made contact with the Mamluk sultan Baybars. Baybars was a formidable figure both militarily and politically, and the Mamluks (slave soldiers) who formed his army were a strong military force, the only army, in fact, which was capable of resisting the Mongols in open battle. In 1260, at the Battle of Ayn Jalut in Palestine, they had put an end to Mongol ambitions to invade Egypt. The Mamluks set up a quasi-dynastic rule in Egypt and Syria which was to last until the Ottoman conquest of 1517 and was the strongest and most stable state in the Islamic world in this period. However, in spite of his powerful position, Baybars was also vulnerable and lacking in a convincing claim to the sultanate. The Mamluks, after all, by origin were no more than Turkish slaves, newly imported from the steppes of what is now southern Russia. They had no ancient status in the Muslim world, no legitimating discourse to convince Muslims of their right to lead. Furthermore, Baybars himself had only become ruler after the murder of his Mamluk predecessor Qutuz.

The arrival of the fugitive Abbasid was therefore an opportunity not to be missed. He was appointed caliph in 1262, Baybars and his courtiers taking a *bay'a* to him, and was given the caliphal title of Hākim. He in turn preached a sermon praising the sultan and exhorting Muslims to obey him and support him in the Holy War against both Crusaders and Mongols. Hākim on the Nile enjoyed very little of the pomp his predecessors had had on the Tigris. He had no court of his own, no vizier, no military guard, just a tower in the citadel to live in and tutors to improve his religious education. He became in effect a part of the Mamluk sultan's entourage, enjoying some respect but no real power.

Hākim reigned (but did not rule) for forty years until his death in 1301, long after Baybars and his immediate successors had perished. He was succeeded by a continuous line of some seventeen Abbasid caliphs until the last one was deported to Istanbul in 1517 at the time of the Ottoman conquest.

Clearly successive Mamluk sultans felt that to have an Abbasid caliph at court was useful, but what exactly did this functionary do? His main purpose was to legitimize the accession of a new sultan. The Mamluk sultanate was never formally hereditary (unlike, of course, the Abbasid caliphate) and frequently passed from one ruler to another through violence and assassination. The caliph's function was basically to approve a usurper. In most cases the new ruler took a *bay'a* to the caliph, though sometimes, especially in the fifteenth century, it seems to have been the caliph who took a *bay'a* to the sultan, a curious reversal of the traditional protocol. The caliph's other function was to impress other Muslim leaders, as when Berke, khan of the Golden Horde (the Mongol rulers of Russia) and a new convert to Islam, sent a delegation to the court at Cairo in 1257. The caliph delivered a *khutba* in Berke's name and a diploma of investiture was passed to his ambassadors.

Only on one occasion did a caliph actually acquire a political role, and that was when, in 1412, a group of Mamluk emirs bidding for power set up the Abbasid caliph Musta'īn as sultan. Needless to say, when the caliph attempted to wield power himself, his backers hastily sent him packing back to his luxurious quarters in the citadel.

The caliph's role was significant, but did not amount to very much. He was God's representative on earth and divinely appointed ruler, and he alone could bring legitimacy to a sultan. However, as a fifteenth-century commentator, Khalīl al-Zāhiri, describes, his duties while in office were otherwise rather mundane:

> His appointment is to concern himself with scholarship and to have a library. If the sultan travels on some business, he is to accompany him for the benefit of the Muslims [presumably to impress them with the sultan's legitimacy as ruler]. He has numerous sources of revenue for his expenses and fine dwellings.

The conquest of Baghdad and the death of the last Abbasid caliph in 1258 also left the field open for other claimants, or rather for other Muslim rulers to use the title. The great historian and thinker Ibn Khaldūn (d. 1406) writes that the caliph is much more than a king, whose only concern is with the well-being of men on earth, whereas the caliph is divinely appointed and guides according to *sharī'a*. Ibn Khaldūn also argues that the caliph should come from Quraysh because they were the most respected and influential tribe in Arabia at the time of the Prophet. He traces what he sees as the changing nature of the caliphate. Under the Orthodox caliphs the caliphate was a religious institution for the guiding of the faithful and the observance of religious laws. Under the Umayyads it became a despotic monarchy which ruled by military might. Soon after the death of Hārūn al-Rashīd it declined in power until it was little more than an empty title and the office had effectively ceased to exist.[1] Ibn Khaldūn's views probably represent those of many Muslims in the later Middle Ages for whom the great days of the caliphate were firmly in the past and the puppets in Cairo and the other pretenders had no real right to the title.

At that time a number of monarchs used the title more or less convincingly. Shah Rukh (1409–47), grandson of Tamerlane and ruler of much of Iran, claimed the title and was addressed by other rulers who sought his favour as caliph and 'the shadow of God on earth'. Yet when he wrote to a Mamluk and an Ottoman ruler demanding that they should accept investiture from him as caliph and strike coins in his name, his pretensions were unceremoniously rejected. After the disappearance of the Almohad caliphate, the Hafsid rulers of Tunisia used the title, as did the Turkman rulers of eastern Anatolia in the fifteenth century and the Shaybani Uzbeg rulers of Bukhara in the sixteenth.

The Ottoman Caliphate

The claims of these rulers to the title of caliph were never widely acknowledged and were in any case much less important to them than the title of sultan or khan. Only the Ottoman dynasty attempted to make their caliphate a reality, though they never used the other ancient title of Commander of the

Faithful. The Ottomans were a Turkish family who had risen to power in north-west Anatolia in the fourteenth century, leading Muslims against the enfeebled Byzantine Empire. From 1354 onwards they also began the conquest of south-east Europe and in 1453 they seized Constantinople, a project which had first been attempted by the Umayyad caliphs seven centuries before. By the end of the fifteenth century they were the most powerful Muslim rulers in the Middle East and when they conquered Egypt from the Mamluks in 1517 their pre-eminence was unchallenged. It is not clear how the Ottoman sultans came to claim the caliphal title, although the title of sultan was always the most important to them. Murad I (1360–89) seems to have been the first of his dynasty to assume the title after he took Edirne and Plovdiv from the Byzantines in around 1362, when he wrote to lesser emirs in more eastern parts of Turkey that God had chosen him to assume the dignity of the caliphate. He called God to witness that 'from the date of his coming to the throne, he had not taken a moment's rest but had devoted himself day and night to the waging of war and *jihād* and always had his armour on to serve the well-being of the Muslims'.[2] Some of his successors used the title, though not the great Mehmet II, whose conquest of Constantinople in 1453 might have been thought to give him an excellent claim.

In 1517 Selīm the Grim (1512–20) seized Cairo, putting an end to the Mamluk sultanate and taking possession of the puppet caliph Mutawwakil III along with what was claimed to be the regalia of the caliphate: the mantle of the Prophet, his staff and his seal. A legend, which seems to have been elaborated at the end of the eighteenth century, recounts that the last Abbasid transferred the caliphate to the Ottoman sultan, but this is no more than a piece of fiction concocted to justify the Ottomans' renewed interest in the caliphal title at that time. A contemporary notes that 'the caliph, Commander of the Faithful Mutawwakil, has been sent by sea to Istanbul' and three years later he is said to still be living in the capital. After the accession of Sulayman the Magnificent in 1520, Mutawwakil was allowed to return to Egypt where he died in 1543, the last and final claimant of a line which stretched back to Saffah in 750.

Selīm assumed not the title of caliph but that of *Khādim al-haramayn al-sharīfayn* (Servant of the Two Noble Sanctuaries). Since the end of the Abbasid caliphate in 1258, a number of Muslim monarchs had competed for the right to guard Mecca and Medina, which was understood to include the right to have one's name mentioned at the *khutba* in Mecca, and hence to have one's status confirmed in front of the pilgrims from all over the Muslim world at the time of the *hajj*. Powerful rulers like Timur's grandson Shah Rukh had coveted the honour, but the simple fact was that whoever ruled Egypt could maintain his right to the title because the Holy Cities were dependent on Egypt for the grain which kept their people alive. In the late fifteenth century an added urgency was given to this office by the appearance for the first time of Portuguese warships in the Red Sea and the Gulf. Muslims were right to fear that these new infidel invaders would attack Mecca. It was no empty honour that Selīm assumed.

From Selīm's time until the First World War, it was the Ottomans who protected the great *hajj* caravans setting out from Damascus and Cairo and the Ottomans who provided the *kiswa* each year. This probably did more than anything else to encourage Muslims, wherever they came from, to regard the Ottomans as leaders of the Muslim world. Despite this, Selīm never seems to have called himself caliph or to have been mentioned as such on coins or in documents; he was always known as sultan. By the reign of Sulayman the Magnificent (1520–56), it was generally accepted that the Ottomans were caliphs as well as sultans. The title of caliph was only really used in relations with other Muslim powers, like the rulers of Morocco, who were not under the direct authority of the Ottomans. The Saʿdi rulers of Morocco (1510–1668) accepted the status of the Ottomans as the protectors of Islam but only as representatives of the true caliphs, who had to be members of the tribe of Quraysh, and they themselves claimed to be descendants of Alī and Fātima. Other Muslim potentates also appropriated the title, as for instance the Mogul emperor Akbar (1556–1605) in distant Delhi, but it was never more than a vague honorific.

In around 1553 the Ottoman grand vizier Lutfi Pasha wrote a pamphlet in which he tackled the issue of the sultan's right to be caliph. He does this, he explains, in response to scholars who have maintained that only a member of Quraysh can be caliph. His argument is that a caliph is absolutely necessary, based on the ancient and widely known Tradition which states that if there is no acknowledged caliph 'the condition of the Muslims is a matter of uncertainty when they die without having known the imam [caliph] of their time and their death is the death of the Jāhiliyya [that is, Muslims would die like those who had not known the Prophet and would therefore go to hell]'. He then cites numerous authorities, including the great historian Tabarī, to the effect that the title of sultan belongs to a ruler who holds the power, while the imam is 'the one who maintains the Faith and governs the kingdoms of Islam with equity'. The caliph is 'he who commands the good and prohibits the evil [that is, maintains the *sharī'a*]'. If the conditions mentioned above, that is conquest, power of compulsion, maintenance of the faith with justice, commanding the good and forbidding the evil, are combined in one person then he is a sultan who can justly claim the titles of imam, caliph, *wālī* and emir without contradiction. He points out: 'Our *ulama* have said that a man becomes sultan by two things: the first by the swearing of allegiance to him and the second is that he can effectively execute his decisions', and then adds that not one of the legal authorities he has consulted has ruled or asserted that the caliph 'should be of Quraysh, nor of Hashimi descent, nor appointed by the Abbasid or any other person'. For him, the statement that the imam should be of Qurashi origin applies to the beginnings of the caliphate, when the Quraysh asserted their rights over the *ansār* of Medina, and was not relevant in the present day.

Lutfi's fundamental argument is that the caliphate belongs to the one who effectively leads and protects the Muslim people. The qualifications for the office are power and competence. Inheritance or kinship have no part in this. This is an argument which, in a sense, goes back to the Zaydi idea that the caliphate belongs to the man who takes action and seizes power in the name of the Family of the Prophet, except that the Zaydis insist on the Qurashi descent of the caliph. There are also echoes here of the discussions of

Juwaynī and Ghazālī in the eleventh century, for whom power was the main qualification for the office of caliph. In Ottoman times it seems to have been generally accepted that the power and authority of the Ottoman sultan justified his taking of the title of caliph, but in doing so the force of the title was largely lost, subsumed in the wider rhetoric of Ottoman power. There was no authority that the sultan gained as caliph which he did not already have as sultan and the office therefore added little to his standing.

In the eighteenth century, with the Muslim world in general and the Ottoman Empire in particular increasingly threatened by European powers, there was a renewed interest in the idea of the caliphate. The first example of this seems to have been in the Treaty of Kucuk Kaynarca of 1774, in which the Ottoman sultan Abd al-Hamīd I (1774–89) was obliged, to all intents and purposes, to cede the sovereignty of the largely Muslim Crimea to Catherine the Great of Russia, and where the sultan was described as 'the imam of the believers and the caliph of all those who profess the unity of God [that is, Muslims]'. This seems to be a face-saving formula to allow him to claim to be the spiritual leader of the Muslims of Crimea and to avoid the shame of allowing Muslims to be ruled by infidels. After this, the idea of the caliphate was increasingly developed by the Ottomans to allow them to claim a spiritual leadership of Muslims beyond their political borders. This introduced a distinction between the political and military leadership (the sultanate) and the spiritual leadership (the caliphate), which was essentially new to Muslim political thought but served useful purposes in the diplomacy of the time.

Abd al-Hamīd II, Sultan and Caliph

The role of the sultan as caliph was pursued with more consistency and determination by Sultan Abd al-Hamīd II (1876–1909). Abd al-Hamīd came to the throne on the deposition of his brother. He was immediately given the oath of allegiance as sultan and caliph. Apart from the *bay'a*, he based his claim to the caliphate on three well-established principles. The first of these was God's will; the second was hereditary succession as his ancestors were Great Caliphs; and the third was the possession of real political power to defend the Muslims. The only one of the traditional attributes of caliphate he could not claim was, of course, membership of Quraysh, but, as we have seen, this had not prevented earlier Ottomans from claiming the office.[3]

On his accession Abd al-Hamīd was obliged to sign a constitution modelled on western European examples – the first such constitution in the Islamic world. As compensation, perhaps, for his loss of temporal power, his role as caliph was developed. In Article 3 of the constitution it is stated that 'The August Ottoman Sultanate, the office of the supreme Islamic Caliphate, must devolve upon the oldest of the members of the [Ottoman family]', a clear enunciation of hereditary succession. Article 4 states that 'the Sultan, in his capacity as Caliph, is the protector of the Muslim religion'. The constitution was soon suspended and did not come into force until 1909, but Abd al-Hamīd clung to and developed the idea that the Ottoman caliph was the leader of all Muslims, not just those under Ottoman rule.

The personality of the sultan-caliph was one of apparent contradictions. For many outside the Ottoman Empire, in western Europe and Russia, he was 'Abdul the Damned', a devious and bloodthirsty tyrant who mistreated and massacred his Christian subjects and about whom nothing good could be said. He was certainly an autocrat, secretive and deeply suspicious by nature. He believed strongly that it was his responsibility, laid on him by God, to rule and protect the Muslim people, both inside and beyond the borders of the Ottoman Empire. He regarded the constitutionalist movement, led by the westernizing reformer Midhat Pasha, as an attack on the divinely sanctioned political order which would undermine the Muslim world, and his opponents were sent away to exile and death. 'The padishah' (sultan-caliph), he wrote, is

> accountable only to God and history . . . If we want to rejuvenate, find our previous force and reach our old greatness, we ought to remember the fountainhead of our strength. What is beneficial to us is not to imitate the so-called European civilization but to return to the *shari'a*, the source of our strength . . . Almighty God, I can only be Your slave and ask only Your help. Lead us on the right path.[4]

There was no doubt that he was a pious and believing Muslim and these sentiments would be certainly be shared by many contemporary Islamists. At the same time he was keenly interested in the technologies of modernity, which he saw as essential to the survival of the Ottoman state. He encouraged the study of western military technologies, bringing the celebrated Colmar von der Goltz and other German officers to train his armed forces, and the building of railways. Culturally too he was open-minded: he enjoyed western music, especially Italian opera, and his private library at the Yildiz Palace consisted of some 100,000 volumes, not only rare Arabic and Persian manuscripts but western works on philosophy and science. In this he was following the example of the great bibliophile caliphs of the past, the Abbasid Ma'mūn in Baghdad and the Umayyad Hakam II in Córdoba. He ordered his government to participate in the 1893 Chicago World's Fair, where there was a Turkish village with a mosque and a covered bazaar in which products of the Ottoman sultanate were sold. He encouraged the participation of his Christian subjects in the economic and social life of the empire, noting that Muslims and Christians worshipped the same God, but also that some Christians had been led astray by the fanaticism of their priests to seek outside help against his lawful government.

One of the most celebrated examples of his adoption of modern technologies to fulfil the ancient responsibilities of the caliphate was the construction of the Hijaz railway from Damascus to Medina, completed in 1900. This enabled the pilgrims from Ottoman lands to make the *hajj* in the (comparative) comfort of the train as opposed to going on foot or on camels. It also alienated many of the Bedouin who had been used to the protection money that the pilgrims paid them, and they were more than happy to cooperate with the British mission led by T. E. Lawrence in his attempts to destroy the track during the First World War. In doing this Abd al-Hamīd was facilitating the *hajj*, just as Hārūn al-Rashīd and the Abbasids had done 1,100 years before with the construction of the Darb Zubayda.

The reign of the new sultan-caliph began with a disastrous war against the Russians in 1877–8, which led to the loss of Bulgaria and other areas of the Balkans. Many in the Muslim world feared that the Ottoman Empire would completely disintegrate, but perhaps paradoxically this defeat encouraged the idea of reviving the concept of the caliphate as a way of defending Muslims against outside attack.

This was a period when many areas of the Muslim world beyond the frontiers of the Ottoman Empire were coming under increasing pressure from outside powers who sought to take over and colonize them. One of the most important of these areas was Central Asia, where Russian advances were swallowing up the independent Khanates of Khiva, Bukhara and Kokand, while the Chinese were advancing on Kashgar from the east. All these regions were Muslim and Turkish-speaking and the threatened rulers sought the support of the Ottoman caliph in resisting the invaders. Equally dangerous as far as many Muslims were concerned was the British military occupation of Egypt in 1882. Although Egypt had not been part of the Ottoman Empire since Napoleon's invasion of 1798, many Muslims there and elsewhere hoped that the caliph would be able to take action. Even in the distant Comoro Islands, between Mozambique and Madagascar, the Muslim inhabitants, threatened by French occupation, appealed for Ottoman support. But the sultan-caliph was no political adventurer: he would offer moral support and refuge in Istanbul, but his military forces remained firmly inside the Ottoman frontiers.

His role as leader of all Muslims was acknowledged in a number of the treaties made with foreign powers during the slow disintegration of the Ottoman Empire in the late nineteenth and early twentieth centuries. When the Austro-Hungarian Empire annexed Bosnia in 1908, the name of Abd al-Hamīd as sultan-caliph continued to be mentioned in Muslim prayers, and after the Italian conquest of Libya, in 1912, the *qāḍī* of Tripoli continued to be appointed from Istanbul. Abd al-Hamīd also tried to use his prestige as caliph as a way to gain the loyalty of the Arab inhabitants of the sultanate, increasingly attracted by the ideas of Arab nationalism.

Another area in which the later Ottomans used and developed the idea of caliphate was their veneration and display of the holy relics. The sultans established a permanent collection of the relics of the Prophet and many of the early heroes of Islam in the Topkapi Saray in Istanbul. They are housed in a series of four smallish rooms, exquisitely decorated with sixteenth-century Iznik tiles. Originally these rooms were the sleeping quarters of the sultans themselves, but from the seventeenth century they moved their quarters to the nearby harem and the rooms seem to have been kept solely as a repository for the relics, which remain there to this day. It is clearly impossible to date these objects or to have any scientific proof that any of them are what they claim to be. We can, however, be certain that some of them, in particular the *burda* (mantle of the Prophet) the most precious and venerated, were already in the Topkapi collection by the sixteenth century. The relics were a visible and tangible sign of the Ottomans' claims to be both the successors of the early caliphs and guardians of the Holy Cities.

A roughly woven garment, black on the outside and white on the inside, the *burda* is kept wrapped in precious fabrics in a golden chest so that only a small portion of it can be seen. It is mentioned in historical sources of the Abbasid period, most notably in the account of the death of Caliph Amīn in 815 where, along with the *qadīb* or sceptre and the Prophet's ring (*hātim*), it is described as 'being the caliphate'.

It is unclear what relationship, if any, there is between the mantle mentioned in the Abbasid sources and the one preserved in Istanbul. According to the traditional story, the Istanbul garment was worn by Muhammad and presented to the poet Ka'b b. Zuhayr, previously a fierce opponent of the Prophet, when he repented and asked for his forgiveness. The poet in return composed a poem in praise of the Prophet and the mantle. Later Caliph Mu'āwiya bought it from Ka'b's heirs and, it is said, it was preserved by all later caliphs. According to one story the *burda* was burned by Hulegu following the sack of Baghdad in 1258 and the death of the last Abbasid caliph of the city, but others said that survivors of the massacre took it to Cairo whence it was removed to Istanbul at the time of the Ottoman conquest in 1517. It was certainly in the Ottoman relic collection by the reign of Sultan Murad II (1574–95) who had a golden case made for it. It was thought to have a talismanic importance and sultans took it on campaign. When Mehmet III (1595–1603) led his armies on campaign to Eger in Hungary, he took the mantle with him. At one point in the battle it looked as if his army was about to be defeated, but one of his courtiers told the monarch, 'My sultan! As an Ottoman sultan who is caliph on our Prophet's path, it would be appropriate for you to put on the Holy Mantle and pray to God.' The sultan took his advice, donned the mantle and led his soldiers to victory, and an elegant miniature illustrates the sacred garment being carried on the head of a courtier as the sultan looks on and the cannon thunder against the enemy. It is interesting in this account to see the identification of the possession of the mantle with the caliphal office, just as it was in the Abbasid period.

The seal of the Prophet was among the relics kept by the Abbasid caliphs. According to a well-known story, the original was lost in a well by the third caliph, Uthmān, and it is generally agreed that the one displayed Istanbul was a replacement made after that.

Another key exhibit to be found at Topkapi is the Qur'ān of Uthmān. Like the one in Tashkent it is said to have been the very volume he was reading when he was killed and his bloodstains are pointed out. Obviously there is no certainty that it is any such thing but, from the pictures at least, it is clearly a magnificent and very ancient volume.

Among the other relics of the Prophet is his banner, which was paraded in front of the army when military expeditions set out; in 1826 it was brought out and hung on the *minbar* of the mosque of Sultanahmet in Istanbul to serve as a rallying point for the people against the rebellious janissaries. Then there is the Prophet's staff, which is recorded from Abbasid times, though it is generally accepted that the staff in the Topkapi collection was made from a tree which grew near the Prophet's tomb.

There are numerous other relics of the Prophet which seem never to have been part of the caliphal insignia – hairs from his beard, his bow and his footprint, as well as the blouse and veil of his daughter Fātima and the shirt of his martyred grandson Husayn. Also to be found in the Topkapi collection are the cooking bowl of Abraham, the turban of Joseph and the arm of John the Baptist. Many of these items were kept in the Kaʿba in Mecca or the Mosque of the Prophet in Medina until the First World War, when the Holy Cities became threatened by the Arab revolt and British occupation. In 1918 they were put on a train by the orders of the Ottoman governor of Medina, Fakhr al-Dīn Pasha, and taken to Istanbul, where they still remain.

The apotropaic properties of the *burda* and the other relics were very much in evidence at the funeral ceremony for Abd al-Hamīd II, who died in 1918 after thirty-four years as sultan-caliph and nine more as deposed sovereign. His obsequies were later described by one Ahmet Rafik Bey, who attended the ceremony, in an account full of atmosphere and melancholy. We are told that the sultan's body was brought to the apartments of the Holy Mantle where it was washed and laid on a winding sheet in the coffin.

Sultan Abdulhamid had not lost consciousness until the last moment of his life. He requested that a testament prayer be put on his chest and a handkerchief rubbed against the Holy Mantle, as well as a piece of the black Kaʿba cover, he used to cover his face. His request was carried out to the letter. It was a truly heartrending sight: Sultan Abdulhamid lying inside the coffin covered with winding sheets, the testament prayer on his naked chest, the black Kaʿba cover on his face, his white beard, with his

eyes forever closed . . . Sultan Abdulhamid was humbly
going to God, leaving his sins behind.

As the coffin was taken away a respectful crowd gathered
round:

Suddenly, the door to the Apartments of the Holy Mantle
opened. All eyes turned to the door. It was crowded on
both sides. Hearts throbbing, everyone sought a view of the
coffin. Carried by hand and adorned with a diamond belt,
silver-embroidered Ka'ba covers, red satin, and a red fez, it
finally appeared, stately and majestic . . . The head preacher
of the Hamidiye Mosque, dressed in a green, silver-
embroidered robe with an imperial monogram on his chest,
stepped forward and stood on the stone. He looked around
and asked:

'How did you know the deceased to be?'

A sad cry echoed among the cypress trees:

'We knew him to be good.'

It was perhaps fitting that the body of the last great caliph
should be washed and laid to rest surrounded by the relics
which had been preserved, according to widely believed traditions, by his illustrious predecessors since the very beginnings of Islam.[5]

The Ottoman Caliphate in the Wider World

The sultan's policy of reviving the idea of a pan-Islamic
caliphate would not have made much impact if it had not had

a wider resonance in the Muslim world. This was particularly true in British-ruled India. There Muslims saw the Ottoman Empire, with which, traditionally, they had had very little contact, as the one major Muslim power which had maintained its independence, and many embraced the idea of the caliphate as a challenge to the discourse of imperial rule and western supremacy.

Support for the Ottomans' right to the caliphate came from some unexpected quarters. In the late 1870s there was a fierce debate in Britain about the validity of the Ottoman claims. This was largely in response to the obvious enthusiasm in India to the idea of caliphate. In 1877 two retired Indian political officers, Sir George Campbell, ex-governor of Bengal, and George Birdwood, argued that the Ottoman claim was fraudulent, and Birdwood went on to say that it would be to the British advantage to encourage looking to the Sharif of Mecca (the local ruler of the Holy City who was also a descendant of Alī and Fātima) as caliph for 'he would be as completely in our power as the Suez Canal'. This provoked a vigorous response from the pro-Ottoman writer James Redhouse (1811–92). Redhouse had enjoyed a career which was, to say the least, unusual. As a young orphan from London, he had taken service as a cabin boy on a British ship. When the ship berthed in Istanbul in 1826, he absconded and used his education in mathematics and science to make a career in the service of the Ottomans, then battling with the insurgent Greeks and the Egyptian Muhammad Alī. Redhouse became a passionate Turkophile and wrote, among other things, the most scholarly and complete dictionary of Ottoman Turkish ever compiled. He now entered the fray and produced a pamphlet entitled 'A Vindication of the Ottoman Sultan's Title of "Caliph"', in which he dismissed challenges to the Ottoman title as 'erroneous, futile and impolitic', firstly because the sultan's claim to the title was ancient and accepted by 'the whole orthodox world of Islam' and then because the claim that the caliph should be of Qurashi descent, always a difficulty for the Ottomans, had no Prophetic support. In this he was joined by George Badger (1815–88), part missionary, part historian of the Eastern Churches and part Arabic lexicographer, who produced a detailed defence of Ottoman claims, concluding with the clear assertion that the 'the Ottoman Sultan is the legitimate successor to Muhammad while the Sharif of Mecca was a man of no standing, an official who could be dismissed at any time by the Ottoman government'. None of the participants in this debate represented British government policy, but in general the British were content to accept Ottoman claims.

The same period also saw the beginnings of a movement in the Arab provinces of the Ottoman Empire, especially in Syria, to separate the caliphate from the Ottoman sultanate and set up an independent Arab caliphate. The catalyst for this movement was the defeat of the Ottoman armies by the Russians in 1877–8, which seemed to be the prelude to the complete collapse of the empire. Arab notables in both Syria and the Hijaz floated the idea of an Arab caliphate, largely to resist the prospect of a European takeover. The Syrian Arabs even found a possible candidate in the person of Abd al-Qādir al-Jazā'iri, a charismatic Algerian Muslim who had been exiled to Damascus after his vigorous resistance to the French occupation of his country. In the end the movement came to nothing and Ottoman control was restored, but it shows that the idea of a caliphate was still a source of political inspiration to those Muslims who wanted change and sought to revive the ancient power and glory of the Islamic *umma*.

The idea of the caliphate as justification for Arab independence from the Ottoman Empire was kept alive in British political debate by the remarkable figure of Wilfrid Scawen Blunt (1840–1922). Blunt was an eccentric upper-class writer who was at one and the same time a landowner connected with many important people in the political establishment of the late Victorian era and a rebel who set out to confront and oppose British imperialism. His numerous love affairs and his adventurous travels in the Arabian desert both marked him out as a man of romantic and alternative tastes. He began his career in the diplomatic service but resigned in 1868, and in 1877–8 he visited the Arab nomads of the Syrian desert. This and subsequent travels in Arabia impressed him deeply and he became convinced that Turkish rule should be ended and that the Arabs, by whom he basically meant the Bedouin of the Syrian and Arabian deserts, should be allowed to rule themselves under British protection. He turned to the idea of the caliphate, arguing that the caliphate of the Ottomans was essentially illegitimate and rested only on their political and military power rather than any legal rights. He made contact with several Arab Muslim leaders, including the respected Muhammad Abduh (1849–1905), a noted advocate of reform at the Azhar in Cairo and in wider Islamic society. He found Abduh was arguing that the caliphate should be revived as a religious institution, and explained:

On the question of the caliphate he [Abduh] looked at that
time to its reconstruction on a more spiritual basis. He
explained to me how a more legitimate exercise of its
authority might be made to give a new impulse to
intellectual progress and how little those who for centuries
had held the title [that is, the Ottomans] had deserved the
spiritual headship of the believers.[6]

The two men seem to have shared a common ideal of a revived
Arab caliphate leading to a new era of greatness for the Muslim
peoples. Yet the reality was, as Abduh acknowledged, that the
Ottomans were 'still the most powerful of the Muhammedan
princes and able to do most for the general advantage, but
unless they could be induced to take their position more seriously, a new Emir al-Mu'minin might legitimately be looked
for'. Blunt may have found a kindred spirit in Abduh, but, for
all his contacts and access, he failed to convince anyone of
importance in the British government to follow his ideas, and
as Abd al-Hamīd's grip on the Arab provinces of the empire
tightened in the 1880s and 1890s such ideas seemed fanciful
and far-fetched.

Abd al-Hamīd had attempted to make his claim to the
caliphate a basis for strengthening the Ottoman position, not
least against his dissatisfied subjects in Istanbul. With the
deposition of the sultan and the revival of the constitution in
1909, this came to seem increasingly irrelevant. The fiercely
nationalist Young Turks who took control were intent on
creating a Turkish rather than a Muslim empire and, while a
strong sultanate was a possible way of doing this, there was
no real role in this scenario for a caliph. The First World War

led to a certain renewal of interest in the idea because some hoped that the appeal of the sultan as caliph would win over Arab opinion and, an even bigger prize, induce Indian Muslims to rise against their British rulers in the name of the caliph. These hopes proved unrealistic and the Ottoman claims aroused little enthusiasm in the subcontinent.

The End of the Ottoman Caliphate

The end of the war saw the final crisis of the Ottoman sultanate-caliphate. Mehmet V died in July 1918 and it fell to his successor, Mehmet VI, to negotiate an armistice with the British and French. A humiliating surrender was signed at Mudros on 30 October, less than two weeks before the 11 November armistice on the western front. The sultan seems to have believed that by appeasing the western powers he could keep his throne and what was left of the Ottoman Empire. To do so he was prepared to sign the Treaty of Sèvres in August 1920, which left only a rump of the Ottoman state in Anatolia. He also made his opposition to the nationalists gathered in Ankara obvious and, in a completely futile gesture, sentenced the nationalist leader Mustafa Kemal to death (a sentence he was, of course, unable to carry out). It was only a residual reverence for the sultan as the embodiment of the ancient greatness of the empire which allowed him to remain as ruler for the next two years. By 1922 the nationalists were triumphant; the Greeks had been driven out of Turkey and Mustafa Kemal was determined to abolish the sultanate and set up a presidential Turkish republic. On 1 November 1922 the Turkish Grand National Assembly voted to separate the caliphate from the sultanate and abolish the latter. The caliphate was to remain in the Ottoman family, but the state would decide which member of the family should hold the office. The sultan Mehmet VI was deposed and his cousin Abd al-Majīd II appointed as caliph.

The office still enjoyed some support in the new Turkey among conservatives who hoped to revive its ancient grandeur and among some nationalists who were reluctant to lose Turkey's role as the leader of the Muslim world. The new (and last) caliph tried to rally these forces, but Mustafa Kemal was adamant in his opposition. On 24 March 1924 the office of caliph was abolished and a republic was declared with Mustafa Kemal as its first president. It was the end of an ancient tradition and never again has a claimant to the caliphate enjoyed any widespread and general acceptance in the Muslim world.

CHAPTER 11

The Twentieth Century and Beyond

The Ottoman caliphate disappeared in 1924, more with a whimper than a bang. But despite this humiliating end, the abolition of the caliphate was greeted with dismay in Muslim lands far beyond the borders of the Ottoman world. The 1920s saw the high-water mark of European imperialism in the Middle East, with the division of the Ottoman territories into Iraq, Syria, Lebanon and Palestine and the establishment of British and French mandates. Egypt was under British control, Libya under Italian rule, while Tunisia, Algeria and Morocco were firmly governed by the French. Many Muslims felt humiliated by these arrangements and some thought that the revival of the caliphate might provide a ray of hope in this otherwise dismal and depressing political landscape.

There was much less agreement about what sort of caliphate this should be and who should be the new caliph. A swift response came from the sheikhs of the Azhar in Cairo, long the established intellectual leaders of the Sunni world. After a meeting on 25 March 1924, they issued a notice reaffirming the traditional view that the caliphs were the representative of the Prophet in the protection of the faith and the implementation of its laws. They rejected the separation of the political and religious powers of the office implied by the 1922 abolition of the sultanate and asserted that Abd al-Majīd was not a true caliph since he had accepted this. Now the *umma* should set about finding a new holder for the office.

Others argued that the caliphate was a perversion of Islam, a calamity which had no basis in the Qur'ān, and that, far from being essential to the faith, it was in fact an impediment which confused politics with religion in an unhelpful way. Thus, in his book *Islam and the Fundamentals of Ruling*, Alī Abd al-Raziq (1887–1966), an Oxford-educated Egyptian intellectual, argued for a separation of religion and government along the models found in the west. While his views were supported by other secularist intellectuals, like Taha Husayn in Egypt, they were roundly denounced and passionately condemned by more orthodox figures.

Events and personalities combined to prevent any agreement on the revival of the caliphate. The divisions between those who saw the office as providing spiritual leadership for all Muslims and those who looked to a caliph who would renew the political power of the *umma* and unify the Muslims in opposition to their oppressors meant that there was no consensus on how to proceed. Any of the suggested candidates for the office – Sharif Husayn of Mecca, Fu'ad I, the king of Egypt, or Ibn Sa'ud, king of what was becoming known as Saudi Arabia, were all mentioned – immediately aroused fierce opposition or simple ridicule, which ruled them out. There was no widespread popular dismay about the abolition of the caliphate, nor any mass movements among Muslims to work for its restoration. By the 1930s Muslims in the Middle East were more concerned about events in Palestine and were looking to Arab nationalism rather than the caliphate as an ideology which would respond to their hopes and anxieties.

Even in what we might call Islamist circles, the reinstatement of the caliphate was not a priority. The most prominent and influential Islamist revival movement was the Muslim Brotherhood, founded in Egypt by Hasan al-Banna (1906–49). For Banna and his followers the real issues were the revival of religious enthusiasm and commitment to the *shariʿa*. In order for this to happen, the destructive influence of foreigners, the British in the Egyptian context, had to be challenged and removed. To do this, Banna was prepared to work with nationalists and with the Egyptian kings Fu'ad and, from 1936, Farouk, trying to stiffen their resolve against foreign rule. The ultimate objective was a Muslim caliphate, to be sure, but the revival of the caliphate would be the end result of independence and moral reform, a distant aim rather than a first step.

The period after 1945, marked as it was in the Middle East by the end of the French mandates in Syria and Lebanon, the end of the British mandate in Palestine in 1948 and the establishment of the state of Israel, led to much uncertainty and division in the Muslim Middle East and discussions about the future and the revival and development of the area. However, few if any of those leaders involved looked to the caliphate as a way forward. The ideology of nationalism was now increasingly joined by that of socialism. Egyptian President Abdel Nasser's nationalization of the Suez Canal in 1956, and the subsequent humiliation of British and French attempts to take it back, led to the forging of close

links between Egypt and the Soviet Union. For most politically active people in the Arab Middle East, communism
rather than the revival of the ancient caliphate pointed the
way to the future. When I first started travelling in the area
in 1964 it was generally assumed this was where the future
lay. Most people would have accepted that they were Muslims
as well as socialists and nationalists, but the mosques were for
old men, relics of a vanished world, and the caliphate as distant and irrelevant as the Holy Roman Empire in post-war
western Europe.

One Islamist group stood out in opposition to this view.
This was Hizb al-Tahrīr (the Party of Liberation), founded by
a leading Palestinian religious scholar, Taqi al-Dīn Nabhani
(1909–77), from 1952 onwards. Like the Muslim Brotherhood
and related movements, Hizb al-Tahrir argued for spiritual
revival and the unity of Muslims. Where they differed was in
asserting that the revival of the caliphate was to be the
instrument of these changes rather than the result. As Reza
Pankhurst, an authority on the recent history of the idea of
the caliphate, explains:

> The founders of Hizb ut-Tahrir, who were Islamic jurists as
> well as activists, viewed the caliphate both as a *shari‘a*
> obligation and as the necessary political structure required
> to reform and unite the community. Emerging in an era
> when the physical restrictions of colonial control were
> being removed, their *ijtihad* [legal reasoning] led them
> to conclude that the necessary revival was one of an
> intellectual nature, requiring fundamental changes in the
> concepts carried and worldview held by the Muslim

community, and that the caliphate was not the final goal
but rather the vehicle for change in the world.[1]

The party has put forward some more specific proposals
about caliphal government, in addition to more typical views
on such matters as women's dress and the enforcement of
sharī'a. The caliph can be chosen from all male Muslims, that
is he, and it must be he, does not need to be of Qurashi descent. The caliph must operate within the limits of *sharī'a*.
The party rejects the idea of democracy and argues that the
concept of the sovereignty of the people amounts to *kufr*
(unbelief) since sovereignty belongs to God alone. It equally
argues against nationalism and groups who seek to establish
Islamic government according to *sharī'a* in one country. It
does, however, assert that Muslims, male and female, should
be able to choose the caliph by voting and that this choice
should be confirmed by the taking of the *bay'a* in the time-
honoured fashion. Non-Muslims living within the caliphate
must be protected but are effectively prevented from voting
or assuming any positions of responsibility in the government. Another distinctive policy is the return to the gold
standard, with dinars and dirhams modelled on those first
issued around the year 700 in the caliphate of Abd al-Malik.
This, it is argued, will prevent inflation and other economic
abuses.

Hizb al-Tahrir, with its call for a universal caliphate, has
attracted considerable popular support in countries such as
Palestine, the 'stans' of Central Asia, and Indonesia, but despite participating in a number of failed coups it has been
unable to put its ideas of caliphate into practice anywhere.

It is always important to recognize that a call to establish an Islamic state, or to launch *jihād*, is not the same thing as calling for a caliphate with all its universal claims. Some militant Islamist groups have attached less importance to the concept of the caliphate than Hizb al-Tahrīr. For Usāma b. Lādin and Al-Qaeda, the restoration, or creation, of a universal caliphate was a distant, even utopian aspiration which would follow after immediate objectives like expelling westerners and western influence from the Muslim world had been accomplished. Al-Qaeda's Afghan allies, the Taliban, were and still are primarily focused on creating a Muslim state, ruled according to *sharī'a* within Afghanistan rather than a caliphate which could attract the loyalty of all Muslims. Ironically, the idea that Al-Qaeda is working to establish a universal caliphate finds its clearest expression in the polemics of American politicians like George Bush and Donald Rumsfeld, who tried to develop the image of the caliphate as a Muslim totalitarian enterprise which threatens the whole world.

Since the proclamation of their caliphate, the so-called Islamic State (*Dawlat al-Islamiya*) has become the most prominent and influential group advocating the revival of the caliphate and, unlike Hizb al-Tahrīr for example, they have moved to put their ideas into practice. Islamic State is distinguished from other jihadi and salafi groups at the present time by its emphasis on the title and role of the caliph. It is the first of these movements in the twenty-first century to have designated an individual who can be identified as the caliph. While other groups may have called for the restoration or revival of the caliphate, only Islamic State has gone so far as to inaugurate one. It is important to recognize what a radical claim this is and what risks and problems it brings with it.

The establishment of the caliphate was announced in Islamic State's online periodical *Dābiq* on the First of Ramadan 1435 H (29 June 2014; *Dābiq* uses the Muslim calendar and Common Era dates are never mentioned). The new Commander of the Faithful and caliph, Abū Bakr al-Baghdādī, addresses Muslims thus:

> O Muslims everywhere, glad tidings for you and expect good. Raise your head high for today – by God's grace – you have a state and a *khilāfa* which will return your dignity, might, rights and leadership. It is a state where the Arab and non-Arab, the white man and black man, the easterner and the westerner, are all brothers . . . Soon, by Allah's permission, a day will come when the Muslim will walk everywhere as a master, having honour, being revered, with his head held high and his dignity preserved . . . The Muslims today have a loud thundering statement and possess heavy boots. They have a statement to make that will cause the world to hear and understand the meaning of terrorism and boots that will trample the idol of nationalism, destroy the idol of democracy and uncover its deviant nature.

Apart from these general exhortatory proclamations, the writers of *Dābiq* are concerned to prove that the ideas of imamate or caliphate are not simply religious ideals but must also lead to the establishment of an active, working and powerful state, that is to say that they completely reject those strands in Muslim thought, medieval and modern, which suggest that the caliphate can offer Muslims only spiritual and religious leadership:

> These callers to God couldn't grasp the idea that Islam could have a state and an imam nor could they begin to understand what it would cost to achieve this. It was as if they had never studied the history of Islam and learned what this endeavour would require from us in terms of blood.

The discussion then moves on to the Quranic verse describing the imamate which God gave to Abraham[2] and what this imamate might entail. This *imāmah* and the *milla* (religious community) of Abraham which was established become the blueprint for the caliphate as a political organization:

> Moreover the *imāmah* mentioned in the above verse isn't simply referring to *imāmah* in religious affairs, as many would wish to interpret it. Rather it's inclusive of *imāmah* in political affairs which many religious people have shunned or avoided on account of the hardship it entails itself and on account of the hardship entailed in working to establish it. Furthermore, the people of today have failed to understand that *imāmah* in religious affairs cannot be properly established unless the people of truth first achieve comprehensive political *imāmah* over the lands and the people.

The claim of Abū Bakr al-Baghdādī to the caliphate seems to be based on two criteria. The first is descent from Quraysh. While we cannot be certain, there is no reason to doubt his lineage and there must be many tens of thousands of people who could claim Qurashi descent, after all; but, as we have seen, there are, and have been since the eleventh century, many Muslims who have rejected the idea that the caliph has to be from the holy tribe. The second criterion seems to be a more simple assertion that many Muslims have taken the *bay'a* and that he is defending Muslims, by whom he means, of course, only the Muslims who believe the same things as he and his followers do. As we have seen throughout this book, there have been many different discourses for claiming the caliphal title and there is no generally agreed legal position on what constitutes a legitimate caliphate. Baghdādī's claim does not seem to be, in the light of these different traditions, *ipso facto* illegitimate: there is a whole variety of precedents.

IS is emphatic that the caliph must come from Quraysh. At the same time it asserts that all Muslims are equal and that distinctions of race and nationality must be swept away along with the international borders which keep Muslims apart. It is difficult to see how these two ideas can be reconciled.

The ideologues of Islamic State use the history of the caliphate in a ruthless but not entirely unintelligent way. Their propaganda and image are redolent with nostalgia for ancient glory. The adoption of black, and of black banners, is a clear attempt to relate their movement to the Abbasid revolution and appropriate its symbols for their own attempt to remake the Islamic world.

But the world they look back to is above all the time of the Prophet and the first caliphs. Their model rulers are what they imagine the early caliphs to have been. Abū Bakr, the first caliph, plays a large part in this and it cannot be a coincidence that the IS caliph has adopted this same name. IS looks back to his military triumph in the *ridda* wars against the rejectionists which followed the Prophet's death and identifies its Muslim opponents in Syria and Iraq with the *murtadds*, the apostates who opposed the early Muslim state. In the accounts of these campaigns they find justification for treating such opponents as worthy of death: if Abū Bakr put the *murtadds* to death without mercy, then his successors in the new caliphate can, and indeed should, do the same. In the abundant, and historically very unreliable, accounts of the wars of the early caliphs, they can discover almost anything. To take one especially terrible example, the burning alive in an iron cage of the unfortunate Jordanian pilot, in the whole of early Islamic history (in contrast, incidentally, to early modern European history) there is virtually no tradition of burning prisoners alive. However, Islamic State 'researchers' have managed to find one example in which Abū Bakr is alleged to have ordered such a dreadful punishment, and that is enough to justify this barbaric behaviour and, more than that, to publicize and glorify it.

IS continuously looks back to caliphal examples and a romantic view of early Islamic warfare. Its magazine *Dabiq* is full of pictures of iconic figures of black-clad warriors on horses brandishing long curved scimitar-like swords. The texts refer to them as *fursān* (knights), a word redolent with memories of courage and commitment lifted straight from the world of medieval chronicles. The desire to associate themselves with an ancient and purer form of warfare, like the revival of the caliphate itself, is eloquent testimony to the seductive power of this vision.

Its enemies are identified with the enemies of the Prophet, his Companions and the first caliphs in the Islamic tradition. The Murji'in were a group which flourished in the Umayyad period. Essentially non-violent, they believed that it was not up to Muslims to decide that other Muslims who did not share their beliefs were *kuffār*, unbelievers. Allah alone should make that decision. The Murji'in, as such, have not been a force in the Islamic *umma* for centuries and their very existence must have been unknown to most Muslims. For Islamic State the term Murji'in can be applied to all those Sunni Muslims in Syria and elsewhere who are not as hardline as they are. And of course it is possible to find Traditions allegedly passed on from the Companions of the Prophet and precedents from the early caliphate to demonstrate that such people were worthy of death.

There are other examples of how Islamic State uses the political and religious disputes of the early caliphate to establish its righteousness and destroy its rivals in the Muslim world. The history of the caliphate is a fundamental legitimizing tool, alive and, in its hands, deeply dangerous.

Its rise and its use of the idea and ideology of caliphate demonstrate that this ancient idea still has power and authority in the Muslim world, which has taken many by surprise. I hope this book has shown that caliphate is a concept with a wide variety of meanings and interpretations. Its strength lies partly in its flexibility. Its intellectual justification draws on the direct connection with the earliest days of Islam and the glorious era of the Umayyad and Abbasid caliphates. At the same time it can be used, even twisted, to promote ideologies which are sinister and brutal. But the idea of caliphate is not in itself dangerous or threatening. We need not be afraid of it, even if we are fearful of how some have chosen to interpret it.

Glossary

amīr: see emir

amīr al-mu'minīn: Commander of the Faithful, title usually held by caliphs

ansār: literally 'helpers': the inhabitants of Medina who supported Muhammad

ashrāf: see *sharīf*

bay'a: oath of allegiance to caliph or other ruler

dā'ī: missionary, usually of clandestine religio-political movements

da'wa: missionary movement (cf. *dā'ī*)

dawla: dynasty or state, e.g. the Abbasid *dawla* or the Fatimid *dawla*

dīnār: standard gold coin

dirham: standard silver coin

dīwān: originally list of those entitled to state salaries. Also office or department of government.

emir: army commander, provincial governor or ruler of small independent state

fitna: civil war or dispute within the Muslim community

ghāzī: Muslim volunteer who fights in the *jihād*

hadīth: Tradition recording the words of Muhammad

hajj: annual pilgrimage to Mecca

hijra: the emigration of Muhammad from Mecca to Medina in 622, which marks the beginning of the Muslim era

imam: spiritual leader of the Muslim community, often synonymous with caliph

Jāhiliyya: period of ignorance or savagery in Arabia before the coming of Islam

jāriya: female slave. Often singer or poet

jihād: holy war

jizya: poll tax levied on non-Muslims

jund: army; one of the administrative districts of Syria Palestine

kāfir, pl. *kuffār:* unbeliever, non-Muslim

kharāj: land tax

khutba: address in mosque at Friday prayer which included mention of the ruler's name, a sign of sovereignty

kufr: unbelief

mamlūk: slave soldier. This term, occasionally used in early Islamic history, came to replace the term *ghulām* from the fifth/eleventh century onwards.

mawlā, pl. *mawālī:* originally 'client', often non-Arab client of an Arab tribe, hence the use of *mawālī* to describe non-Arab Muslims in the first century of Islam. Later more commonly 'freedmen' in the Abbasid period, the term passes out of general use in the fourth/tenth century.

minbar: pulpit in a mosque

muhājir, pl. *muhājirūn:* one who participated in the Hijra, that is a Meccan who accompanied Muhammad to settle in Medina

murtadd: apostate: used of those who rejected the authority of the Muslims after the death of Muhammad

nass: designation of ruler by his predecessor

qādī: Muslim judge

qalansuwa: tall, conical headgear worn as part of Abbasid court dress

ridda: apostasy from Islam; hence the wars in Arabia which followed Muhammad's death are known as the *ridda* wars

sābiqa: precedence, especially precedence in conversion to Islam, i.e. the earlier a person was converted, the greater his *sābiqa*

sahāba: Companions of the Prophet

sadaqa: the payment of alms enjoined by Muslim law

sharī'a: Muslim religious law

sharīf, pl. *ashrāf*: in Umayyad times, tribal leader, chief. By the fourth/tenth century the title is usually confined to descendants of Alī.

shawkat: political and military power

shirk: polytheism

shūra: council formed to choose a caliph

sikka: the right to mint coins, usually the prerogative of the ruler

sunna: the sayings and actions of Muhammad used as legal precedents

sūq: market

ulama: learned men, especially experts in the Traditions of the Prophet and Islamic law

umma: the Muslim community

List of Caliphs

This list is based on the definitive reference work of
C. E. Bosworth, *The New Islamic Dynasties*, Edinburgh:
Edinburgh, University Press (1996).

THE ORTHODOX OR RIGHTLY GUIDED CALIPHS (632–61)

632	Abū Bakr
634	Umar b. al-Khattāb
644	Uthmān b. Affān
656–61	Alī b. Abī Tālib

THE UMAYYAD CALIPHS (661–750)

661	Mu'āwiya I b. Abī Sufyān
680	Yazīd I
683	Mu'āwiya II
684	Marwān I b. al-Hakam
685	Abd al-Malik
705	Walīd I
715	Sulaymān
717	Umar II b. Abd al-Azīz
720	Yazīd II
724	Hishām

743	Walīd II
744	Yazīd III
744	Ibrāhīm
744–50	Marwān II

THE ABBASID CALIPHS (749–1517)
BAGHDAD AND IRAQ (749–1258)

749	Saffāh
754	Mansūr
775	Mahdī
785	Hādī
786	Hārūn al-Rashīd
809	Amīn
813	Ma'mūn
833	Mu'tasim
842	Wāthiq
847	Mutawakkil
861	Muntasir
862	Musta'īn
866	Mu'tazz
869	Muhtadī
870	Mu'tamid
892	Mu'tadid
902	Muktafī
908	Muqtadir
932	Qāhir
934	Rādī
940	Muttaqī
944	Mustakfī
946	Mutī
974	Tā'ī
991	Qādir

1031	Qā'im
1075	Muqtadī
1094	Mustazhir
1118	Mustarshid
1135	Rāshid
1136	Muqtafī
1160	Mustanjid
1170	Mustadī
1180	Nāsir
1225	Zāhir
1226	Mustansir
1242–58	Musta'sim
1258	*Mongol sack of Baghdad*

CAIRO (1261–1517)

1261	Hākim I
1302	Mustakfī I
1340	Wāthiq I
1341	Hākim II
1352	Mu'tadid I
1362	Mutawakkil I, *first time*
1377	Mu'tasim, *first time*
1377	Mutawakkil I, *second time*
1383	Wāthiq II
1386	Mu'tasim, *second time*
1389	Mutawakkil I, *third time*
1406	Musta'īn
1414	Mu'tadid II
1441	Mustakfī II
1451	Qā'im
1455	Mustanjid
1479	Mutawakkil II

1497	Mustamsik, *first time*
1508	Mutawakkil III, *first time*
1516	Mustamsik, *second time*
1517	Mutawakkil III, *second time*
1517	*Ottoman conquest of Egypt*

THE SPANISH UMAYYAD CALIPHS (929–1031)

929	Abd al-Rahmān III al-Nāsir (emir since 912)
961	Hakam II al-Mustansir
976	Hishām II al-Mu'ayyad, *first reign*
1009	Muhammad II al-Mahdī, *first reign*
1009	Sulaymān al-Musta'īn, *first reign*
1010	Muhammad II, *second reign*
1010	Hishām II, *second reign*
1013	Sulaymān, *second reign*
1018	Abd al-Rahmān IV al-Murtadā
1023	Abd al-Rahmān V al-Mustazhir
1024	Muhammad III al-Mustakfī
1027–31	Hishām III al-Mu'tadid
1031	*Abolition of Umayyad caliphate of Andalus*

THE ALMOHAD CALIPHS IN NORTH AFRICA AND ANDALUS (1130–1269)

1130	Muhammad b. Tūmart
1130	Abd al-Mu'min
1163	Abū Ya'qūb Yūsuf I
1184	Abū Yūsuf Ya'qūb al-Mansūr
1199	Muhammad al-Nāsir
1214	Abū Ya'qūb Yūsuf II al-Mustansir
1224	Abd al-Wāhid I al-Makhlū

1224	Abū Muhammad Abdallāh al-Ādil
1227	Yahyā al-Mu'tasim
1229	Abū al-Alā Idrīs al-Ma'mūn
1232	Abū Muhammad Abd al-Wāhid II al-Rashīd
1242	Abū al-Hasan Alī al-Sa'īd al-Mu'tadid
1248	Abū Hafs Umar al-Murtadā
1266–9	Abū'l-Ulā al-Wāthiq
1269	*Christian conquest of all Spain except Granada; North African lands divided among Abdal-Wādids, Hafsids and Marīnids*

THE FATIMID CALIPHS (909–1171)
NORTH AFRICA (909–69)

909	Ubaydallāh al-Mahdī
934	Qā'im
946	Mansūr
953	Mu'izz (*from 969 in Egypt*)

EGYPT (969–1171)

977	Azīz
996	Hākim
1021	Zāhir
1036	Mustansir
1094	Musta'lī
1101	Āmir
1131	Hāfiz
1149	Zāfir
1154	Fā'iz
1160–71	Ādid
1171	*Ayyubid conquest of Egypt*

Notes

ABBREVIATION

CIS = Kersten, C. (ed.), *The Caliphate and Islamic Statehood: Formation, Fragmentation and Modern Interpretations*, Berlin: Gerlach Press (3 vols.; 2015)

CHAPTER 1: THE FIRST CALIPHS

1. M. Cook, 'Muhammad's Deputies in Medina', *Usūr al-wusta* 23 (2015), 1–67
2. P. Crone and GM. Hinds, *God's Caliph: Religious Authority in the First Century of Islam*, Cambridge: Cambridge University Press (1986), 111–12
3. Ibid., 12–23
4. R. Hoyland, 'The Inscription of Zuhayr, the Oldest Islamic Inscription (24 AH/AD 644–645)', *Arabian Archaeology and Epigraphy* 19 (2008), 210–37
5. E. Gibbon, *The History of the Decline and Fall of the Roman Empire*, ed. W. Smith, London: John Murray (1855), VI, 288
6. A. Marsham, *Rituals of Islamic Monarchy*, Edinburgh: Edinburgh University Press (2009), 100–101
7. P. Crone, *Medieval Islamic Political Thought*, Edinburgh: Edinburgh University Press (2004), 60–61

**CHAPTER 2: THE EXECUTIVE CALIPHATE:
THE RULE OF THE UMAYYADS**

1. Translated and discussed in Marsham, *Rituals*, 86–9
2. Quoted in Crone and Hinds, *God's Caliph*, 6

3. Ibid., 33–42
4. Balādhuri, *Futūh al-buldān*, ed. M. J. de Goeje, Leiden: Brill (1866), 167–8
5. R. Hillenbrand, 'La Dolce Vita in Early Islamic Syria', *Art History* 5 (1982), 1–35
6. Crone and Hinds, *God's Caliph*, 118–26
7. Translated and discussed in ibid., 129–32

CHAPTER 3: THE EARLY ABBASID CALIPHATE

1. Tabarī, *Ta'rīkh al-rusul wa'l-mulūk*, ed. M. J. de Goeje et al., Leiden: Brill (1879–1901), III, 29–33
2. Night 19, *The Arabian Nights*, trans. M. C. Lyons and U. Lyons, London: Penguin Books (2008), I, 123
3. Night 462, ibid., II, 321
4. Tabarī, *Ta'rīkh*, III, 709
5. Miskawayh, Abu Ali, *The Eclipse of the Abbasid Caliphate*, trans. D. S. Margoliouth, London: I. B. Tauris (2015), I, 57–60
6. Ibn Fadlān, *Mission to the Volga*, ed. and trans. J. Montgomery, New York and London: New York University Press, Library of Arabic Literature (2014)

CHAPTER 4: THE CULTURE OF THE ABBASID CALIPHATE

1. Mas'ūdi, *Murūj al-dhahab*, ed. and French trans. C. Barbier de Meynard, Paris: Imprimerie Nationale (1874), VIII, 289–304
2. This was a characteristic tenet of the Mu'tazila, who held that every Muslim has free choice and that if he is guilty of a serious offence and dies without repentance he will endure hell-fire for ever, in contrast to other groups, notably the Murji'a, who held that Muslims might be punished for a while but would ultimately attain paradise (*janna*).
3. S. M. Toorawa, *Ibn Abī Tāhir Tayfur and Arabic Writerly Culture*, London and New York: RoutledgeCurzon (2005), 33–4
4. J. M. Bloom, *Paper before Print: The History and Impact of Paper in the Islamic World*, New Haven and London: Yale University Press (2001)
5. Ibn Khallikan, *Ibn Khalikan's Biographical Dictionary*, trans. M. de Slane, Paris (1842–71), I, 478–9
6. Ibid., V, 315–17

7. The name means 'ugly', which was a name often given to beautiful slaves, perhaps as a joke, perhaps to guard against the evil eye.
8. The caliph's given name, which would only have been used by his closest intimates and lovers.

CHAPTER 5: THE LATER ABBASID CALIPHATE

1. T. W. Arnold, *The Caliphate*, Oxford: Clarendon Press (1924), 65–7
2. This is translated and discussed in A. Mez, *The Renaissance of Islam*, New Delhi: Kitab Dhavan (1937), 268–70
3. Bayhaqi's account can be read in *The History of Beyhaqi*, trans., C. E. Bosworth and M. Ashtiany, Cambridge MA: Harvard University Press (2011), I, 401–24
4. Ibn al-Athir, *Chronicle*, trans. D. S. Richards, Aldershot: Ashgate (2008), I, 108
5. Arnold, *The Caliphate*, 86–7
6. *The Chronicle of the Third Crusade: A Translation of the Itinerarium Peregrinorum et Gesta Regis Ricardi*, trans. Helen J. Nicholson, Aldershot: Ashgate (1997), 53
7. Ibn Wāsil, quoted by K. Hirschler in *Medieval Muslim Historians and the Franks in the Levant*, ed. A. Mallett, Leiden: Brill (2015), 149
8. Ibn al-Athir, *Chronicle*, I, 190–91
9. *The Travels of Ibn Jubayr*, trans. R. Broadhurst, London: Jonathan Cape (1952), 236–9

CHAPTER 6: THREE AUTHORS IN SEARCH OF THE CALIPHATE

1. Al-Māwardī, *The Ordinances of Government*, trans. W. H. Wahba (Reading: Garnet Publishing, 1996) 1–32
2. Ibid., 6–22.
3. W. B. Hallaq, 'Caliphs, Jurists and the Saljūqs in the Political Thought of Juwaynī', *CIS*, II, 210–25 at p. 221
4. C. Hillenbrand, 'Islamic Orthodoxy or Realpolitik? Al-Ghazālī's Views on Government', *CIS*, II, 226–52 at p. 230

CHAPTER 7: THE CALIPHATE OF THE SHI'ITES

1. See the excellent discussion of this work in W. al-Qāḍī, 'An Early Fāṭimid Political Document', *CIS*, II, 88–112
2. See Nasir-ī Khusraw, *Book of Travels*, trans W. M. Thackston, Cosa Mesa, CA: Mazda Publishers, 2001, see pp. 52–76

CHAPTER 8: THE UMAYYADS OF CÓRDOBA

1. See R. M. Menocal, *Ornament of the World: How Muslims, Jews and Christians Created a Culture of Tolerance in Medieval Spain*, New York: Little, Brown (2002)
2. Latin text and English trans. in C. Smith, *Christians and Moors in Spain*, Warminster: Aris & Phillips (1988), I, 62–75
3. Slavs from eastern Europe had been imported to Andalus, via the great slave market at Prague, throughout the tenth century as elite soldiers.

CHAPTER 9: THE ALMOHAD CALIPHS

1. Ibn Sāhib al-Salāt, *Al-man bi'l-imāma*, ed. A. al-Hadi al-Tazi, Beirut (1964), 534
2. Abd al-Wāhid al- Marrākushi, *Al-Mujib*, ed. M. al-Uryan, Cairo (1949), 238–9

CHAPTER 10: THE CALIPHATE UNDER THE MAMLUKS AND OTTOMANS

1. Arnold, *The Caliphate*, 74–6, 107–8
2. Ibid., 130
3. Ṣ. Tufan Buzpinar, 'Opposition to the Ottoman Caliphate in the Early Years of Abdülhamid II: 1877–1882', *CIS*, III, 6–27
4. Quoted in K. H. Karpat, *The Politicization of Islam: Reconstructing Identity, State, Faith, and Community in the Late Ottoman State*, Oxford: Oxford University Press (2001), 161, 162. 'Padishah' was an ancient title of Persian origin, sometimes used by the Ottoman sultans

5. For the full text and a beautifully illustrated account of the relics, and of Abd al-Hamīd's funeral, see H. Aydin, *The Sacred Trusts: Pavilion of the Sacred Relics, Topkapi Palace Museum, Istanbul*, Clifton, NJ: Tughra Books (2014)

6. Buzpinar, 'Opposition to the Caliphate', 20

CHAPTER 11: THE TWENTIETH CENTURY AND BEYOND

1. R. Pankhurst, *The Inevitable Caliphate?*, London: Hurst and Company (2013), 99

2. Qur'an, 2 (*Surat al-Baqara*), verse 124

Further Reading

GENERAL

- Arnold, T. W., *The Caliphate*, Oxford: Clarendon Press (1924)
- Crone, P., *Medieval Islamic Political Thought*, Edinburgh: Edinburgh University Press (2004)
- Kennedy, H., *The Prophet and the Age of the Caliphates*, London: Routledge (3rd edition, 2015)
- Kersten, C. (ed.), *The Caliphate and Islamic Statehood: Formation, Fragmentation and Modern Interpretations*, Berlin: Gerlach Press (3 vols; 2015). A valuable collection of essays on all aspects of the caliphate, cited hereafter as *CIS*
- Montgomery Watt, W., *Islamic Political Thought*, Edinburgh: Edinburgh University Press (1968)
- Rosenthal, E., *Political Thought in Medieval Islam*, Cambridge: Cambridge University Press (1962)
- Tyan, E., *Institutions du droit public musulman, vol. I: Le Califat*, Paris: Siney (1956)

THE FIRST CALIPHS

- Afsaruddin, A., *Striving in the Path of God: Jihād and Martyrdom in Islamic Thought*, Oxford: Oxford University Press (2013)
- Donner, F. M., *The Early Islamic Conquests*, Princeton: Princeton University Press (1981)

FURTHER READING

- Hoyland, R. G., *In God's Path: The Arab Conquests and the Creation of an Islamic Empire*, Oxford: Oxford University Press (2015)
- Kennedy, H., *The Great Arab Conquests*, London: Weidenfeld and Nicolson (2007)
- Madelung, W., *The Succession to Muhammad: A Study of the Early Caliphate*, Cambridge: Cambridge University Press (1997)

THE UMAYYAD CALIPHS

- Crone, P., and Hinds, M., *God's Caliph: Religious Authority in the First Centuries of Islam*, Cambridge: Cambridge University Press (1986)
- Hawting, G. R., *The First Dynasty of Islam: The Umayyad Caliphate, A.D. 661–750*, London: Routledge (2nd edition, 2000)
- Marsham, A., *Rituals of Islamic Monarchy: Accession and Succession in the First Muslim Empire*, Edinburgh: Edinburgh University Press (2009)
- McMillan, M. E., *The Meaning of Mecca: The Politics of Pilgrimage in Early Islam*, London: Saqi Books (2011)

THE EARLY ABBASIDS AND ABBASID COURT CULTURE

- Bennison, A. K., *The Great Caliphs: The Golden Age of the Abbasid Empire*, London: I. B. Tauris (2009)
- Bowen, H., *The Life and Times of Ali b. Isa, the Good Vizier*, Cambridge: Cambridge University Press (1928)
- Caswell, F. M., *The Slave Girls of Baghdad: The Qiyān in the Early Abbasid Era*, London: I. B. Tauris (2011)
- Gutas, D., *Greek Thought, Arabic Culture: The Graeco-Arabic Translation Movement in Baghdad and Early Abbasid Society*, London: Routledge (1998)

- Kennedy, H., *The Court of the Caliphs: The Rise and Fall of Islam's Greatest Dynasty*, London: Weidenfeld and Nicolson (2004). Published in the USA as *When Baghdad Ruled the Muslim World*, Cambridge, MA: Da Capo (2005)

- Kennedy, P. F., *Abu Nuwas: A Genius of Poetry*, Oxford: Oneworld Publications (2005)

- Turner, J. P., *Inquisition in Early Islam: The Competition for Political and Religious Authority in the Abbasid Empire*, London: I. B. Tauris (2013)

- Van Berkel, M., El-Cheikh, N., Kennedy, H., and Osti, L., *Crisis and Continuity at the Abbasid Court: Formal and Informal Politics in the Caliphate of al-Muqtadir (295–320/908–32)*, Leiden: Brill (2013)

THE LATER ABBASID CALIPHATE

- Donohue, J., *The Buwayhid Dynasty in Iraq 334 H./945 to 403 H./1012*, Leiden: Brill (2013)

- Hanne, E. J., *Putting the Caliph in His Place: Power, Authority, and the Late Abbasid Caliphate*, Medison NJ: Fairleigh Dickinson University Press (2007)

- Mez, A., *The Renaissance of Islam*, New Delhi: Kitab Dhavan (1937)

THREE AUTHORS IN SEARCH OF THE CALIPHATE

- Hallaq, W. B., 'Caliphs, Jurists and the Saljūqs in the Thought of Juwaynī', *CIS*, II, 210–25

- Hillenbrand, C., 'Islamic Orthodoxy or Realpolitik? Al-Ghazālī's Views on Islamic Government', *CIS*, II, 226–51

- Māwardī, Alī b. Muhammad, *The Ordinances of Government*, trans. W. Wahba, Reading: Garnett Books (1996)

FURTHER READING

THE UMAYYAD AND ALMOHAD CALIPHATES IN THE WEST

- Brett, M., and Fentress, E., *The Berbers*, Oxford: Blackwell (1996)
- Constable, O. R. (ed.), *Medieval Iberia: Readings from Christian, Muslim, and Jewish Sources*, Philadelphia: University of Pennsylvania Press (1997)
- Jayyusi, S. K. (ed.), *The Legacy of Muslim Spain*, Leiden: Brill (2 vols; 1992)
- Kennedy, H., *Muslim Spain and Portugal: A Political History of al-Andalus*, London: Longman (1996)
- Menocal, M. R., *The Ornament of the World: How Muslims, Jews, and Christians Created a Culture of Tolerance in Medieval Spain*, Boston WIA: Little Brown (2002)

THE CALIPHATE OF THE SHI'ITES

- Al-Qādī, W., 'An Early Fatimid Political Document', *CIS*, II, 88–112
- Daftary, F., *The Isma'ilis: Their History and Doctrines*, Cambridge: Cambridge University Press (1990)
- Halm, H., *Shi'ism*, Edinburgh: Edinburgh University Press (2nd edition, 2004)
- Halm, H., *The Empire of the Mahdi: The Rise of the Fatimids*, Leiden: Brill (1996)
- Jafri, S. H. M., *The Origins and Early Development of Shi'a Islam*, London: Longman (1979)
- Sanders, P., *Ritual, Politics, and the City in Fatimid Cairo*, Albany NY: State University of New York Press (1994)
- Walker, P. E., *Exploring an Islamic Empire: Fatimid History and Its Sources*, London: I. B. Tauris (2002)

THE CALIPHATE UNDER THE MAMLUKS AND OTTOMANS

- Aydin, H., *The Sacred Trusts: Pavilion of the Sacred Relics, Topkapi Palace Museum, Istanbul*, Clifton, NJ: Tughra Books (2014)

- Finkel, C., *Osman's Dream: The Story of the Ottoman Empire*, New York: Basic Books (2005)
- Gibb, H. A. R., 'Lutfi Pasha on the Ottoman Caliphate', *CIS*, II, 171–8
- Hourani, A., *Arab Thought in the Liberal Age*, London: Oxford University Press (1962)
- Karpat, K. H., *The Politicization of Islam: Reconstructing Identity, State, Faith, and Community in the Late Ottoman State*, Oxford: Oxford University Press (2001)
- Longford, E., *A Pilgrimage of Passion: The Life of Wilfrid Scawen Blunt*, New York: Knopf (1980)
- Rogan, E., *The Fall of the Ottomans: The Great War in the Middle East, 1914–1920*, London: Allen Lane (2015)
- Tufan Buzpinar, Ş., 'Opposition to the Ottoman Caliphate in the Early Years of Abdülhamid II: 1877–1882', *CIS*, III, 6–27

THE TWENTIETH CENTURY AND BEYOND

- Pankhurst, R., *The Inevitable Caliphate? A History of the Struggle for Global Islamic Union, 1924 to the Present*, London: Hurst and Company (2013)
- Sayyid, S., *Recalling the Caliphate: Decolonisation and World Order*, London: Hurst and Company (2014)
- Taji-Farouki, S., *A Fundamental Quest: Hizb al-Tahrir and the Search for the Islamic Caliphate*, London: Grey Seal (1996)
- Tufan Buzpinar, Ş., 'Opposition to the Ottoman Caliphate in the Early Years of Abdülhamid II: 1877–1882', *CIS*, III, 6–27

Index

The European Union:
A Citizen's Guide
Chris Bickerton

Who rules the EU and how does it work?

Who are the winners and losers of European integration?

Is the EU a threat to democracy?

Chris Bickerton is a lecturer in politics at the University of Cambridge and a fellow of Queens' College, Cambridge. He has taught at the universities of Oxford, Amsterdam and Sciences Po, Paris. One of his previous books, *European Integration*, was described by Professor Wolfgang Streeck, emeritus director of the Max Planck Institute for the Study of Societies, as 'the most innovative contribution to the study of European integration I have seen in decades'.

A PELICAN
INTRODUCTION

Revolutionary Russia, 1891–1991
Orlando Figes

What caused the Russian Revolution?

Did it succeed or fail?

Do we still live with its consequences?

Orlando Figes teaches history at Birkbeck, University of London and is the author of many acclaimed books on Russian history, including *A People's Tragedy*, which *The Times Literary Supplement* named as one of the '100 most influential books since the war', *Natasha's Dance*, *The Whisperers*, *Crimea* and *Just Send Me Word*. The *Financial Times* called him 'the greatest storyteller of modern Russian historians'.

A PELICAN INTRODUCTION

Who Governs Britain?

Anthony King

Where does power lie in Britain today?

Why has British politics changed so dramatically in recent decades?

Is our system of government still fit for purpose?

Anthony King is Millennium Professor of British Government at the University of Essex. A Canadian by birth, he broadcasts frequently on politics and government and is the author of many books on American as well as British politics. He is co-author of the bestselling *The Blunders of Our Governments*, which David Dimbleby described as 'enthralling' and Andrew Marr called 'an astonishing achievement'.

A PELICAN
INTRODUCTION

Greek and Roman Political Ideas
Melissa Lane

Where do our ideas about politics come from?

What can we learn from the Greeks and Romans?

How should we exercise power?

Melissa Lane teaches politics at Princeton University, and previously taught for fifteen years at Cambridge University, where she also studied as a Marshall and Truman scholar. The historian Richard Tuck called her book *Eco-Republic* 'a virtuoso performance by one of our best scholars of ancient philosophy'.

A PELICAN INTRODUCTION